Clear and
Present Thinking

Project Director

Brendan Myers (CEGEP Heritage College)

Contributors to the first edition

Brendan Myers, Charlene Elsby (Purdue University Fort Wayne) Kimberly Baltzer-Jaray (University of Waterloo) Nola Semczyszyn (Franklin & Marshall College) Natalie Ellen, editor (University of Guelph)

Contributors to the second edition

Brendan Myers (lead author)
Charlene Elsby (contributor, chapter 7)
Alex Zieba
(CEGEP Heritage College, contributor, chapter 10.1.)

Editor / Proofreader

Melinda Reidinger
(Anglo-American University of Prague)

Layout and Design

Nathaniel Hébert, winterhebert.com

For all other enquiries,
please visit *brendanmyers.net*

Published by Northwest Passage Books
Gatineau, Québec, Canada
2017.

ISBN

978-0-9939527-9-1

Clear and Present Thinking

A handbook in logic and rationality.

Second edition,
2017

Northwest
Passage Books

Table of Contents

Chapter Six: Science and Scientific Reasoning 115

Chapter Seven: Fallacies 131

Chapter Eight: Reasonable Doubt 143

Chapter Nine: Moral Reasoning 175

Chapter 10: Activities! 189

Acknowledgments

This second edition was financially supported by the
contributions of over 170 people, through
the Kickstarter.com fundraising website, including:

Joshua Smith
Richard Shea
Robert Tharp
Ellen Seebacher
Bernd Buldt
Deanna Smith
Mike Little
Debbie Goldsmith
Joe Roy
trit
Eric Hortop
Anthony Coppola
Jussi Myllyluoma
Steffen Nyeland
Kay M Purcell
John Beckett
Tom
Devin Kibler
Bart Salisbury
Graham Engel
Steven Hosford
Holly Bird

Truls Bjørvik
Chris Wityshyn
Rafael Dellamora
Tristan Knight
Shirelle Capstick
Karen MacLeod
Ben Rossi
Glenn McCrimmon
JD Ferries-Rowe
Cynthia Savage
Christopher White
Nayel hakim
Ellen Behrens

Non-linear thinking

Introduction: What is thinking?

It may seem strange to begin a logic textbook with this question. 'Thinking' is perhaps the most intimate and personal thing that people do. Yet the more you 'think' about thinking, the more mysterious it can appear. Do our thoughts appear in our minds because of the electro-chemical workings of our brains? Or do thoughts come from something that can't be described by science, such as a soul? Are there deeper levels to the scientific explanation of thinking, for instance involving sub-atomic quantum effects? Or do our thoughts come from pure magic? Does it fit the case to say that our thoughts 'come from' some place? Or that they 'appear' in our minds? Are the workings of the mind very different from the workings of the heart? Or are emotions and feelings only another kind of thinking? Might the same be said of intuitions, or inspirations, or dreams?

Let's say, as a starting place, that thinking is an activity of the mind. We can direct this activity towards all kinds of different purposes, from everyday questions like how to spend your money or what to have for dinner tonight, to the highest and deepest matters like the meaning of life. You are thinking, right now, as you read this sentence. Knowing that you are thinking is a bit like knowing what the colour red looks like, or knowing the taste of an apple: you're sure you know what it is, but you might find it difficult to explain to others.

Thinking about thinking can also be complicated in other ways. Many people believe, for instance, that thinking is a very different matter from feeling; and that the mind and the heart are always going to move you in fundamentally different ways. Some people believe that computers, or animals, are capable of thinking, even if their way of thinking is somehow different from that of humans. Some people believe there are things that the thinking mind cannot discover on its own, and that there are other forms of knowing: intuition, or religious faith, or some sort of inspiration. And some might say that the question 'what is thinking?' cannot be answered at all. We could also ask personal questions about the nature of thinking, such as: 'who is it that knows that *he or she knows?*' Who is it that is aware of thinking? And is not that awareness of thinking itself a kind of thinking?

It's a little bit beyond the purpose of this book to investigate those questions. But if you happen to find yourself curious about some of those questions, or wondering how do you know that you know something, or if you find yourself thinking about the nature of thinking itself, you may be well on your way toward becoming a philosopher! We, the authors and contributors of this book across two editions, would like to show you how it is possible to reason about everything. More than that: we'd like to show how it's possible to reason clearly, systematically, logically, and most of all *helpfully*, about everything; and that doing so can be quite personally satisfying, and even pleasurable.

Logic, as we shall define it for this book, is the study of thinking. Or, to be more precise, it is the study of the procedures of *good* thinking. And reason, as we shall define it here, is organized curiosity. You can probably see how these two terms are related to each other. And you can probably see how there's nothing especially strange, or frightening, or emotionally cold, or un-spiritual about them. Logic and reason, taken together, form the most powerful and historically successful source of knowledge ever devised. It is the foundation of science and technology; it enables clear communications in politics, economics, and social relations; it is the standard of excellence in education; it dwells in the heart of the world's most inspirational art and religion. And it belong to everyone.

Is logic difficult?

You might hear people say that they are no good at math, or at computer programming, or at some other kind of activity that requires a lot of concentration. When I was in high school, I used to believe that I was very bad at math. I resented going to math classes, and so I didn't study, and (therefore!) scored poorly on tests and exams. But one day I found myself making my own video games on my Commodore 128 computer, with no other help besides the dictionary of commands. Then a few years later I was coding HTML scripts by hand, which I learned to do by reading the source codes of other people's web sites. I eventually realized that I was actually rather good at logic, or rather that I could be really good at it if I wanted to be.

Thinking rationally and critically is much the same thing. It's actually fairly easy, once you get into the habit of doing it. Most people are born with an ability to perform complex computational tasks built right into their brains. It's true that we often make mistakes when we try to calculate big numbers in our heads, or when we try to calculate probabilities without much information to start with. Nonetheless, the ability to think deliberately, precisely, and analytically is a large part of what it is to be human. Indeed, every human language, all 8,000 or so of them, have complex computational operators built right into the grammar and syntax, which we use to speak and be understood about anything we may want to talk about. When we study logic, we study (among other things) those very operators as they work themselves out, not only in our thinking, but also in our speaking to each other, and

in many of the ways we relate to each other and the world. Logic examines not what people ought to think, but it examines how we actually do think – when we are thinking clearly!

Here's a very short exercise which may help to show you that you already have within your mind everything you need to understand logic and critical reasoning. (It's similar to an exercise that was used by the philosopher Aristotle, and modern philosophers still use it as a way of saluting our predecessors.) Consider the following two sentences:

1. All men are mortal.
2. Socrates is a man.

As almost anyone can see, these two sentences have a relationship to each other. For one thing, there's a topic of discussion that appears in both of them: 'men'. Both sentences also follow the same grammatical structure: they name an object and they name at least one property that belongs to, or can be attributed to, that object. But they also have another, more subtle relation to each other. That subtle relation tells you what should follow next. Here are three possibilities:

a. Therefore, we're having Greek tonight!
b. Therefore, Socrates is a nerd.
c. Therefore, Socrates is mortal.

To most people, the answer is so obvious that I don't need to state which one it is. That's because logical and rational thinking, as already mentioned, is something we all naturally do, all the time.

That example, it may interest you to know, was used by the philosopher Aristotle more than two thousand years ago, and it is still a favourite among philosophy teachers today: we use it as a way of tipping the hat to our predecessors.

Let's look at three other examples, which might show a little more of how that subtle relation works.

1. All the houses built in that neighbourhood are post-

war bungalows.

2. My house is in that neighbourhood.

3. Therefore –

    a. My house is a rotting, decrepit shack.

    b. My house is a grand chateau.

    c. Long John Silver was a rotten businessman.

    d. My house is a post-war bungalow.

1. Every morning, if it is going to be a sunny day, the rooster in the yard crows.

2. Tomorrow is probably going to be a sunny day, just like the last few days.

3. Therefore –

    a. That rooster is more reliable as the TV weather man.

    b. One of these days, I'm going to kill that horrible creature!

    c. My old clock on the wall is a family heirloom.

    d. Tomorrow morning, that rooster will probably crow again.

1. If the surprise birthday present is a Harry Potter book, it will be a great gift.

2. The surprise birthday present is a Harry Potter book.

3. Therefore –

    a. I'm going to hide in my bedroom for a few hours.

    b. I really owe the person who gave it to me a big thank-you!

    c. I have to fix the leaky roof over the kitchen today.

    d. It's a great gift.

In each of these examples, the best answer is option D. So long as the first two statements are true, then the third one, option D, *must* be true. You also know that in both examples, option C doesn't belong. It has nothing to do with the two statements that came before it. To claim that option C should come next *is not logical*. Perhaps option C would make sense if it was part of a joke, or a very complicated discussion of housing development plans for pirates, or inheritance laws involving clocks and farm animals, or how author J.K. Rowling doesn't like leaky houses. But in these examples, we do not have that extra information.

Going only with the information that we have been given, option C cannot be the correct answer. The best answer, in each case, is option D. Of all the four options offered here, option D has the strongest support from the statements that came before it.

But look again at the options A and B in all three examples. These options were not as silly as option C. They *might* follow correctly and logically from the statements that came before them, if only we had a little bit more information. Without your deliberate, conscious awareness, your mind probably filled in that extra information with statements like these ones:

1. Maybe all the postwar bungalows in this neighbourhood are rotting, decrepit shacks.

2. Maybe the rooster has never got it wrong so far, unlike the TV weatherman, who makes mistakes all the time.

3. The reason I'll be hiding in my bedroom is because I will want to read the book in a place where no one will disturb me.

4. People who give great gifts deserve to be thanked.

None of these statements appeared among the initial premises of the argument. Nothing in the initial premises told you anything about these possibilities. They come from outside the argument as presented so far. But that subtle relation between statements allowed you to add something consistent and plausible to the argument in order to move the argument from the premises you had, to conclusions A or B. You might even fill the space with more than one sentence to make the move, as we did in the third possibility above.

Logic is the study of relations among ideas like these. If you could handle these three examples here with ease, then you can handle *everything else in this textbook* just as easily.

Many people believe that philosophy is something rather vague, wishy-washy, or simplistic. You'll hear people quote a line from a popular song or movie, and then they'll say, 'That's my philosophy'. But there's a lot more to it than that; and a person who merely repeats a popular saying and calls it philosophy has not been doing enough work. Philosophical questions are often very *difficult* questions, and they demand a lot of effort and consideration and time. That much deserves to be acknowledged. However, if you learn to think logically, and if you grow into the habit of thinking logically, you will find that the difficulty of philosophical questions becomes no longer frightening. Indeed you may find that kind of difficulty an interesting invitation. And this will spread to other areas of your life. Are you planning to start a new business, and the barriers to entry seem dauntingly high? Are you arranging the seating at a wedding reception where a third of the guests hate each other? Got some other super-hard problem to solve? Challenge accepted!

Linear and Non-Linear Thinking

Many people associate logic with 'linear' thinking, and treat it as the opposite of 'nonlinear' thinking: intuition, creativity, free association, the emotions, and the arts. An often-cited paper in management studies says this about it:

> …we further define linear thinking style as a preference for attending to external data and facts *and* processing this information through conscious logic and rational thinking to form knowledge, understanding, or a decision for guiding subsequent action. We also further define nonlinear thinking style as a preference for attending to internal feelings, impressions, intuition, and sensations; *and* for processing this information (both consciously and subconsciously) to form insight, understanding, or a decision for guiding subsequent actions.[1]

This distinction may have some occasional usefulness. But it can give people the mistaken impression that intuitions, feelings, imagination, and the like, have nothing to do with logic, or even that they are somehow contrary to logic. Looking at the distinction drawn in the quote above, it seems clear to me that what is typically called nonlinear thinking is actually thinking which arrives at an unexpected result by means of a process one is unable or unwilling to ex-

plain. So instead of explaining that process, we mystify it away with hard-to-define words like 'intuition' and 'sensation'. The very word 'nonlinear thinking' allows people to pretend they can transcend or dispense with logic, as if logic somehow limits or oppresses them. But what passes for nonlinear thinking is in fact logical thinking applied more seriously and, at the same time, more playfully. It may reach for the non-obvious or even the fantastical, for instance by re-framing a given problem, looking for non-obvious possibilities, or advancing some kind of sporting proposition (basically a kind of 'what if—?'). But it does so by launching itself from the known and the probable; and there is nothing especially nonlinear about that. It may create relations between things that appear to have no logic, but it does so by experimenting with new logics of its own.

Even fantasy fiction, one of the most imaginative and nonrealistic of human creative activities, requires a few principles of logic in order to pass that experimental test and so convince audiences to suspend their disbelief: principles like consistency, subtlety, simplicity. For example, imagine if J.K. Rowling released a new *Harry Potter* book which revealed that all magic wands were actually technological devices given to the wizarding community by aliens. It's likely that no reader would accept this twist in the story: it is *not logical* according to the story's established worldview.

There are, obviously, several different kinds, or ways, of thinking. The philosopher Plato, back in the 4th century BCE, described at least four different kinds of thinking: *eikasia*, imagination (in the sense of making an image, a representation, of something); *pistis*, belief; *dianoia*, thinking that follows some principle of logic; *noesis*, thinking about the principles of logic.[2]

More recently, the educational psychologist Benjamin Bloom (1913-1999) identified four types of knowledge (factual, conceptual, procedural, and metacognitive) and six types of cognitive processes (remembering, understanding, applying, analyzing, evaluating, and creating), arranged in a taxonomy which school teachers can use to plan lessons and activities.[3] So when I say there's no such thing as nonlinear thinking, I am not claiming that there's only one

1 C. Vance, K. Groves, Y. Paik, & H. Kindler, "Understanding and Measuring Linear-NonLinear Thinking Style for Enhanced Management Education and Professional Practice. <u>Academy of Management Learning & Education</u>, 2007, vol.6, No.2, p.170

way to think. Clearly, there are many. But take a look at the different ways of thinking distinguished by Plato, and by Bloom. You will notice that none of them are especially or necessarily 'nonlinear'. Not even creativity, the sixth of Bloom's cognitive processes, is without a critical or systematic side, as we shall see when we discuss Imagination as a good thinking habit.

By declaring up-front like this that there's no substantial difference between linear and nonlinear thinking, indeed that the very distinction is very probably a false dichotomy, I realise that I am going against what most people take to be common sense. I'm also going against more than half a century of pop culture and peer pressure reinforcement; Think of characters like Spock, from *Star Trek*, the man whose commitment to logic requires him to suppress his emotions. My hope is that after you have read this book, the next time someone tells you that your thinking is too linear and that you should learn to think more creatively, or more 'different' somehow, 'out of the box' or 'out of your comfort zone', you will be able to reply by showing that you have been doing so all along, and that you know how to do so better than them.

Why is good thinking important?

The really important distinction is not between logical and non-logical thinking. It's between good thinking and bad thinking. Yet some people might feel personally uncomfortable, or even threatened, by this distinction. Your thoughts are probably the most intimate and the most precious of all your possessions. Your mind, indeed, is the only part of you that is truly 'yours', and cannot be taken away from you. Thus if someone tells you that your thinking is muddled, confused, unclear, or just plain mistaken, then you might feel hurt or offended.

Some people resist learning how to reason because they find their intuitive beliefs make them feel good, and they don't want anything to interfere with those feelings. Or, perhaps they worry that if they think about their beliefs very deeply, then they may have to change their beliefs, and as a result perhaps change their lives. But notice that these are all still *reasons* for

why people don't like reasoning. It always happens that when people explain why they don't like to intellectually examine their beliefs, their explanation becomes, itself, an intellectual examination of their beliefs.

But your thinking certainly *can* be muddled or confused. Normally, bad quality thinking happens when your mind has been 'possessed', so to speak, by old comfortable habits, or by the influence of other people. This can happen in various ways.

In your life so far, you have gathered a lot of beliefs about a lot of different topics. You believe things about who you are, what the world is like, where you belong in the world, and what to do with your life. You have beliefs about what is good music and bad music, what kind of movies are funny and what kind are boring, whether it's right or wrong to get a tattoo, whether the police can be trusted, whether or not there is a God, and so on. These beliefs came from somewhere. Most of you probably gathered your most important beliefs during your childhood. You learned them from your family, especially your parents, your teachers at school, your piano instructor or your karate instructor, your religious leader, your medical doctor, your friends, and just about anybody who had any kind of influence on your life. There is nothing wrong with learning things from other people this way; indeed, we probably couldn't get much of a start in life without this kind of influence. But if you have accepted your beliefs from these sources, and not done your own thinking about them, then they are not your beliefs, and you are not truly thinking your own thoughts. They are, instead, someone else's thoughts and beliefs, occupying your mind. If you believe something only because someone else taught it to you, and not because you examined those beliefs on your own, then in an important sense, you are not having your own thoughts. And if you are not having your own thoughts, then you are not living your own life, and you are not truly free.

My view is that everyone will benefit if more and more people learn how to reason, and how to reason *well*. Rationality can benefit your life in so many ways:

---

2 See the Parable of the Divided Line, in Plato, The Republic, book 6, 509d-511e
3 Krathwohl, D.R. "A revision of Bloom's Taxonomy: An Overview." Theory Into Practice, 41(4), 2002, pp. 212-218.

- You will be in greater conscious control of your own mind and thoughts.
- It will be harder for advertising, political propaganda, peer pressure, scams and confidence tricks, or other forms of psychological manipulation, to affect you.
- When your actions or motives are questioned, you will be much better able to explain yourself effectively and persuasively.
- You will be able to understand difficult, complex, and challenging ideas a lot easier, and with a lot less anxiety.
- You will be able to understand things in a more comprehensive and complete way.
- You will be better able to identify the true sources of your problems, and better able to handle or solve those problems.
- You will feel much less frustrated or upset when you come across something that you do not understand.
- You will be better able to plan for the future, compete for better paying or more prestigious jobs, and to gather political power.
- You will find it easier to stand up to governments, employers, and other authorities when they act unjustly.
- Tragedies, bad fortune, stress, and other problems in life will be easier to deal with.
- You will find it easier to understand other people's feelings and other people's points of view.
- Differences in opinions between you and others will not lead to conflict as often.
- You will get much more pleasure and enjoyment from the arts, music, poetry, science, and culture.
- You may even enjoy life more than you otherwise would.

Let me add (again!) that the use of reason doesn't shut out one's feelings, or the benefit of the arts or of human relationships, or any of the apparently non-logical things that make life enjoyable and fun. Indeed, in classical and mediaeval philosophy reason was said to be the very presence of God within the human soul. It is by means of reason that a human being could get inside the mind of God, and obtain an experience of eternity. Reason can be a spiritual thing. But, alas, I'll have to discuss that prospect in more detail another time.

Probably the most important fields in human life where words display their power, are the fields of politics, economics, religion, education, and the like— the public realms where words configure the power relations that obtain between people. This edition of this book was prompted by the author's observation that the words configuring the power-relations in the western world's public realms were becoming increasingly *weaponized*, especially by people who are immersed in a culture of anti-intellectualism. (Perhaps this is also happening in other parts of the world, but I don't know enough about that to say.) We in the various 'Western' countries live in a social and cultural environment where "alternative facts", "post truth", and "fake news", has replaced truth, snarkiness and hurtful forms of comedy have replaced serious progressive debate, and the word *reality* itself serves only to get attention for various artificial contrivances: "reality TV", "virtual reality", "real fruit flavour!".

Over the centuries, thoughtful individuals and their associates used reason, evidence, argument, scientific observation and persuasion, to work for a more free, peaceful, wise, and just society. Consider a few examples:

WANG ANSHI (11TH century): Chinese economist who transformed the civil service examination system to prevent nepotism. He instituted various reforms in government to protect the rights of the poor, especially poor farmers.

MARTIN LUTHER (1483—1546): Christian monk from Saxony, who translated the Bible into German so that ordinary people could read it and decide for themselves what it meant. His public condemnations of corrupt practices in the Roman Church (especially including the sale of indulgences) led to the creation of a new kind of Christianity: Protestantism.

NELLIE McCLUNG (1873—1951): Canadian politician who, together with four associates (the 'Famous Five'), campaigned to change Canadian law so that women would be recognized as persons. This allowed women to vote, and to hold political offices including appointment to the Senate.

EDWARD R. MURROW (1908—1965): American journalist and broadcaster. He was one of the first reporters to describe to the world the crimes against humanity, which took place at the Buchenwald Nazi concentration camp. He also systematically exposed, and effectively stopped, the Communist conspiracy paranoia promoted by Wisconsin Senator Joseph McCarthy.

WILLIAM WILBERFORCE (1759—1833): British evangelical Christian who was the most influential voice in the movement to abolish slavery in the British empire in 1807.

VACLAV HAVEL (1936—2011): Playwright, poet, and political activist who campaigned against unjust prosecutions. Eventually becoming President of Czechoslovakia, he oversaw the dismantling of communism in his country, and of the Warsaw Pact military alliance.

FLORENCE NIGHTINGALE (1820—1910): Military nurse during the Crimean War, who secularized and expanded the profession of nursing, and who campaigned for the improvement of public health in the British Empire.

In their own time, many of these people were ridiculed or persecuted. Some of them were, and still are, controversial figures, because of other things they did. But all of them changed the world for the better, in great or small ways, and at great personal risk, through the courageous use of their intelligence. I'm going to be bold here and claim that every successful social reformer the world has ever known has also been a rational and critical thinker and speaker. Regardless of their profession, every successful social and political reform was made possible by people who carefully and logically observed, examined and judged the world around them. Even great religious prophets and their supporters had to show that their teachings could withstand rational scrutiny, and were not simply, nor only, a matter of revelation.

By studying logic and critical thinking, you will be equipping yourself with the same skills that enabled them, and people like them, to become heroes. As an exercise, see if you can think of more people to add to this list, and give a few reasons to support why they belong there.

About the Organization Of This Book

The chapters of this book roughly follow a path that I shall refer to as 'The Process of Reasoning'. This process has four steps, as follows:

- OBSERVE AND QUESTION. This first stage requires us to gather as much information as we can about one's situation and one's problems. This stage is studied in chapters two and three, where we discuss questions, and various good and bad thinking habits.
- EXAMINE POSSIBILITIES. This stage teaches a few techniques and skills that can help us tell the difference between good and bad answers to your questions. We study these skills in chapters four through to seven, when we look at arguments and fallacies.
- MAKE YOUR DECISION. The process of reasoning almost always ends with some kind of judgment or choice, or decision to be made, whether it's a decision about what to believe or about what to do. This stage is covered in chapters eight and nine, when we look at reasonable doubt and moral reasoning.
- OBSERVE AND QUESTION AGAIN. The last stage is like a return to the first stage. It involves looking at one's decisions, and perhaps also the consequences that may have followed from them, as new events in the world which can be observed and questioned alongside any other events.

Also, you'll notice some words and phrases are printed in boldface. These are terms that are defined in the glossary, at the end of the book.

All right—prologue done. Now, here we go!

Chapter One:
An Outline History of Logic

THE PRINCIPLES OF LOGIC are often taught as if they are universal, timeless, a discovered feature of the world and of the human mind comparable to the principles of physics and other sciences. However, they had a history; they emerged from the lives of people in various times and places who faced various philosophical, social, personal, and intellectual problems, and who gave their solutions to the world. Over time these solutions embedded themselves in academia and in culture, such that many of them them are now taken to be common sense. But what looks like common sense today was in the past not so common, and not seen as obviously sensible. More often than not, somebody somewhere had to struggle for it. Here's a very brief history of that struggle: how the concepts of logic unfolded over the centuries, and how our ideas about the nature and purpose of logic also changed.

1.1. We Usually Say It Began in Greece...

The Pre-Socratics (6ᵗʰ century BCE–4ᵗʰ century BCE)
Thales of Miletus (c. 600 BCE)
Pythagoras of Samos (c. 570–500 BCE)
Xenophanes of Colophon (c. 570 BCE)
Parmenides of Elea (c. 500 BCE)
Heraclitus of Ephesus (c. 500 BCE)
Zeno of Elea (c. 475 BCE)

Philosophy, and the principles of reason, begin with curiosity and wonder. For Western civilization, it began somewhere before the beginning of its recorded history, reaching back to the time of authors like

Homer and Hesiod, the nameless composers of stories like *The Epic of Gilgamesh,* and those who produced the very earliest books of the Torah. In this period, philosophical questions tended to ask: Which god was responsible for this or that feature of the world, and why? What must we do to please the gods, or to placate their anger if they are not pleased with us?

Somewhere in the sixth century BCE, some people in Greece decided that the old stories no longer satisfied their needs. They still felt awe at the immensities of the universe, but they also experienced an intellectually curious kind of feeling that was not widely attested in earlier Greek poetry and literature. They began asking *naturalistic* questions, such as: What force, or what substance, is responsible for the way things are? Is the universe ultimately one big thing, or is it a collection of many separate things? Is there a rationally understandable process that governs why things come into being and why they pass away? What happens to us when we die?

Well, some of those questions were perhaps already ancient. The elaborate Paleolithic burial mounds are perhaps evidence that ancient people wondered about the soul, the nature of the world, and so on. Calendar stones like the one at Newgrange, Ireland, or the solar alignments in stone circles like Stonehenge, England, similarly attest to Neolithic people's analytic abilities. But what was new, with the advent of philosophy, was a *naturalistic* way of looking at things—a way of investigating the world with an eye for natural, material explanations instead of supernatural or mythological explanations.

Here's an illustration. There's a story in one of Aristotle's books, the *Metaphysics*, about how the people of Miletus, a trading town on the east coast of the Aegean Sea, discovered that the shape of the coast had slowly changed over time, such that their harbour ended up landlocked. Instead of asking why the god of the sea might be angry, they asked why the land might have changed shape on its own. They concluded that the river Meander (the English word *meander* comes from the name of this river, because of its wandering, snake-like path) had carried sand and stones in its current and deposited them at the mouth, slowly over time, but consistently enough to push back the edge of the sea several yards away from where it had been when the town was established. The first philosopher in the history of Western civilization whose name survives to this day came from that same town. His name was Thales, and his most important theory was that the substance of the world was somehow alive. Aristotle quoted him as saying the soul 'is mixed in the whole, and perhaps this is why Thales thought all things are full of gods'. Thales thought that soul was what made it possible for things to move. So, if things like magnetic rocks, or amber with its static-electric properties (the Greek word for amber is *ēlektron*), could make things move, they must have soul. Water, in particular, interested him: He thought that the earth rests on water in much the same way that wood floats. Aristotle said of him: 'Maybe he [Thales] got this idea from seeing that the nourishment of all things is moist… and the seeds of all things have a moist nature; and water is the principle of the nature of moist things'.[1] Now, you might think the idea that water is somehow responsible for the shape of the world is a little silly. But it is, at least, a naturalistic explanation of things. If you want to disprove it, you have to reason along with it to find the flaws in its logic, or else find a logically stronger alternative. If you make a habit of reasoning about things that way, you might end up a philosopher. (Oh, dear!)

By the way, the town of Miletus still exists, and the coast is now ten kilometres away!

It's from early thinkers like Thales—we call them the Pre-Socratics now, because they came before

Socrates—that we have inherited some of the basics of logic. I'll draw attention to only a few here, to give you an overview:

Pythagoras invented several basic mathematical axioms such as the theorem about the sides of triangles that bears his name. He may also have been the first to use the term *philo-sophus*, the love of wisdom.

Xenophanes introduced the distinction between certain knowledge and mere opinion, especially when it comes to knowledge of the gods.

Parmenides is the first recorded idealist. He believed that Being cannot come from Non-Being, i.e. things that exist cannot have emerged out of nothing, nor can things that exist pass into non-existence: 'What is, is; what is not, is not'. Since this is contrary to what our senses tell us, he argued that our senses deceive us. The world is ultimately 'one' and it is through thinking instead of sense-experience that we discover that it is one: 'For to think is the same as to be'.

Heraclitus, who is often treated as a counterpoint to Parmenides, argued that all the world was a 'fire' that was constantly kindling and going out at the same rate. However, by 'fire" he did not mean a substance or type of energy. Rather, this is a dynamic process that maintains stability through constant flux. Another of his expressions of this idea is 'one cannot step into the same river twice'. Moreover, in his thinking, all change in the world is governed by a single natural law, which he called the *Logos*.

Zeno invented several logical **paradoxes**, the most famous of which is the paradox of Achilles and the Tortoise. Suppose the Homeric hero Achilles was in a running race with a tortoise, and the tortoise was given a head start. When they begin, Achilles must run up to the place where the tortoise had begun. But by the time he gets there, the tortoise has moved on, and remains ahead of him in the race. Achilles must now run up to it again, but as before, by the time he reaches the place where the animal once was, it has already moved on. And this goes on forever—so it's impossible for Achilles to ever catch the tortoise. Yes, I know it seems absurd: that's what makes it a paradox. The idea is to show that there's something wrong with the conceptions people were coming into this exercise

---

1 Fragments of Thales cited in Curd & McKirahan, A Presocratics Reader, (Indianapolis: Hackett, 1995) pp. 10-11.

with.

1.2. ...With Men Like Socrates of Athens (469–399 BCE)

Socrates is the first Greek philosopher whose life story and logical methods have survived mostly intact. He's also noteworthy for claiming to be uncommitted to any of the big world-building theories that came from the philosophers before him. Instead of saying he knew the answers to the big questions, he'd say he knew *that he did not know* the answers. Statements of this kind are now called **Socratic wisdom**. Unlike his predecessors who mostly inquired about nature, Socrates usually asked questions about ethics and human affairs, such as: What is piety? What is the true value of money and wealth? What is our duty to the community or the state? What is love? What is justice? What is art and beauty? What does it take to lead a truly worthwhile life?

Socrates did not spell out his method in detail. Of course, that's because he didn't write down any of his philosophy at all; everything we know about him comes from the writings of others, especially his student Plato. Still, it's possible to infer his method by paying attention to how he does things. Mostly, Socrates would ask someone philosophical questions like the ones above, and then examine their answers in order to discover hidden ambiguities or contradictions. This method has come to be known as Socratic dialogue. Although it has its limitations, this method has the great advantage of helping everyone involved in the activity to achieve more precision in their search for answers, and it promotes intellectual honesty in the search. At the end of this book there is a more detailed description of how this works, and you and your friends can try it yourselves.

Socratic dialogue, and philosophical debate in general, became important in classical Greek society for two main reasons. The first, and perhaps the more obvious reason, is that it was a method for seeking the truth of things which relied only on one's own intelligence. With philosophy, you didn't have to rely on what you were told by priests, ancient traditions,

Socrates is noteworthy for claiming to be uncommitted to any of the big world-building theories that came from the philosophers before him. Instead of saying he knew the answers to the big questions, he'd say he knew that *he did not know* the answers. Statements of this kind are now called *Socratic wisdom*.

or politicians if you didn't want to. Philosophy also provided an enjoyable way to for people exercise their minds together. *In* a time before television, newspapers, radio, and the internet, philosophical debate was a common dinner party entertainment. Guests might have been asked to come to the party prepared to discuss, or even give short speeches on, a question that had been chosen in advance. A dinner party debate was called a *symposium*; and to this day, some academic conferences are still called symposiums.

The other reason it became important is that around 508 BCE, Athens invented a new-fangled form of government that enabled all citizens, not just aristocrats, warlords, or priests, to participate in public decision making. That form of government was called democracy—rule by the people. And for a democracy to work, all citizens had to be involved—in fact, some of the important government offices were chosen by lottery. (Though we remind the reader that the citizenry of ancient Athens did not include women, slaves, or resident foreigners.) The Greeks had a word for people who refused to partake in politics: *idiotes*, from which we get the modern English word *idiot*. So, studying philosophy (or if not philosophy, then at least rhetoric and oratory) looked to many Athenians like a kind of civic necessity. If you wanted people to agree with your ideas for how things should be done, you had to know how to persuade and influence them. And to do that, you had to know how to think, and how to speak convincingly.

But Socrates, after having used this method in debates for some time, eventually came to believe that nobody really knew what they thought they knew. He also believed that only he knew that he didn't know anything, and it was therefore his duty to publicly point out that most people didn't know what they claimed to know. And this, as you can imagine, really angered some people. From their point of view, the humility of Socratic wisdom looked more like a sophisticated kind of hubris. Socrates was eventually arrested, charged with 'corrupting the youth' and other crimes, found guilty, and executed. He thus became philosophy's first documented martyr.

1.3. But It Also Began in China...

Lao Tzu (6th–5th century BCE)
Confucius (551–479 BCE)
Mencius (372–289 BCE)
Chuang Tzu (369–286 BCE)
Hui Shih (380–305 BCE)

At about this point in the story, some of you might be wondering whether anyone in other parts of the world was also inventing logic. The answer is yes—although what was developed elsewhere might not look like the same kind of logic they had in Athens. Here's one reason why:

> Practically all major ancient Chinese philosophical schools were greatly concerned with the relationship between names and actuality, whether for its social and moral significance (as in Confucianism), for its metaphysical import (as in Taoism), or for political control (as in Legalism). None of them was interested in the logical aspect of the problem...The only school that was primarily devoted to logical considerations was the Logicians, who constituted one of the smallest schools and exercised no influence whatsoever after their own time...They represent the only tendency in ancient China toward intellectualism for its own sake.[2]

About those Logicians, then: their leader was a man named Hui Shih, whose teachings mostly consisted of various paradoxical and contradictory sayings that he and his students would debate for fun. Here are a few of them:

> The egg has hair.
> A chicken has three legs.
> Ying (the capital of Ch'u) contains the whole world.
> A dog can be a sheep.
> The horse has eggs.
> The frog has a tail.
> Fire is not hot.
> Mountains produce mouths.
> The wheel never touches the ground.
> The eye does not see.

2 Wing-Tsit Chan, A Source Book in Chinese Philosophy, (Princeton University Press, 1963) pp. 232-4.

A puppy is not a dog.

The pointing of the finger does not reach [a thing]: the reaching never ends.

Take a stick one foot long and cut it in half every day and you will never exhaust it even after ten thousand generations.[3]

Notice how the last two sayings listed here are remarkably similar to some of Zeno's Paradoxes.

As noted above, the right use of words and language were important in all three of the main branches of ancient Chinese philosophy: Confucianism, Taoism, and Legalism. A central principle of Confucianism, for instance, is called 'The Rectification of Names'. This is a demand for clarity and precision in one's speech, especially when moral and political principles are being discussed. Here's how Confucius himself introduced the concept and explained its importance:

> Tzu-lu said, 'The ruler of Wei is waiting for you to serve in his administration. What will be your first measure?' Confucius said, 'It will certainly be the rectification of names…If names are not rectified, then language will not be in accord with truth. If language is not in accord with truth, then things cannot be accomplished. If things cannot be accomplished, then ceremonies and music will not flourish. If ceremonies and music do not flourish, then punishment will not be just. If punishments are not just, then the people will not know how to move hand or foot. Therefore, the superior man will give only names that can be described in speech and say only what can be carried out in practice. With regard to his speech, the superior man does not take it lightly. That is all.'[4]

And here's Confucius describing the importance of what Western philosophers call Socratic wisdom:

> Confucius said, 'Yu, shall I teach you [the way to acquire] knowledge? To say that you know when you do know, and to say that you do not know when you do not know – that is the way to acquire knowledge.'[5]

The antithetical position was expressed by Lao Tzu in the cryptic first lines of the *Tao Te Ching*: 'The Tao that can be told of is not the eternal Tao. The name that can be named is not the eternal name'.[6] Lao Tzu was saying that there are some things or events in the world whose meaning cannot be expressed in words; or if some part of their meaning can be expressed, the totality of their meanings cannot. This 'Tao' itself is the prime example of such a word. It's notoriously untranslatable; the nearest English equivalent concept would be 'the way of nature'. Lao Tzu's point seems to be that the words for things and events are not the same as the things and events in themselves. Moreover, words and language have limitations, but these limitations need not be the same as the limitations of our knowledge. But this is an ancient debate, and I won't pretend to solve it here.

Confucius led a rather adventurous live for a career intellectual. His first important job was Minister of Crime (kind of like an Attorney General) in the state of Lu, which was a kingdom during China's Warring States period. He was so effective in this job that crime was nearly extirpated during his tenure. So, feeling confident in his ideas, he persuaded his boss, Duke Deng, to order the demolition of the walls surrounding three cities in the kingdom. This would compel those cities to trust each other, and it would make it harder for those cities to rebel. One of them refused, which forced Deng to lay siege to the city (to assert his authority), and Confucius had to resign his post and go into exile. He took a small crowd of students with him, and while they were on the road they copied his teachings into books. Those books went on to inspire nearly all of Chinese religious and political thought to the present day.

Alas, most of we know about philosophy and logic in ancient China comes in fragments. Between the years 213 and 206 BCE, long after important thinkers like Confucius, Lao Tzu, Mencius, and Chuang Tzu had lived and died, the leadership of the Qin dynasty attempted to erase all previous dynasties from history. Therefore, they burned books, destroyed schools, and killed scholars. As a result, although we know *that* work had been done on the rules of reasoning in

---

3 ibid. pp. 234-8.   **4** Analects 13:3, cited in ibid. p. 40.   **5** Analects 2:17, cited in ibid. p. 24.   **6** ibid. p. 139

The sages searching in their hearts with wisdom, found out the bond of being in non-being. Their ray extended light across the darkness: But was the One above or was it under? Creative force was there, and fertile power: Below was energy, above was impulse. *Who knows for certain?*

ancient China, we have a hard time knowing exactly *what*, exactly, it was.

1.4. ...And in India, As Well.

The Vedas (first composed between 1700–1100 BCE) Siddhartha Gautama, a.k.a. The Buddha (563–483 BCE)

The loss or destruction of documents also prevents us from knowing exactly how logic developed in ancient India. Thus, we tend to know more about the *conclusions* reached by ancient Indian and Chinese philosophers than we know about the *methods* they used to reach them. But for all that, we know that in ancient India there was a culture of questioning and of using reason to find answers. The Vedas, India's ancient holy books, provide evidence for it. Here's a selection:

> The sages searching in their hearts with wisdom,
> Found out the bond of being in non-being.
> Their ray extended light across the darkness:
> But was the One above or was it under?
> Creative force was there, and fertile power:
> Below was energy, above was impulse.
> Who knows for certain? Who shall here declare it?
> Whence was it born, and whence came this creation?
> The gods were born after this world's creation:
> Then who can know from whence it has arisen?
> None knoweth whence creation has arisen;
> And whether he has or has not produced it. [7]

Along with the poetically-expressed philosophical questions, we can see something which, to my eyes, resembles Socratic wisdom: the idea that nobody, not even the gods, knows the nature of the world, nor does anyone know how it was created.

Nor is it the only example of Indian philosophy independently deliberating on the same ideas as Westerners. The Nyaya School of orthodox Hinduism held that 'Perception, inference, comparison and word (verbal testimony)' are 'the means of right knowledge'. [8] There is some circumstantial evidence that Nyaya School ideas influenced 19th-century Western logicians

7 'Hymn of Creation' x.129.4, cited in Radhakrishnan and Moore, Indian Philosophy, p. 23.
8 Cited in Radhakrishan & Moore, Indian Philosophy, p. 359. **9** Jonardon Ganeri (2001). Indian Logic: A Reader, Routledge. pp. vii; 5; 7.
10 Kisor Kumar Chakrabarti (June 1976). 'Some Comparisons Between Frege's Logic and Navya-Nyaya Logic'. Philosophy and Phenomenological Research.
 International Phenomenological Society. 36 (4): 554–563.

including Babbage, DeMorgan, and Boole.[9] There is also evidence that this school hit upon the distinction between the sense and the reference of the meaning of words, in much the same way that Gottlob Frege did in the early 20TH century.[10]

Elsewhere in ancient India, the philosopher Siddhartha Gautama encouraged autonomous reasoning in his teachings. In a famous address to a people called the Kalamas, he said:

> Do not go upon what has been acquired by repeated hearing; nor upon tradition; nor upon rumor; nor upon what is in a scripture; nor upon surmise; nor upon an axiom; nor upon specious reasoning; nor upon a bias towards a notion that has been pondered over; nor upon another's seeming ability; nor upon the consideration, 'The monk is our teacher.' Kalamas, when you yourselves know: 'These things are bad; these things are blameable; these things are censured by the wise; undertaken and observed, these things lead to harm and ill,' abandon them.[11]

This text is regarded by Buddhists as a kind of manifesto for independent critical thinking, and is admired by many non-Buddhists as well. It encourages us not to automatically believe something just because various people or social forces around may be encouraging us to believe it. Instead, it says we should believe or not believe on the basis of whether we find the belief acceptable. Elsewhere in the same text, there's a discussion of why it is wise to lead a moral life even if some common features of Indian religion, such as karma and reincarnation, turn out to be wrong. To me, this argument strongly resembles the **game theory** used in **Pascal's Wager**.

Much like Confucius and Socrates, Prince Siddhartha also led an adventurous life. Born the son of a king, he renounced his wealth and privilege to become a spiritual seeker. He travelled around northern India, studied under various teachers, and lived in a kind of voluntary poverty, in order to prevent distraction from his purpose. He eventually found a solitary place in the heart of a forest where he could work out the answers to important philosophical questions such as

'Why do we suffer?' and 'What must we do to find true happiness?' Having found satisfactory answers to these, he became the first Buddha—one who has awakened from the sleep of ignorance and ended the cycle of suffering—and his answers became the foundational teachings of Buddhism.

Sometime around the 5TH century CE, just less than a thousand years after the Buddha was alive, Indians built one of the world's first universities: Nalanda, in what is now Bihar province. Comparable in its aims to Plato's Academy, the Ancient Library of Alexandria, and Baghdad's House of Wisdom, Nalanda was a Buddhist university that attracted students and scholars from all over Asia, even from as far away as Indonesia. Some reports say the university's library building was nine stories tall, and besides classics of Buddhism, it also held works on logic, sciences (especially astrology and astronomy), literature, and medicine. Some versions of the story of Nalanda say was destroyed in 1193 CE during a Muslim invasion of the area. A Turkic warlord, who had fallen ill and was cured by a scholar from Nalanda, felt ashamed that his Muslim medicine was not as advanced as Buddhist medicine, and so he ordered the library destroyed. Other stories suggest that it was already in ruins when the Muslims arrived, having been sacked three times and rebuilt twice.[12] But in 2014, a newly revived Nalanda University, in the nearby town of Rajgir, accepted its first students.[13]

1.5. Plato of Athens (c. 424—348 BCE)

Socrates' best student, Plato, became the most influential philosopher in the history of Western civilization. For him, logic and reason were something divine: they could make the shapes and movements of our thoughts follow the shapes and movements of the universe as a whole. There are many passages in his books which attest to this view of the purpose of reason: here's one which appears in *Timaeus*, Plato's dialogue on cosmology and the creation of the world:

> The motions which are naturally akin to the divine principle within us are the thoughts and revolutions of the universe. These each man should follow, and correct

11 'Kalama Sutta: The Buddha's Charter of Free Inquiry', translated from the Pali by Soma Thera. Access to Insight, 7 June 2010.
12 Bhatt, Rakesh Kumar. History and Development of Libraries in India. (New Delhi, India: Mittal Publications, 1995)
13 Shreya Pareek, "The Ancient University Which Is Taking Students Again After 800 Years" The Better India, 2nd September 2014.

the courses of the head which were corrupted at our birth, and by learning the harmonies and revolutions of the universe, should assimilate the thinking being to the thought, renewing his original nature, and having assimilated them should attain to that perfect life which the gods have set before mankind, both for the present and the future.[14]

This is an essentially *mystical* view of the reason why we reason (!) We do it so we can govern our lives in a way similar to how the Divine Reason governs the cosmos. This view had its critics in the next few decades following Plato's time, notably the Epicureans, who were among the world's first organized atheists. Nonetheless, this mystical notion of the purpose of reason remained at the centre of western philosophy for more than a thousand years.

1.6. Aristotle of Stagira (384–322 BCE)

Plato's student Aristotle made the next major contribution to the history of logic (in the West), with what is now known as categorical logic. Aristotle thought that we could reason more precisely and more efficiently by using words in a more systematic way. His method involved identifying classes of things and then discussing statements about the relations between the members of those classes. If 'all cats are mammals' is true, for instance, it does not logically follow that therefore 'all mammals are cats'. But if 'some tables have four legs', it *must* follow that 'some tables do not have four legs'. There's more to it than that, of course, and we'll see more of it in the chapter on argumentation.

Aristotle also developed a theory of scientific explanation. In his theory, a scientific explanation is a movement from knowledge of the facts to knowledge of the reasons for the facts. If you had complete knowledge of what something is and why that's what it is, then you would know its essence. An essence, for Aristotle, is that which something ultimately *is*; or to be more precise, it is the *formal proposition* which expresses that which something ultimately is. It therefore becomes extremely important to use your words with wisdom-loving care.

The first thing one must do as an Aristotelian scientist is to describe the facts as precisely and completely as possible. There are ten categories; i.e., ten ways to describe something. For an example of how this works, suppose I was describing a certain car that I can see from my window. I would have to describe the:

- *Substance* (the thing you are describing): The individual car itself.
- *Quantity*: Three meters long, nearly twelve thousand kilograms.
- *Quality*: Red.
- *Relation*: Bigger than a bread box; smaller than a house.
- *Place*: In the parking lot across the street.
- *Time*: Now.
- *Position*: Upright, balanced on its wheels.
- *Condition*: A little muddy, some rust around the edges of the wheel wells.
- *Action*: Slowly moving forward.
- *Affection*: Is being heated up by the sun.

Having gathered all the facts like this, the next thing to do is consider the reasons why these facts are as they are. Aristotle thought there are only four ways to do this, and these four ways taken together have come to be called the doctrine of the four causes. The four causes are:

The *efficient* cause: what agent or force is responsible for shaping or putting together or bringing about the thing? This corresponds to our usual way of understanding the word 'cause'. The other three causes require us to think of the word 'cause' a little differently. If I was still studying the car I mentioned above, the efficient cause would be the manufacturing plant where the car was assembled, all its machinery and workers, perhaps also the factory's corporate management and stockholders, etc.

The *material* cause: what material or 'stuff' is the thing made of? The material cause of my car would be the metal, rubber, plastic, upholstery in the seats, and so on.

---

14 Timaeus 90d; cited in The Dialogues of Plato, trans. B. Jowett, (NY: Random House, 1892-1920) Vol.2, p. 66.

The *formal* cause: what form, or shape, is the thing in? What 'species' does it belong to? Note that this 'form' is seen with the eye of the mind, not the eye of the body. The word being translated here is *eidos*, which is also the word for 'species'. It derives from the verb *idein*, 'to see', from which we get the English word 'idea'. This works in Latin, too: the English word 'species' comes from *speculare*, 'to see'. [15] The formal cause of the car would be not simply the physical shape and measurable dimensions, but also the idea of a car, which it shares in some curious way with all other cars.

The *final* cause: why does this thing exist? Does it have a purpose, a function, or a job to do, or is there some other *reason* why it's here? The final cause of a car could be 'because people need transport', 'because investors in car companies want a return on their investment', 'to bestow social prestige upon the owner, in the manner of other conspicuously expensive consumer products', or the like. Notice the final cause tends to be general in nature, and not an explanation of any particular individual car.

Aristotle's system of logic became the dominant model of scientific method in Europe for the next thousand years.

Before we leave Athens, I should mention Chrysippus of Soli (280–206 BCE), who built upon the Aristotelian model of logic to invent another one, which we now call propositional logic. His system treated simple statement-sentences as the basic unit of logic: these are statements that might not be about categories (though they could be), which cannot be divided into simpler sentences, such as 'The cat is sleeping', or 'the book is open'. He also developed a set of indicators to build more complex propositions such as 'if/then', 'and', 'either/or', and 'more/less likely'. These allow us to treat compound statements like 'If there's wine in the jug, then we should drink it' as if they are single statements. Chrysippus was also a leader of the Stoic tradition of philosophy: a tradition which was, at the time, a rival of the Academy, the school that was carrying on the teachings of Plato. It is possible that Chrysippus developed propositional logic as a

means to defend Stoicism from the arguments of other philosophers.

1.7. The Great Library of Alexandria (c. 295 BCE)

Theon of Alexandria (335–405 CE)
Hypatia of Alexandria (?–417 CE)

After finishing his studies at the Academy, Aristotle went back to Macedonia to take up a job tutoring the son of King Philip II of Macedon. The boy would grow up to become Alexander the Great, who conquered nearly everything between Greece and what's now Pakistan. Along the way he also conquered Egypt, and on an island near the mouth of the Nile he established a city that bears his name to this day: Alexandria. Perhaps remembering his teacher's influence, or the accounts of the many educated Greeks who visited Egypt to study their books (including Herodotus the historian, Theophrastus, and Eudoxus, as well as Plato), Alexander wished to establish a library in this city, to collect as much knowledge as possible in a single place. Alexander died before the library was properly begun. But his successor as ruler of Egypt, Ptolemy I Soter, with the assistance of a Greek philosopher named Demetrius of Phaleron (who had just lost political favour in Athens and was looking for a new job), established the Library around the year 295 BCE. The project was ambitious. As one contemporary account put it:

> Demetrius…had at his disposal a large budget in order to collect, if possible, all the books in the world…to the best of his ability, he carried out the king's objective. [16]

The scholars searched every ship that came to the city, buying or borrowing (for the purpose of making copies) all the books they found on board. The library eventually came to be housed in two main buildings: The Great Library, which was located somewhere on the island of Alexandria near the dockyards, and an expansion building on the mainland attached to a temple called the Serapeum. Some accounts say the

---

15 This analysis by way of Greek and Latin is derived from J. Lavery and J. Mitscherling, An Outline History of Western Thought, unpublished manuscript in my possession, p. 16.
16 Letters of Aristeas, pp. 9-10.

library boasted around 200,000 books by the end of the reign of Ptolemy I. There are other accounts, however, which say that the library housed only half that number by the time of Ptolemy's successor, Ptolemy II. It has been claimed that by 47 BCE, some 700,000 of the library's books were destroyed in a fire, when Julius Caesar got involved in a civil war between Queen Cleopatra and her brother Ptolemy XIII. [17] However, there is some evidence that the books in the Serapeum survived. In the 4th century CE, when Alexandria was a province of the Roman empire, the head librarian was a man named Theon of Alexandria, who was probably a philosopher in the Neoplatonic tradition. His daughter Hypatia of Alexandria became one of the most famous names associated with the library in its entire history. Most of the evidence shows that she was well respected as a public intellectual, and one account of her life says:

> Hypatia was born and educated in Alexandria. Since she had greater intelligence than her father, she was not satisfied with his instruction in mathematical subjects and she devoted herself diligently to philosophical studies. This woman used to put on her philosopher's cloak and walk through the middle of town. She publicly interpreted Plato, Aristotle, or the works of any other philosopher for everybody who wished to hear her. In addition to her expertise in teaching she rose to the pinnacle of civic virtue. [18]

By this time, however, the Roman empire was internally divided along religious lines. Christians in Alexandria disapproved of her promotion of science and free thought, and they strongly disapproved of women as public intellectuals. Here's how one of the bishops described her:

> And in those days, there appeared in Alexandria a female philosopher, a pagan named Hypatia, and she was devoted at all times to magic, astrolabes and instruments of music, and she beguiled many people through satanic wiles. [19]

Most accounts of her life say that a religious fanatic named Peter the Reader incited the riot in which Hypatia was murdered. But there's another story, which says she may have been murdered because of a math problem. The Roman and Alexandrian churches disagreed about how to calculate the correct date for Easter. This disagreement was more serious than it may appear to us today, because the study of astronomy and mathematics (a science that was needed to calculate the equinox and hence the correct date for Easter) was still associated with paganism. It's also possible that the Roman calculation was too similar to the Jewish calculation for the Alexandrian church's liking. What's more, if one church was wrong about when to celebrate Easter then it might be wrong about other things too, including matters of doctrine and salvation. As a top-tier mathematician, Hypatia may have called in to settle the matter. Perhaps she concluded that the Roman calculation was correct, so (perhaps) the Alexandrians murdered her for it. [20] The evidence for this version of events is partially circumstantial, but nonetheless intriguing.

Hypatia is the last scholar of the Great Library whose name has survived to our time. Yet the library itself, or at least the Serapeum, may still have been preserved a little longer. In the year 641 CE the city was besieged by Arabs during the expansion of the Muslim empire into Egypt. The general who conquered the city, 'Amr ibn al-'As, wrote back to his caliph in Baghdad to ask what to do with the books. The caliph, Omar, ordered him to burn them. And so,

> …The books were distributed to the public baths of Alexandria, where they were used to feed the stoves which kept the baths so comfortably warm. Ibn al-Kifti writes that 'the number of baths was well known, but I have forgotten it' (we have Eutychius's word that there were in fact four thousand). 'They say', continues Ibn al-Kifti, 'that it took six months to burn all that mass of material.'
> Aristotle's books were the only ones spared. [21]

But by this time the Library was probably a mere shadow of its former glory. The city had been sacked and damaged several times in the previous centuries,

17 F.G. Kenyon, ed. Books and Readers in Ancient Greece and Rome, 2nd edition (Oxford: Clarendon Press, 1951) p. 27.
18 The Suda (Byzantine Encyclopaedia) cited in Hecht, J. Doubt: A History p. 207. **19** John of Nikiu (fl. 696), Chronicle, 84.87-103.
20 Ari Belenkiy, 'An Astronomical Murder?' Astronomy & Geophysics, Volume 51, Issue 2, 1 April 2010, pp. 2.9–2.13.

most notably in 391 CE when Emperor Theophrastus ordered the destruction of the pagan temples—which included the Serapeum. Furthermore, the Greek texts, the language in which most of the books were written, were likely 'crawling with errors, for Greek was increasingly a forgotten language'. [22]

In the year 2002, the government of Egypt established a new library in the city, the *Bibliotheca Alexandrina*. In addition to books, the new library also houses thousands of films and television programs, and millions of web sites, in English, French, and Arabic. But that's getting far ahead of ourselves. Our history of logic and knowledge now moves to:

1.8. The Arabs and the Persians

Al-Khwarizmi (780–850)
Al-Farabi (872–950)
Ibn Sīnā, aka Avicenna (980–1037)
Al-Ghazzali (1058–1111)
Averröes (1126–1198)

From here, our brief history of logic moves to the Arab world—for the Roman empire, inheritor of the knowledge of Greece and most of the Mediterranean world, entered a decline phase leading to a period which some historians call 'The Dark Ages'. The empire's dissolution took at least two, maybe three centuries; but one noteworthy date for our purpose is 529, the year Emperor Justinian ordered all philosophy schools to close. It's probable that some of the philosophers fled to the Arab world. One source I consulted while researching this work said that a philosopher named Simplicius, one of the last heads of Plato's Academy, fled to a town called Harran, which lies in what is now southeast Turkey.[23] Maybe he and his followers influenced Arab ideas. But it is also possible (and between us, I think more likely), that Arab philosophers had figured out the basics of reasoning on their own, just as the Indians and the Chinese had. What can be claimed with certainty, and is paradoxical, given the zeitgeist in which I presently live, is that Westerners have the Muslims to thank that Western philosophy did not disappear under the boot of one or another of Europe's

From here, our brief history of logic moves to the Arab world—for the Roman empire, inheritor of the knowledge of Greece and most of the Mediterranean world, entered a decline phase leading to a period which some historians call 'The Dark Ages'.

21 Martin Ryle, trans. Luciano Canfora, The Vanished Library: A Wonder of the Ancient World (Berkeley: University of California Press, 1990) p. 99.
22 ibid, p. 87.
23 Richard Sorabji, (2005), The Philosophy of the Commentators, 200–600 AD: Psychology (with Ethics and Religion), p 11.

own history-destroying tyrants. The philosophers Al-Farabi and Ibn Sīnā (better known in the west as Avicenna), are the outstanding figures here. Al-Farabi wrote commentaries on the works of Aristotle: He was so impressed by Aristotle that he often referred to him as 'The Teacher'. Al-Farabi himself came to be known as 'The Second Teacher'.

These and other Arabic intellectuals were associated with a Great Library of their own: the *Bayt al-Hikma*, the 'House of Wisdom'. Founded in the 8th century by Caliph Harun al-Rashid of the Abbasid dynasty, it became the world's most important centre of learning for the next five centuries. The evidence suggests that it was a vibrant, progressive, and multicultural institution. Scholars of both sexes from all over Europe, India, and the Arab world were invited; besides Arabic they spoke Greek, Latin, Farsi, Hebrew, and Hindi. There were purpose-built galleries for philosophy, science, math, literature, medicine, and other subjects, as well as an astronomical observatory. By the way, it's possible that this was the first library in the world where the majority of books were written not on vellum or leather, but on paper—the technology to make paper having been recently imported from China.

The mathematician Al-Khwarizmi deserves a special mention here. While working at the House of Wisdom he invented *al-jabr*, 'completion', which you probably know by the name of *algebra*. (It's also possible that he did not invent it whole cloth, but codified it from several separate sources.) He also hired seventy geographers to help him compile the world's first general atlas, *The Face of the Earth*; in his time, wrote the most accurate tables for predicting the motion of the planets; and composed the first general-purpose math textbook. Most importantly, he wrote *On the Calculation of Hindu Numerals*, the book that introduced the decimal system and the 'Arabic' numerals that we use today—though those numerals were probably Hindu in origin and Al-Khwarizmi himself was Persian and not an Arab. Eventually, his ideas would influence twentieth-century computer scientists. In 1936 Alan Turing published *On Computable Numbers*, a paper that describes a procedure to automate certain kinds of

problem-solving and decision-making tasks. Soon after, his associates named the procedure the *algorithm*, after the Greek word for numbers, *arithmos*, and the Latin version of Al-Khwarizmi's name: *Algoritmi*.

The House of Learning lasted until about 1258, when the Mongol king Hulagu, grandson of Genghis Khan, sacked and destroyed the city of Baghdad. Today, although the city of Baghdad still exists, nothing of the Abbasid dynasty still remains there.

1.9. Then Suddenly, It Was the Middle Ages…

Leonardo Bonacci (1175–1250)
Peter Abelard (1079–1142)
Roger Bacon (1219–1292)
William of Ockham (1287–1348)
Francis Bacon (1561–1626)
Baruch 'Blessed' Spinoza (1632–1677)

Philosophy returns to Europe around the ninth and tenth centuries, and there are two characters who are perhaps the most responsible for restoring it. One is Leonardo Bonacci, better known as Fibonacci, whom you may know from the series of numbers that bear his name. He also translated several of Al-Khwarizmi's books into Latin and thus popularized the decimal system in Europe. The other main figure here is Peter Abelard, a scholar who gained fame for himself as 'the only undefeated philosopher in the world' and for having a secret marriage with his lover Héloïse d'Argenteuil. He wrote what is probably the first general textbook in his field, *Logic for Beginners*, as well as a compilation of the works of Aristotle, called the *Organon* ('the Instrument') and several texts on theology. Abelard is closely associated with a tradition of philosophy called scholasticism, the dominant intellectual tradition of the period. These scholars aimed to bring Christian theology together with Greek and Roman philosophy, and they insisted on a strictly deductive kind of logic, avoiding contradictions on the quest for certainty. Scholasticism also followed in the tradition of Plato, which holds that the point of studying logic is to become enlightened.

We should also remember Roger Bacon, a Franciscan monk and English philosopher who anticipated later movements toward empiricism, experimental methods, and the creation of encyclopaedias. In the year 1267 Bacon sent a proposal for reforming the university education curriculum to Pope Clement IV. He called this *Opus Majus*, 'The Greater Work', perhaps because it was over 800 pages long. (He also included a summary of it, called *Opus Minor*, 'The Lesser Work'.) It covered topics including language, mathematics, and the design of experiments; a section on optics and the structure of the human eye that shows the influence of Arabic scholarship; and a section on alchemy that included the earliest European recipe for gunpowder. Bacon may thus seem like a mediaeval scholar with a modern mind. Yet his text also discusses occultism and magic, and it places theology as the ultimate foundation of all knowledge, and these moves place him securely within the Scholastic tradition of his own time. Still, people like Bacon, Ockham and Abelard show that before the advent of mass public education, there were still a few places where the love of learning was kept alive.

Another Scholastic philosopher we should bring to mind here is William of Ockham, who wanted to make theology and metaphysics more efficient. He is best known today for the logical rule of thumb which bears the name of his hometown in Surrey, England: Ockham's razor, the idea that there should be 'no unnecessary repetition of identicals', or as it is often phrased today, 'the simplest explanation tends to be the truth'.

By about the year 1250, Aristotle's works were re-established as the basis of philosophical teaching in almost all European universities and monasteries. The trouble with Scholastic philosophy is that while it's a powerful way to unpack the implications of ideas that you already took for granted (or, for that matter, which you read in a theology book), it doesn't do much to help you discover things that no one else already knows. That was the problem which Francis Bacon (no relation to Roger) set about to solve. In 1620 he published *Novum Organum* ('New Instrument'), one of the first works, and certainly the first popular one in

its time, on the principles of science. In it, he regarded Aristotle's scientific method as only a procedure for solving logic puzzles. It could help you to think clearly about things you already know, but is not helpful for discovering new knowledge. Bacon's work initiated a new tradition of philosophy, empiricism: the theory that our most important knowledge comes mainly from the experience of our physical senses. Evidence gained through *experiments is particularly valued*; especially when the experiments yield observable and mathematically quantifiable results. Bacon is also the first (documented) philosopher to suppose that we do not pursue knowledge only for enlightenment, as Plato had supposed. We also pursue it in order to *do* things: '*Nam et ipsa scientia potestas est*'—'And thus knowledge itself is power'.

By the way: in one of his private notes, Bacon described himself as having a disposition especially suited to philosophy; this moment of self-awareness is widely treated as an early definition of critical thinking:

> I found that I was fitted for nothing so well as for the study of Truth; as having a mind nimble and versatile enough to catch the resemblances of things (which is the chief point), and at the same time steady enough to fix and distinguish their subtler differences; as being gifted by nature with desire to seek, patience to doubt, fondness to meditate, slowness to assert, readiness to consider, carefulness to dispose and set in order; and as being a man that neither affects what is new nor admires what is old, and that hates every kind of imposture. So I thought my nature had a kind of familiarity and relationship with Truth.[24]

Probably the last philosopher in the Western tradition to use the old Scholastic method was Baruch 'Blessed' Spinoza. He published a book called *Ethics*, that was actually mostly about metaphysics and said very little about ethics. He followed what he called a 'geometric' kind of argumentation that started with basic axioms and then worked out their implications to reach conclusions. The Jewish community of Amsterdam, of which he was a member, decided that

---

24 De interpretatione naturæ prœmium, Works, III, pp. 518–520; cited in Ward & Trent, et al. The Cambridge History of English and American Literature. (New York: G.P. Putnam's Sons, 1907–21 / New York: Bartleby.com, 2000).

The Enlightenment thus became the period in European history in which the last remaining features of the mediaeval world were swept away *(sometimes violently)* and replaced with 'modern' ideas about the power and promise of human reason. These were desired so people could understand and master both the natural world and the human world of society and government.

his book was too pantheist and therefore heretical, so they excommunicated him. Rather than trying to earn re-admission to his community, as would have been expected of him, he withdrew to a nearby town and carried on with his usual day job as if nothing happened. (He was a lens grinder for telescopes and spectacles. However, this was a dangerous occupation: reathing the glass dust from this work gave him a lung disease that killed him when he was only 45.)

But aside from last-gasp Scholasticism like Spinoza's, Empiricism would quickly dominate European thinking. In it we find the beginning of the modern relationship between science and technology, as well as the beginning of a shift in the view of what the study of logic ought to be used for. It became less about contemplating and understanding the world, and more about *controlling* the world: less reason-as-mysticism, and more reason-as-instrument. We reason in order to prevent disease, prolong life, build bigger and longer-lasting buildings, travel longer distances in less time, and to bring about greater justice and fairness in politics and economics. And also to gain power, money, fame, beauty, sex, and nearly anything else that people may want for themselves.

1.10. ...Followed by Early Modernity, and the Enlightenment.

René Descartes (15961–650)
Blaise Pascal (1623–1662)
The Great Lisbon Earthquake (1 November 1755)
Voltaire (1694–1778)
Denis Diderot (1713–1784)
David Hume (1711–1776)
Immanuel Kant (1724–1804)

Starting around 1650, philosophers combined the empiricism of the scientists with the humanism of the Italian Renaissance, and the movement that emerged from this synthesis is generally called the Enlightenment. Probably the best manifesto of its values is the first paragraph of Immanuel Kant's essay from 1784, 'What is Enlightenment?'

Enlightenment is man's release from his self-incurred tutelage [*Unmündigkeit;* nonage, childhood, immaturity]. Tutelage is man's inability to make use of his understanding without direction from another. Self-incurred is this tutelage when its cause lies not in lack of reason but in lack of resolution and courage to use it without direction from another. *Sapere aude!* 'Have courage to use your own reason!'—that is the motto of enlightenment.[25]

The Enlightenment thus became the period in European history in which the last remaining features of the mediaeval world were swept away (sometimes violently) and replaced with 'modern' ideas about the power and promise of human reason. These were desired so people could understand and master both the natural world and the human world of society and government. Now, what they meant by 'Enlightenment' was not the same as what Plato might have meant. The thinkers associated with the movement were interested in using logic to solve scientific, moral, and political problems, rather than in promoting metaphysical or religious understandings. This is the period when scientists like Isaac Newton, Robert Hooke, and Anton and Marie Lavoisier came to prominence. It's the time of political thinkers like Locke, Rousseau, and the authors of the American constitution, all of whom were also influenced in various ways by indigenous societies in North America. (American federalism, for instance, was inspired by the Haudenosaunee Confederacy. See also the discussion of the 'state of nature' thought experiment, in chapter 9.) This is also the period when mercantilism, the system of economics that dominated the Renaissance, gave way to capitalism. Enlightenment ideas were not adopted universally across all sectors of European society, or implemented at the same rate: the movement overlaps in time with a counter-movement called Romanticism, as well as with the worst period of Europe's witch-hunting craze. Nonetheless, this was when modern values like individualism, equality, freedom, universal human rights, and democratic responsible government first gained prominence. The Enlightenment's second motto could be the one announced by the French writer Voltaire: '*Ecrasez l'Infame!*' 'Let us

crush the corrupt!')

As we usually tell the story, the first philosopher of the period is René Descartes. He is also the mathematician who invented the Cartesian Plane that you learned about in primary school, as well as the use of exponents to write large numbers in shorthand. Descartes is the one who said those famous five words everyone quotes: 'I think, therefore I am.' About those five words: Descartes was looking for the foundation of all human knowledge; so, in that respect he was looking for the same thing as everyone else I've mentioned here. But he invented a new method to find it, which he called methodological doubt. To be brief and perhaps overly simplistic about it, methodological doubt involved looking at everything he thought he knew, and declaring that if he had any reason to doubt it, no matter how small and silly that reason might be, he should declare it unfounded. If, by doing this, he could eventually hit upon a belief which he could not doubt, that belief would have to be the foundation of all the rest of his knowledge. He eventually decided that the one thing he could not doubt was his own existence. By the way, a major plank in his argument, the famous 'evil genius' who might be deceiving him in such a way as to leave him unable to tell that he is being deceived, was not his original idea. It also appears in the work of the Spanish nun Teresa of Ávila (1515–1582), whose book *Interior Castle* (1588) was tremendously popular in the early 1600s.[26] (Was he a plagiarist, or a participant in an intellectual tradition? I invite you to do the research and decide for yourself.)

About the middle of the 19th century, philosophers began pointing to the publication of Descartes' publication of his *Meditations on First Philosophy* (1647) as the beginning of modern philosophy. This was not only because of the application of methodological doubt: they pin it here because of his emphasis on the individual knower, and his shifting of philosophy's main questions away from metaphysics (that is, questions about God, the soul, etc.) and towards epistemology (that is, questions about knowledge, truth, and logic). Metaphysical speculations still played a part here: for instance, he argued that he couldn't doubt the existence of God because God wouldn't deceive him

25 Kant, 'What is Enlightenment?' cited in Isaac Kramnick, ed. The Portable Enlightenment Reader (Penguin, 1995), p. 1. The German original term and its translation is my own insertion. 26 Mercer, C. "Descartes' Debt to Teresa of Ávila, Or Why We Should Work on Women in the History of Philosophy" Philosophical Studies, Vol.174, Iss.10, pp. 2539-2555 (2017).

about God's existence. In that argument, God's existence is presupposed from the beginning, so it's a case of **circular fallacy**. But I can't hold it against him too much, given the way the power-relations of his world were configured. His *Meditations* begins with a letter to the theology professors at the University of Paris, apologising in advance for any errors he might make and asking for their help in correcting them. I think Descartes believed that as an intellectual Christian he had a responsibility to show that reason and faith were compatible. Nevertheless, he was probably bearing in mind what happened to Giordano Bruno (1548–1600) and was keen to avoid the same end.

Not long after Descartes, a group of anonymous writers who called themselves The Port Royal Logicians published the first popular and widely distributed textbook on reasoning: *Logic or the Art of Thinking* (1662). This group included Blaise Pascal, a mathematician who is best known today for inventing a working mechanical calculator (while still a teenager!), for some clever experiments with mercury barometers, and for establishing one of the first public transit systems in the world. Most of all, he's known for inventing Pascal's wager, an early form of game theory which made a non-mystical, *mathematical* argument for why people should believe in God. His idea is that the consequences of not believing in a God who does exist (such as spending an infinity in hell after death), are worse than the consequences of believing in a God who doesn't exist (such as missing out on the—finite—pleasures of one's vices). There are some straightforward criticisms of this argument. Can religious feeling can be dispassionately selected? Does the argument, or some close variation of it, also support believing in a different religion, or a different God? Is his argument so deeply embedded in his own theology that if someone were to reject or doubt some part of that theology, however small, then the whole thing would be logically unsound? Does his use of infinity, as a feature of the argument's logic, render the game incoherent? We may also wonder what Pascal's final version of the argument would have looked like. For it appeared in a book which he did not publish; it was found in a desk drawer after his death, still

unfinished. His friends published it under the title *Pensées* ('Thoughts').

Many more books on general knowledge, and on logic, were published in the decades that followed, including *Logick or the Right Use of Reason* (by Isaac Watts, 1725), *Logic* (Richard Whately, 1826) and *A System of Logic* (by John Stuart Mill, 1843). Among these books, I would like to draw special attention to *L'Encyclopédie* (first edition 1751), by Denis Diderot. The idea behind this book was to collect all human knowledge in one place, so that anyone who could read would be able to acquire a base of knowledge in anything that interested her. (Much like the Great Library of Alexandria, or the Baghdad House of Wisdom—anyone sensing a trend here?) In addition to 'high culture' topics like science and theology, *L'Encyclopédie* also included topics from 'low culture' like handicrafts and farming practices, to show that the things studied by working people were just as important as those studied by aristocrats and clergy. The text also questioned the historical truth of events described in the Bible and doubted the scientific veracity of miracles. And although Theology was the first entry in the table of contents, it was classified together with divination and superstition, and the entry on the Catholic Eucharist is cross-referenced with the entry on cannibalism! The book was blacklisted by the Catholic Church for a few years for this, and Diderot was sent to jail for several months. He got released because one of his admirers and supporters was Madame de Pompadour, probably the age's most important political lobbyist for Enlightenment values (and as an aside, she was also the mistress of King Louis XV). Moreover, as we know today, notoriety is one of the best forms of marketing: the banning of this work and jailing of its chief editor actually helped to make it more popular.

Before moving on, I want to draw attention to a natural disaster that took place in this period. As mentioned above, the mystical view of the purpose of logic had been in decline at least since the early 1600s. If there was a definitive moment in history when that slow decline bent into a sharp drop, it would have been 1 November 1755, the day of the Great Lisbon Earthquake. Thousands of people were killed during

---

25 Kant, 'What is Enlightenment?' cited in Isaac Kramnick, ed. The Portable Enlightenment Reader (Penguin, 1995), p. 1. The German original term and its translation is my own insertion.

the event itself, then thousands more perished in the tidal wave and the wildfire that followed. Some people argued that the earthquake was sent by God to punish people for their sins, Old Testament style. Enlightenment writers including Voltaire and Kant pointed out that plenty of ostensibly moral and God-fearing people also died in the fire. They concluded that the earthquake was evidence that God was *not* ethically reliable, *not* generally involved in the day-to-day maintenance of the world, and possibly did not exist at all. Therefore, there is no point in guiding one's life according to the Platonic 'Divine Reason' or anything else along those metaphysical lines. Even the non-mystical arguments for God, such as Pascal's Wager, no longer seemed persuasive. This earthquake also changed the language people used when they analysed arguments: philosophers began saying that a good argument was 'firm', 'well grounded', or 'solid'—rather like the earth when there isn't an earthquake in progress. Similarly, a bad argument was 'shaky' or 'unstable' or 'without foundation', rather like the earth during a quake.

1.11. David Hume (1711–1776)

David Hume, an empiricist in the tradition of Bacon, is the next character you should meet in this tour: not only because he was an important figure of the Enlightenment, but also because he threw several wrenches into the Enlightenment's gears. I'll draw your attention to two of those wrenches. The first is called the naturalistic fallacy, which is also sometimes referred to as 'the is–ought problem'. This is a type of bad argument that appears to reason from premises about facts to premises about morality: One thing is the case; therefore, something else ought to also be the case. People reason like this all the time, when they say things like 'It's natural for people to be compassionate; therefore, you ought to be more compassionate', or 'God exists; therefore, you should follow God's laws.' Hume showed that there's a missing premise in these arguments, and that without it, the conclusion is, perhaps not provably false, but definitely not *proven to be true*.

Hume's second wrench in the gears is called the

problem of induction. This occurs when we reason from the way things have been in the past towards conclusions about the way things will be in the future. 'The sun has risen in the east every morning'; therefore 'The sun will rise in the east again tomorrow'. There's a missing middle premise here too. That premise must be: 'The course of nature always continues uniformly the same'[27]—or to put it another way, 'The future will be like the past.' We could claim to know that the future will be like the past because in the past the future turned out to be like the past. But if we took *that* proposition as the support for the conclusion 'The future will be like the past' we have a case of **circular fallacy**. The problem of induction seemed to make scientific prediction impossible, and it was not solved until the early 20th century. As for the naturalistic fallacy: well, it's still a fallacy.

Hume was possibly the greatest doubter in Western philosophy. In addition to doubting the foundations of ethics and of scientific reasoning, he also doubted the existence of God, the significance of miracles, the existence of reality beyond appearances; and (more radically than Descartes), he doubted the existence of the self. If you know anything about Buddhism, that might sound familiar, and there's some terribly speculative but at least plausible evidence that Hume might have been exposed to Buddhist ideas. In the 1700s, very few Europeans had visited Buddhist countries. However, one of them was a certain Jesuit missionary, Charles Francois Dolu, who had been part of a French embassy to Siam (today Thailand) and retired to the Royal College of La Flèche (a smallish town in France, just west of Paris) in 1723. Twelve years later, Hume visited the same town, and while there he wrote most of his book *A Treatise on Human Nature* (first published 1739). Dolu would have been 80 years old by then, and Hume was in his 20s, but it's entirely possible the two men met each other and discussed Buddhist ideas. Hume may also have read works by other Jesuits who had visited Buddhist countries and passed through La Flèche on their way home.[28] As I said, this is terribly speculative, but it's also very intriguing.

26 Mercer, C. "Descartes' Debt to Teresa of Ávila, Or Why We Should Work on Women in the History of Philosophy" Philosophical Studies, Vol.174, Iss.10, pp. 2539-2555 (2017). **27** Hume, Treatise on Human Nature, § 89.
28 A. Gopnik, 'Could David Hume Have Known About Buddhism? Charles Francois Dolu, The Royal College of La Fleche, and the Global Jesuit Intellectual Network.' Hume Studies Vol. 35, No. 1&2, 2009, pp. 5-28.

1.12. Immanuel Kant (17241–804)

Over in Germany, Immanuel Kant read Hume's book, and then told his friends 'Hume awoke me from my dogmatic slumbers'. This is possibly the highest praise any philosopher can give to another—especially since Kant would eventually become one of the top-ten most influential philosophers of all time. Kant felt sure that Hume was wrong about certain important points of logic, but he laboured for a long time to explain exactly what those mistakes actually were. These struggles resulted in the publication of *The Critique of Pure Reason* (1781), the aim of which was to find out whether pure reason alone, apart from the evidence of the senses, can produce any new knowledge. Here's a very short version of what he found.

Logical propositions can be of two types:

Analytic, in which there's only one idea being expressed, and
Synthetic, in which two or more ideas are combined (synthesized) together.

The truth or falsehood of any proposition can come from two sources:

a priori ('before experience'); that is, from pure logic alone, and
a posteriori ('after experience'); that is, from the evidence of our bodily senses.

It's easy to see how analytic propositions can be shown true or false *a priori*. A proposition like 'All bachelors are unmarried men' is true just because of the meanings of the words. It's also easy to see how *a posteriori* propositions tend to be synthetic in character. 'The apple is green' contains two ideas: apples, and the property of green-ness, put together by the copula verb 'is'. You can find out whether or not that proposition is true just by looking at the apple. It still works with more complex concepts: 'the apple is tasty' is still an *a posteriori* proposition even if people disagree about whether the apple is truly tasty. (The *type* of proposi-

tion has no bearing on whether or not it's true.) The big challenge is showing whether there can be such a thing as a *synthetic a priori*: a proposition that brings together two or more ideas and derives its truth from the logical relation between them. Kant decided that mathematical propositions, like 5+7=12 (his own example), are *synthetic a priori*. So, we really can discover new things which have nothing to do with what our senses tell us. Such is Kant's first minor victory over Hume's empiricism.

Next, recall Hume's problem of induction. Kant thought that it made scientific research impossible, for it made basic scientific principles like cause and effect look like mere habits instead of natural laws. Kant found a novel way to make science possible again: A kind of balance between Hume's empiricism and the rationalism of people like Descartes and Leibniz. As Kant put it: The *material* of our experience of the world comes from our physical senses (*a posteriori*), and the *form* of our experience comes from the structure of your mind—particularly from what he called 'the conditions of sensibility': *Space and time*. So, unlike Hume and the empiricists, our concepts do not conform to our experiences of things in the world. Rather, in Kant's view, our experience of things in the world conforms to our concepts. Kant might have agreed with the famous quote from American poet Anaïs Nin: 'We do not see things as they are, we see them as *we* are.'[29] This makes his idea look simpler than it really is, but it gets the point across.

Kant called this his 'Copernican hypothesis' because it reversed the empiricist view of knowledge, much in the same way as Copernicus had reversed our view of the relation between the sun and the earth. But alas, Kant's hypothesis left a huge problem. It required a distinction between the phenomena of objects (i.e., what they appear to be), and the things-in-themselves (i.e., what they actually are). So, if Kant is right and all we ever know of the world is what we see of it, combined with the concepts we bring to the act of seeing, we will never know the world as it actually is. We will never know the thing-in-itself.

That unsolved **aporia** in Kant's work, the impossibility of knowing the thing-in-itself, would trouble

---

29 Nin, Seduction of the Minotaur (Chicago: Swallow Press, 1972 [first published 1961]), pg. 124. Nin herself attributed the quote to the Talmud; the only similar statement in the Talmud appears in Tractate Berakoth, Folio 55b: "A man is shown in a dream only what is suggested by his own thoughts."

all the German idealists for at least the next century.

1.13. Georg Wilhelm Friedrich Hegel (1770–1831)

Among the philosophers who were troubled by Kant's conclusion, an honourable mention must go to G.F.W. Hegel. In his effort to show that we *can* know the thing-in-itself, he argued that rationality was like a force in the world, a kind of world-soul, which he called by various names, such as Geist (spirit), or the Absolute. Hegel can be read as a last gasp of the ancient Platonic idea of reason-as-mysticism; the idea that there's an eternal, timeless, and unchanging Truth out there, and it's the job of philosophy to find it. Along with advances in science (notably by Tycho Brahe, who lived from 1546–1601 and discovered a supernova, measured its parallax, and thereby proved that the realm of the fixed stars was not eternal and unchanging), as well as with the writers of the German Romantic period (1790–1830; this movement includes the Brothers Grimm), people began to suspect that all human endeavour, including philosophy, was subject to the changing influence of history. Therefore, there might not be a timeless and eternal Truth out there for philosophy to find. One can read Kant and Hegel side by side as two different attempts to grapple with the relativist consequences of that historical view. Kant tries to limit its influence by establishing an *a priori* foundation for science; Hegel says that what looks like relativism is actually all part of the big rational plan.

The book in which this worldview appears is called *The Phenomenology of Spirit* (1807). By the way, at the same time and only a few miles away from the room where Hegel wrote its last pages, another kind of history was being made: Napoleon's army was attacking the Prussians in the Battle of Jena, on 14 October 1806. The ongoing conversation of philosophy might have gone differently if the battle caused his manuscript to get lost in the mail.

History, Hegel argued, is really the story of how the Absolute becomes aware of itself. It does this through a process called the dialectic of the absolute.

Among the philosophers who were troubled by Kant's conclusion, an honourable mention must go to G.F.W. Hegel. In his effort to show that we can know the thing-in-itself, he argued that rationality was like a force in the world, a kind of world-soul, which he called by various names, such as Geist (spirit), or the Absolute.

A popular simplification of Hegel's dialectic describes it as a pattern of 'thesis → antithesis → synthesis', or perhaps 'being → nonbeing → becoming', where 'thesis' is the appearance of some idea, 'antithesis' is the appearance of that idea's contrary, and 'synthesis' is the reconciliation or the merging of the idea and its contrary into a single new idea – which then becomes the thesis for the next iteration of the cycle. That pattern isn't a completely wrong interpretation of Hegel's text, but a better one would look like this: 'Logic → Nature → Spirit.' These are the stages that Hegel thinks the Absolute must progress through, in order to manifest itself with greater authenticity and self-awareness. Here's how it works. In the first step of the dialectic, the Absolute becomes aware of itself (or reveals itself) through concepts and the logical relations among them. When this step is complete, the Absolute breaks out of the realm of logic and becomes aware of itself and/or reveals itself into the world of nature. So, if you are a scientist, Hegel might say you are not really studying nature: You are studying the spirit of the Absolute as embodied and revealed in the natural world. This second step culminates in emergence from nature of the human being, 'the crown of creation'; this is a being who is able to recognise nature as a mirror of the logical, and is therefore the highest form of embodied spirit. That recognition initiates the third step, in which logical potentiality and natural embodiment are united, and the Absolute is finally able to recognize itself *as* pure spirit. Ya, I know it's weird. You'll get used to it.

Hegel thought he could map out all of history with this dialectic; here's a small sample of how he thought that schema worked itself out.

1. Logic, the idea *in* itself
    a. Being
    b. Essence
    c. The Notion
2. Nature, the idea *for* itself
    a. Mechanics
    b. Physics
    c. Organics (i.e., processes of life)
3. Spirit, the idea *in and for* itself
    a. Subjectivity
    b. Objectivity

    c. The Absolute
        i. Art
        ii. Religion
        iii. Philosophy [30]

That third step, by the way, has many more sub-steps (and sub-sub-steps) than I have sketched here. And some of them are shot full of observer bias: For instance, Christianity becomes the absolute religion, the Prussian state becomes the absolute political order, and the final move in this biography of spirit is the development of Hegel's own system! So you might be wondering whether his system has a place for people with disabilities, uneducated people, or people from other cultures. But this brief schematic should be enough to give you the general idea. Philosophy, for the rest of the 19th century, would be about how to answer the problems posed by Kant, and how to challenge the dominance of Hegel. In the 20th century his idea would influence various forms of political-historical determinism, including Nazism, Soviet communism, and American exceptionalism and manifest destiny.

1.14. They Made Words Like Numbers, and Built Thinking Machines.

Gottfried Wilhelm Leibniz (1646–1716)
Charles Babbage (1791–1871)
George Boole (1815–1864)
Augustus De Morgan (1806–1871)
John Venn (1834–1923)
Gottlob Frege (1848–1925)

The next major problem logicians faced arises from ambiguities in language. Words, the logician's tools-in-trade, often have multiple meanings, and the exact meaning of a given word often depends on contexts like grammar, or the speaker's intention, which can make it hard to reason about things with the kind of precision philosophers would like to have. The German mathematician and philosopher Gottfried Wilhelm Leibniz therefore developed a symbolic language system, to solve this problem by making reason more like a kind of mathematical calculation. He proposed a universal logic calculator, the *Calculus*

---

30 For this scheme of Hegel's dialectic, and this discussion of Hegel in general, I referred to Lavery and Mitscherling, <u>An Outline History of Western Thought,</u> unpublished MS in my possession, 2001.

ratiocinator, as well as a universal language of concepts, *the characteristica universalis*. Then he built a machine to perform those calculations using that language, which he called the *Stepped Reckoner*. This is now widely regarded as the first attempt to build a modern digital computer. By the way, Leibniz also claimed to have invented calculus, the mathematics of moving bodies, before Isaac Newton. But Leibniz kept his notes private, and Newton published his notes immediately. Thus, a common question given to students of math and logic is: Who *really* invented calculus first? And the best answer still might be that it was neither of them. An astronomer from India, Madhava of Sangamagrama (1340–1425) may have beaten them both by 300 years!

After Leibniz's computer, I should also mention Charles Babbage, the British philosopher and inventor who built the first general-purpose computer containing an arithmetic logic unit. Called the *Analytical Engine*, it received input in the form of punch-cards; it stored memory with other kinds of punch cards or with pegs on rotating drums, and its output came from a printer and a bell. After Babbage, I should also mention Ada Byron Lovelace (1815–1852), daughter of the poet Lord Byron, and Babbage's long-time collaborator. She saw the potential of this machine more clearly than he did: For instance, she recognized that the numbers it crunched could represent not only quantities but also concepts, or musical sounds, or anything at all. She also devised the first procedural algorithm for the machine to compute—in effect, she became the world's first programmer (though the word *algorithm* had not yet been defined as we define it now). Alas, Babbage did not have a machine large enough for her to test her program, nor a budget large enough to build one.

There are several other names to mention in connection with early endeavours to make reason look and work more like mathematics. One is George Boole, who developed the system of Boolean operators and their symbols. His intention was to show that the laws of thought (which is also the title of one of his books, published in 1854) were just as precise and rigorous as the laws of mathematics. He noticed that there were interesting similarities between mathematical operators and logical relations. For instance, he saw

that a sentence like 'A or B' is interchangeable with 'B or A' in the same way that the mathematical expression '1+2' is interchangeable with '2+1'. He also noticed that if you treat propositions as either true or false, it is the same as saying a variable in algebra can be either 1 or 0. We still refer to words like 'And', 'Or', 'Not' as Boolean operators, not only in philosophy but also in other fields such as set theory and computer programming. He created a group of symbols to represent these operators:

An upward pointing wedge $\wedge$ for 'and'
A downward pointing wedge $\vee$ for 'or'
A line with a downward tick mark $\neg$ for 'not'.

He also used letters to represent simple propositions, in much the same way mathematicians use letters to represent variables. When typewriters became more widespread, people substituted a tilde (~) for 'not' and a dot (•) or an ampersand (&) for 'and'. Later logicians would add more symbols:

A hook $\supset$ later replaced with an arrow $\rightarrow$ for 'If / then'.
Three dots $\therefore$ or a tack $\vdash$ for 'Therefore'

Another name to mention here is John Venn, who invented the Venn Diagram, a way of determining the soundness or un-soundness of categorical arguments by drawing two or more overlapping circles. To entertain himself on the side, Venn also built a machine that throws cricket balls. It struck out the top cricket player of the day, four times in a row.

Then in 1847, Augustus De Morgan published *Formal Logic*, in which he pointed out a major error in the usual way of handling Aristotelian syllogisms. If the propositions 'Some Ps are Qs' and 'Some Ps are Rs' are both true, you couldn't deductively say there's any relation between Qs and Rs because you don't have enough information. There might be some Ps that are neither Qs nor Rs. However, De Morgan demonstrated that if the propositions are about definite numerical quantities, it is possible to say there is a relation. For example, if there was a library with 100 books, in which sixty of the books are green, and fifty of them are hardcovers, we could conclude that at least ten of

Another name to mention here is John Venn, who invented the Venn Diagram, a way of determining the soundness or un-soundness of categorical arguments by drawing two or more overlapping circles. To entertain himself on the side, Venn also built a machine that throws cricket balls. It struck out the top cricket player of the day, four times in a row.

the books are green hardcovers. He called arguments using these kinds of propositions numerically definite syllogisms. De Morgan also found several ways in which certain kinds of complex propositions could be exchanged with simpler ones, without affecting the logical structure of an argument: He called these *equivalences*. There are many kinds of equivalences, and some of them now bear his name: De Morgan's theorems. Here they are:

$\sim(P \lor Q)$ is the same as $\sim P \lor \sim Q$
$\sim(P \bullet Q)$ is the same as $\sim P \bullet \sim Q$

Don't worry if you don't understand these statements yet. You can return to them after you've read the chapter on formal logic.

Finally, the German philosopher Gottlob Frege developed a system of quantification, and a symbolic logic of predicates to go alongside the already well-known symbolic logic of propositions. This allowed him to handle a huge pile of deductive arguments more efficiently and accurately. He also distinguished the sense and reference of nouns, and distinguished necessary conditions from sufficient conditions. Frege also provides an example of the notorious 'can we separate the man from his ideas?' problem. This is because although he was a brilliant and game-changing logician, Frege was also a notorious anti-Semite. In 1924 he wrote in his diary that he wished all the Jews 'would get lost, or better would like to disappear from Germany.'[31]

Before we leave the 19th century, a date you might want to remember is 24 June 1833. This is the day when the third meeting of a group now known as The British Association for the Advancement of Science was held. Early in this meeting, the poet Samuel Taylor Coleridge told the assembly they should stop calling themselves 'natural philosophers', as had been the practice for centuries. Philosophers, he argued, pursue the truth only through pure reason; they don't get their hands dirty doing experiments, and therefore the members of the assembly should come up with a new name for who they were and what they were doing. Out of the noisy and angry debate that followed, William Whewell (who was a close friend of Babbage, from their student days) proposed as follows:

---

31 Yvonne Sherratt, <u>Hitler's Philosophers</u>, (Yale University Press, 2013), p. 60.

'If "philosophers" is taken to be too wide and lofty a term…[then] by analogy with *artist* we may form *scientist*.'[32] The root word was taken from the Latin *scientia*: 'knowledge', and this was the first documented occasion when the word 'scientist' was spoken aloud in public.

1.15. The Early Twentieth Century

Charles Sanders Peirce (1839–1914)
Edmund Husserl (1859-1938)
The Austrian School
Karl Popper (1902–1994)

When we come to the twentieth century, we find several attempts to almost re-invent logic anew. The American philosopher Charles Sanders Peirce, for example, invented a new theory of what *truth* means: Where previously truth was regarded as a property of statements which logically fit with other statements (coherence theory), or as a property of statements which accurately represent the observable world (correspondence theory), Peirce showed that truth could also be a property of statements which happen to be useful things to believe, whatever the logical coherence or the correspondence with reality might be. This view is now called **pragmatism**. And in Austria, Edmund Husserl invented a new kind of Cartesian methodological doubt that he called **epoché**, an ancient Greek term meaning 'suspension' or 'reduction', in the sense of 'leading back' to original principles. This is the practice of studying the world by looking at how things appear to your perceptions, while suspending judgments about them, including the judgment that they exist at all. It is thus a way to study one's own mind from the inside, perhaps to find the structure of human thought. This method, he said, 'made spirit as spirit the field of systematic scientific experience, thus effecting a total transformation of the task of knowledge.'[33] Husserl's work inspired a new branch of philosophy, called **phenomenology**. Other philosophers who worked on this with him, including his teacher Franz Brentano (1838–1917), and some of Brentano's students, including Alexius Meinong (1853–1920) and Carl Stumpf (1848–1936), and together

they came to be called the Austrian School.

The differences between these two approaches to logic, pragmatism and phenomenology, will become important later in the century. But before we get there:

The twentieth century also gives us Karl Popper and his solution to the problem of induction. His idea was that scientists should not look for confirmation of their theories; instead, they should look for falsification. To explain: You cannot have deductive certainty that a theory is true; you can only have varying degrees of probability that it's true. But you *can* have absolute deductive certainty that a theory is *false*. The theory we take to be true is simply the one which has so far survived every attempt to falsify it. Falsification was one of several values which he called the epistemic values of science, and in Popper's view, science had to follow those values or else whatever they were doing would not be science.

1.16. The Quest for a Logically Perfect Language

Bertrand Russell (1872–1970)
Alfred North Whitehead (1861–1947)
Kurt Gödel (1906–1978)
Ludwig Wittgenstein (1889–1951)
Moritz Schlick (1882–1936) and the Vienna Circle.

In the 20th century we also find several heroic efforts to compose all these different themes together into a single integrated masterwork. The most influential and successful of these efforts was the *Principia Mathematica* by Bertrand Russell and Alfred North Whitehead, both of whom were Cambridge professors at the time. It took them ten years to write it, and it was published in three volumes between 1910 and 1913. Their aim was to show that all logic and mathematics, and indeed all human knowledge, could be 'reduced', or simplified without loss of meaning or logical integrity, into a kind of mathematically perfect language that followed a small number of basic rules. However, this supremely ambitious project would face stiff criticism from other geniuses of the time. One of these was Kurt Gödel, a German mathematician who was possibly the only person in history who read the thousands upon

32 Laura Snyder, <u>The Philosophical Breakfast Club</u> (Broadway Books, 2012), p. 3.
33 Husserl, <u>Crisis of European Humanity</u>, pt. II.

thousands of pages of the *Principia* entirely from cover to cover. He showed how any formal system of axioms, such as the one Russell and Whitehead were trying to develop, must still contain some axioms that can't be defined in the same system's own language, and there is no way to ever cover up this gap. This discovery is now called Gödel's **incompleteness theorem**, and it seems to show that there is still some impossible-to-purge weirdness in mathematics and logic, after all. Gödel, by the way, became so obsessed with solving the great problems of mathematics that he eventually lost his mind. Terrified by the (completely false) belief that someone wanted to poison him, he would only eat food prepared by his wife. When she became ill for six months and couldn't cook for him, he starved himself to death.

The other major critic of Russell and Whitehead's project was Ludwig Wittgenstein, a former student of Russell's, who is now widely regarded as one of the greatest logicians to have ever lived. After Whitehead said that all of European philosophy is 'a series of footnotes to Plato', his students added, 'until Wittgenstein.'[34] Wittgenstein began writing his *Tractatus Logico-Philosophicus* (1921) while he was a soldier in the First World War (where he was otherwise sitting in the foxholes and trenches, getting shot at). The book had a very ambitious concern: He wanted to find out the absolute limitations of human thought. Concluding that the limitations of thought were the same as the limitations of language, he declared that what can be said should be said clearly and that what cannot be said should be 'passed over in silence'. For all our philosophical problems arise, he thought, from talking about things that fundamentally cannot be talked about—especially metaphysical things like God, or Hegel's world-soul, or Plato's Divine Reason.

Wittgenstein came from Vienna, Austria, as did Karl Popper; Wittgenstein from a wealthy family, and Popper from the working class. When they met for the first time, at a seminar in Cambridge supervised by Bertrand Russell, there was an incident of a sort, involving a fire poker. It might entertain you to look it up.

Though he is among the greatest of logicians,

Ludwig Wittgenstein is also one of philosophy's great tragic figures. He struggled with his mental health for much of his life: He was troubled by depression, loneliness, and lingering guilt and fear about his homosexual feelings (sodomy was still illegal in Britain). He often travelled to isolated and sparsely-populated places like the west of Ireland, to get away from people and to think. He built a cottage in a Norwegian fjord and lived in it alone for three years.

Wittgenstein's ideas found their most eager audience in a group of logicians based in Vienna, Austria, who called themselves the Vienna Circle (Note: This is *not* the same as the aforementioned Austrian School). It began when Moritz Schlick, who had studied both philosophy and physics, became head of the *Naturphilosophie* department at the University of Vienna in 1922. He wanted to bring his philosopher friends (Gödel among them) and his scientist friends together. They gathered at Schlick's house, and later at university halls, ate and drank together, and became friends. The brand of philosophy that emerged from their gatherings was called logical positivism. In 1929 they published a manifesto, and then they organized conferences in various cities in Europe. They adopted Wittgenstein's anti-metaphysical position; they held that statements could be meaningful only if they can be shown either true or false (the 'Verification' criterion); and like Russell in Cambridge they also sought a logically perfect language. They were so strongly empiricist that they rejected Kant's category of synthetic a priori judgments, as such statements were, in their view, impossible to verify with observable facts. The members' insistence on these and related principles made them unpopular among other German-speaking philosophers of the day, most of whom were Hegelian idealists. Friendly critics, including Popper, pointed out that the criterion of verification was itself unverifiable according to its own rules. By the way—the Circle once invited the great Wittgenstein to give a lecture to them. He arrived, faced the blackboard with his back to the audience, and read them poetry. Not quite what his admirers expected, I'm sure.

But what really brought the Circle down was the members' political activism. They saw the

34 Whitehead, Process and Reality (Pt.2, Ch.1, Sec.1); the addendum 'until Wittgenstein' is attributed to Wasfi Hijab, one of Wittgenstein's students and the secretary of the Moral Science Club at Cambridge.

38

anti-Semitism and the general anti-intellectualism strengthening in their society and entrenching itself in the laws, and they spoke out against it. You might think there's nothing politically radical about the ideas that words should have clear meanings and arguments should follow a few simple logical rules. But those ideas could be used to show that the fascists, with their beliefs about historical destiny and about the different intrinsic natures of people from different races, were wrong. The Vienna Circle could have potentially been a stronger force for rationality in European culture, but on 22 June 1936, Schlick was murdered by one of his students. His killer, Johann Nelböck, thought that Schlick's anti-metaphysical ideas were dangerous: He said they 'interfered with his moral restraint'. (However, another version of the events says Nelböck had been jilted by a woman he loved, and came to believe that Schlick was responsible.) The case became a theme for the fascists, who portrayed Nelböck as defending society against the moral degeneracy of the Jews. Schlick was not Jewish, but many other Vienna Circle members were, and that's all the fascists cared about.

By that time, most of the Vienna Circle members had already fled to the UK or America. When Germany annexed Austria, Nelböck was released, after having served two of the ten years of his sentence.

A final comment about the search for a logically perfect language: Later in his life Wittgenstein became his own sharpest critic. He came to believe that the language of ordinary people, rich with ambiguities and roughness, might be more valuable than a mathematically perfect language. He also later considered that the things which cannot be spoken of might turn out to be the most important things of all. However, he didn't mean anything metaphysical by this. Rather, he meant that some things that cannot be spoken of because they can only be *shown*; for example, things like the sense of propositions, the meaning of signs and symbols, ethical virtues, and the beauty in works of art.

1.17. Western Philosophy Today: A House Divided

After Wittgenstein, most logicians thought that it was either not possible, or else not desirable, to create a logically perfect language. And some of the leftover problems from Kant and Hegel were still unsolved, such as how to provide solid logical foundations for knowledge and for science. Much of the rest of the 20th century was therefore given over to figuring out what to do next. Two main options appeared—and by the way, Wittgenstein is often claimed by analytics as a member of their camp, but actually he is the last philosopher who is common to both traditions.

The first option was to follow Russell, Frege, the Pragmatic school, and the Vienna Circle. This leads to a logic that emphasizes pragmatism, empiricism, epistemology, Utilitarian ethics, and the analysis of concepts underlying our beliefs and practices. The majority of philosophers in English-speaking countries eventually joined this camp. We now call this type of philosophy the **analytic tradition.** For the analytics, truth is a property of sentences: A boring thesis, perhaps, but certainly a highly useful one. Among its notable figures and accomplishments:

- John Langshaw Austin (1911–1960), described the logic of speech-acts;
- Paul Grice (1913–1988) described the rules of conversational implicature;
- Carl Hempel (1905–1997) and Nelson Goodman (1906-1998) identified new versions of the old problem of induction: Hempel's 'Raven paradox', Goodman's 'Grue and Bleen paradox'.
- John Searle (b.1932) invented the famous 'Chinese Room' thought experiment, which seemed to show that machines are not conscious and they do not 'think' in any way comparable to human consciousness or human thinking;
- Willard Quine (1908–2000) and Pierre Duhem (1861–1916), were the creators of The Quine-Duhem Thesis on the philosophy of science, which did for science what Gödel did for math. It showed that even in hard sciences like physics and chemistry, things are still a little bit 'socially constructed'.
- and finally, Edmund Gettier (b. 1927) described the 'Gettier Problems' concerning knowledge and the 'justified true belief' that there's a cow standing in a field. I know it sounds silly. But it did drop the bottom out of analytic epistemology for a few decades.

The second option was to follow Husserl and his associates in the Austrian School, as well as existentialists like Soren Kierkegaard and iconoclasts like Karl Marx and Friedrich Nietzsche. The logic here emphasizes introspection, the structure and context of personal experiences, and the interpretation of phenomena. Today this branch is called the **Continental tradition**, although that is a bit of a misnomer. The name was coined in the 1950s as a term of disparagement by British philosophers who thought the philosophers 'on the European continent' (i.e., anyone who did Western philosophy in a language other than English) were not doing real philosophy. For the Continentals, truth is an event in the world: A revealing (*aletheia*) of the Being-in-the-world (*Dasein*) of things. This is a much more interesting thesis, but it's terribly difficult to discuss it with the kind of clarity that analytic philosophers demand.

The Continental tradition produced influential thinkers including:

- Martin Heidegger (1884–1976), a student of Husserl's. His book *Being and Time* (1927) almost completely changed the vocabulary of phenomenology. The terms *aletheia* and *Dasein*, noted above, were his. During World War II he was an enthusiastic supporter of the Nazi party, and after the war refused to discuss his involvement with it. Unresolved questions remain about whether his postwar ideas were still influenced by his Nazi experience.
- Hannah Arendt (1906–1975), Jewish philosopher and former student of Heidegger's (and his former lover—yeah, I know!) and political theorist, best known for exposing the logical and moral bankruptcy of totalitarianism and fascism.
- Emmanuel Levinas (1906–1995), Lithuanian-born French-Jewish philosopher, who attempted to make ethics take the place of epistemology as 'first philosophy'. In order to do this, he described the principle of 'Otherness' in ethics and social life.
- Simone de Beauvoir (1908–1986), a feminist author who is most noted for her book *The Second Sex* (1949) which, some twenty years after publication, set off the second wave of feminism.

- Jean-Paul Sartre (1905–1980), author of *Being and Nothingness* (1943); the most influential populariser of the philosophy of existentialism; sometimes Simone de Beauvoir's lover; and the only person ever to decline a Nobel Prize he was to be awarded.
- Jacques Derrida (1930–2004), inventor of a method of literary criticism called deconstruction (notice there's no capital letter: That's not an accident), which involves examining a text with special attention to the problems (or even outright contradictions) which inform the creation and reception of the text, and which draws attention to the deferred meanings and the 'violence' that underlies its assumptions.
- Hans-Georg Gadamer (1900–2002), who invented a new branch of philosophy: Hermeneutics (the study of how we interpret things), in his work *Truth and Method* (1960).
- Paul Ricoeur (1913–2005). As a reply to reductive notions of personal identity that were popular among analytic philosophers, Ricoeur produced a theory of personal identity based on hermeneutics and narrative storytelling.
- Jean-Francois Lyotard (1924–1998) was commissioned by the Canadian province of Quebec to write a report on 'the state of knowledge' in the world. He found that technological progress had rendered the grand worldviews of western civilization, especially the worldview of the Enlightenment, impossible for most people to believe. In the place of those grand worldviews there could now be found only 'incredulity toward metanarratives'; i.e., general distrust of overarching worldviews, distrust of universal 'capital-T' truths, and a widespread acceptance of relativism. His book that describes this state of affairs, *The Postmodern Condition* (1979), more or less began the postmodern movement in Continental philosophy, and it spread from there to society, politics, art, and culture.

1.18. Summary Remarks

From out of all this history, I hope that you can see that the quest for knowledge is long and complicated, yet also joyful, and has taken some surprising turns. There's as much adventure here, and madness, and cultural crossover, and love, and even murder, as there is in the history of art or literature or religion. If there is any common spirit inhabiting all of those who have contributed to it, that spirit might be something like a kind of confidence in the use of human intelligence to solve the hardest problems; confidence that we mortals really can understand our world. It also gives me great satisfaction to know that the history of logic and the quest for knowledge is still in progress.

Still, we have a few remaining unanswered questions about logic and its history. Here are a few of them which occurred to me as I wrote this chapter.

- Indian and Chinese philosophy developed logical methods uncannily similar to methods developed in the West, and yet it appears they developed them entirely on their own. Could that mean that the principles of logic are *discovered*, and not invented?
- If most logicians today do not regard logic as something mystical, does it make sense to say that the quest for knowledge is the same now as it was in Plato's time? How does this different way of thinking about logic change the quest for knowledge?
- Similarly: What new views of the nature and aim of logic replaced the old Platonic view of logic-as-mysticism? We saw Bacon's view of knowledge-as-power, and Russell's search for the logically perfect language. How successful were they? Are there any others?

- Why are there so few women in the history of logic?
- Do "intellectual" characters from books, film, and television accurately represent what logical thinking is really like? (Examples: Sherlock Holmes, Hercule Poirot, Miss Marple, Nancy Drew, the Vulcans of *Star Trek*, the Mentats of *Dune*, Tyrion Lannister, Hermione Granger, Phryne Fisher, the cast of *The Big Bang Theory*, Stewie from *Family Guy*.) Are the portrayals of these characters any more or less accurate than the portrayal of artists, lovers, working class people, and so on?
- Many people today believe there is a strict division between 'mind' and 'heart', and that thinking and feeling are different activities that may be either opposed or complementary. But is this division real? Is it represented in the work of any historical logician? Or is it only a trope, reinforced by popular culture?
- You might have noticed an overlap between the history of logic and the history of mathematics, the physical sciences, and computer science. What is the relationship among them? Which one leads the way? Are there other fields of knowledge whose histories also overlap with the history of logic?
- Some 20th-century philosophers thought 'philosophy is dead.' Why did they say that? Has history borne them out?

Still, we have a few remaining unanswered questions about logic and its history...

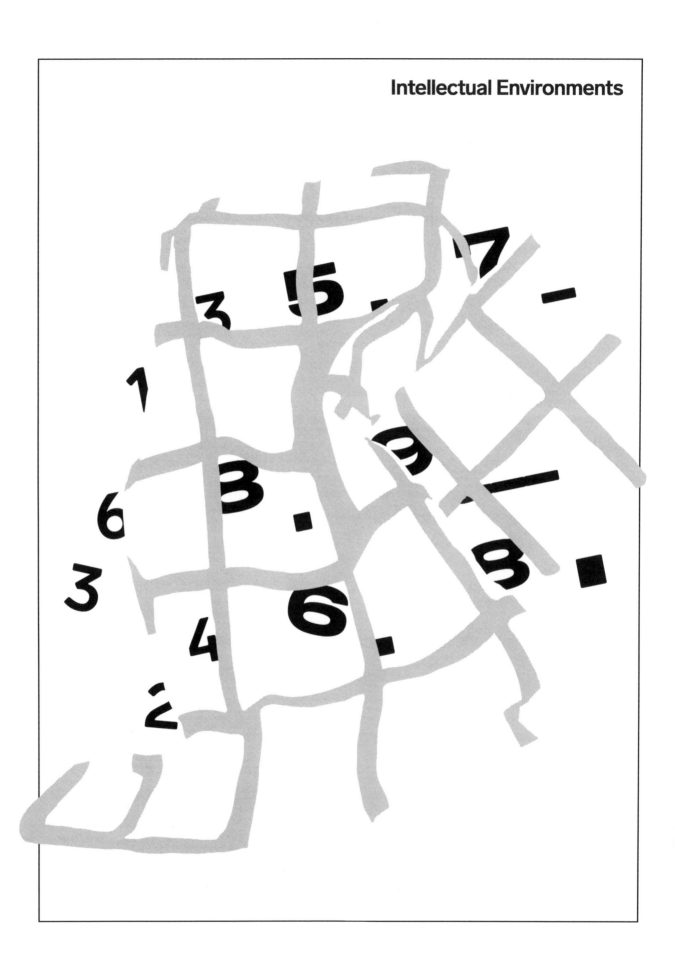

Chapter Two: Informal Logic—Questions, Problems, and Worldviews

BEFORE GETTING into any of the more analytic details of logical reasoning, let's consider the ways ideas 'play out' in the world, and how we arrive at most of our beliefs. Most textbooks on modern logic assert that the basic unit of logic is the proposition—a simple sentence which can be either true or false. (And we will get to that, in a later chapter.) But it seems to me that propositions do not emerge out of nothing, and they have to come from somewhere. The most obvious places where ideas are born are one's intellectual environments, one's problems, and the questions that one tends to ask in the company of others in the same community. However, better ways of thinking begin in situations that prompt the mind to think differently about what it has thus far taken for granted.

2.1. Intellectual Environments

Where does thinking happen? This may seem at first like a rather silly question. Thinking, obviously, happens in your mind. But people do more than just think their own thoughts to themselves: They also share their thoughts with one another. We have conversations, write letters or essays or social media posts, make art and music, publish books, and invent symbols and signs. In those ways, our thoughts do not remain confined within our own brains: They also *express themselves* in words and actions. I'd like to go out on a bit of a limb here and externalize the process: It seems to me that thinking happens not only in a person's own mind, but also in any place where two or more people gather to communicate and share ideas. In

such exterior spaces, ideas are expressed, shared, traded, moved around, examined, criticized, affirmed, rejected, modified, and argued about, which can result in some participants changing their ideas, or formulating new ones. Of course, with our thinking externalized like that, it's possible that someone might manipulate the environment in various non-necessarily-logical ways in order to influence the conversation. For instance, someone might provide food and drink to the other participants, show off expensive or prestigious objects, make sexual advances, or make a dramatic outburst of emotion. But that is only to say that *good* thinking is fragile, and vulnerable non-logical influences, not to say that it isn't (at least partially) social.

The importance of dialogue in reasoning is perhaps most important, and also most obvious, when we are reasoning about moral matters. The Canadian philosopher Charles Taylor said:

> Reasoning in moral matters is always reasoning with somebody. You have an interlocutor, and you start from where that person is, or with the actual difference between you; you don't reason from the ground up, as though you were talking to someone who recognized no moral demands whatever.[1]

What Taylor says about moral reasoning also applies to other things we reason about. Whenever you have a conversation with someone about whether something is right, wrong, true, false, partially both, and so on, you do not start the conversation from scratch. Rather, you start from your own beliefs about

1 Taylor, Malaise of Modernity, p. 32.

such things, and the beliefs held by your partner in the conversation, and you start from the extent to which your beliefs are (assumed to be) the same, or different, as those of the other person. It is not by accident that Plato, one of the greatest philosophers in history, wrote his books in the form of dialogues between Socrates and his friends. Similarly, the French philosopher Michel Foucault observed that—especially among Roman writers—philosophy was undertaken as a *social* practice, often within institutional structures like schools, but also in the context of informal relations among friends and family members. This social aspect of one's thinking was considered normal and even expected:

> When, in the practice of the care of the self, one appealed to another person in whom one recognised an aptitude for guidance and counselling, one was exercising a right. And it was a duty that one was performing when one lavished one's assistance on another…[2]

So, to answer the question 'Where does thinking happen?' we can say: 'Any place where two or more people can have a conversation with each other about the things that matter to them'. And there are lots of such places. While the Romans might have listed the philosophy schools and the political forums among those places, along with their bath houses and public toilets, we could add:

- Movies, television, pop music, and the entertainment industry
- Internet-based social networks like Facebook, Twitter, and YouTube
- Streets, parks, and public squares
- Pubs, bars, and concert venues

- Schools, colleges, and universities
- Religious communities and institutions
- Theatres, art galleries, and cultural institutions
- Science and technology labs
- Corporate offices
- Courtrooms and legal offices
- Political settings, on a small or large scale
- The marketplace, both local and global
- Your own home, with your family and friends

Can you think of any more places like this?

In each of the places where thinking happens, there's a lot of activity. Questions are asked, answers are explored, ideas are described, teachings are presented, opinions are argued over, styles and aesthetics are displayed and developed, and so on. Some questions are treated as more important or relevant than others, and some answers meet with greater approval than others. It often happens that in the course of this huge and complicated exchange, some ideas become more influential and more prevalent than others. You find this in the way certain words, names, phrases or definitions get used more often. And you find it as certain ways to describe, define, criticize, praise, or judge things are used more often than others. The ideas that are expressed and traded around in these ways and in these places, and especially the more *prevalent* ideas, form the intellectual environment that we live in.

Most of the time, your intellectual environment will roughly correspond to a social environment: That is, it will correspond (at least loosely) to a group of people, or a community that you belong to. Think about all the groups and communities that you are a member of now, or have belonged to at some time in the past:

Alisdair MacIntyre: "Traditions, when vital, embody continuities of conflict."

2 Foucault, The Care of the Self, p. 53.

- Families
- Sports teams
- The student body of your college or high school
- The members of any social club you have joined
- The people at your workplace
- Your religious group (if you are religious)
- People who live in the same neighbourhood of your town or city
- People who speak the same language as you
- People who are roughly the same age as you
- People who come from the same cultural or ethnic background
- People who like the same music, movies, or books as you
- People who play most of the same games as you
- Can you think of any more?

Each of these groups and communities will have its own intellectual environment—its own collection of ideas which become prominent among the many ideas that are shared and traded around when people in the group interact.

An intellectual environment will have a character of its own. That is, in one place or among one group of people, one idea or group of related ideas may be more prevalent than other ideas. In another place and among other people, a different set of ideas may dominate. Most likely, you move around in more than one social environment, so you are probably hearing different sets of ideas. Some of your groups may have very similar intellectual environments, but when they only partially overlap or differ considerably, this can sometimes generate tensions.

One or more particular intellectual environments (along with their prevalent ideas) surround everyone almost all the time, and they influence the way people think. Here, we learn most of our basic ideas about life and the world, starting at a very early age. There will be a handful of stock words and phrases that people can use to communicate and be understood right away. This is not to say that people get all of their thoughts from their environments. Obviously, they can still do their own thinking wherever they are. And this also is not to say that the contents and practices of your

intellectual environment will always be the same from one day to the next. As observed by the philosopher Alisdair MacIntyre: "traditions, when vital, embody continuities of conflict", and the conflict is "in part about the goods which constitute the tradition."[3] But this is to say that wherever you are, and whatever community you happen to be living in or moving through, the prevalent ideas that are expressed and shared by the people around you will influence your own thinking and your life in profound ways that you are often unaware of.

By itself, this fact is not something to be troubled about. Indeed, in your early childhood it was very important for you to learn from the people around you. For instance, it was better for a parent to tell you not to touch a hot barbecue with your bare hand than for you to put your hand there yourself and find out what it feels like. But as you grow into adulthood, it becomes more and more important to recognize what your intellectual environment is really like. It is very important to know what ideas are prevalent there, and to know the extent to which those ideas influence you. For if you know the character and content of the intellectual environment in which you live, you will be much better able to do your own thinking. You may end up agreeing with most of the prevalent ideas around you—but you will have agreed with them for your own reasons, and not (or not primarily) because you have passively absorbed them from the people around you. And as already discussed, that will make an enormous difference in your life.

Some intellectual environments are actually hostile to reason and rationality. In these circles. people become angry, feel personally attacked, or will deliberately resist the questioning of certain ideas and beliefs. Indeed, some intellectual environments hold that intellectual thinking is bad for you and for others! Critical reasoning sometimes takes great courage, especially in times and places where one person or class of people reserve for themselves the right to do all the thinking, and where they defend that right with various forces, from peer pressure, to control over the legal system, to violence and the threat of violence.

3 MacIntyre, <u>After Virtue</u>, 2nd Edition (London: Duckworth, 1985) p. 222.

2.2. Worldviews

Eventually, the ideas that you gathered from your intellectual environment, along with a few ideas that you developed on our own, come together in your mind. There they take shape as a kind of plan, a picture, or a model of what the world is like, how things work, and so on. This plan helps you to understand what's going on around you and make decisions. Philosophers sometimes call this plan a worldview.

Think for a moment about some of the biggest, deepest, and most important questions we ask ourselves. They might include:

- What should I do with my life? Where should I go from here?
- Should I get married?
- What kind of job do I want?
- Should I travel far away to get a good job?
- Where is my place in the world? How do I find it? How do I create it?
- What about a Divine Being? What is God like? Is there one god, or many gods? Or no gods at all? And how do I know if any such thing exists? And if it does not, how do I know that?
- Why are we here? Why are we born? Is there any point to it all?
- What is my society really like? Is it just or unjust? And what is Justice?
- Who am I? What kind of person do I want to be?
- What does it mean to be an individual? What does it mean to be a member of society?
- What happens to us when we die?
- What do I have to do to pass this course?
- Just what are the biggest, deepest and most important questions anyway?

These are philosophical questions. (Well, all but one of them.) Your usual way of thinking about these questions, and others like them, is your worldview. Obviously, most people do not think about these questions all the time. We are normally dealing with more practical, short-term problems. What will I have for dinner tonight? If the traffic is bad, how late might

The greatest of the spirit's tasks is to produce a theory of the universe. What is meant by a theory of the universe? It is the content of the thoughts of society and the individuals which compose it, about the nature and object of the world in which they live, and the position and the destiny of mankind and of individual men within it.

I arrive? Is it time to buy a new phone? What's the best way to train a cat to use its litter-box?

But every once in a while, what's called a limit situation will appear, and it will prompt us to think about higher and deeper things. And then the way that we think about these higher and deeper things ends up influencing the ways that we live, the ways we make choices, the ways that we relate to other people, and the ways we handle almost all of our problems. The sum of your answers to those higher and deeper questions is called your 'worldview'.

The word 'worldview' was coined by the German philosopher Albert Schweitzer in a book called *The Decay and Restoration of Civilization*, first published in 1923. Actually, the word that Schweitzer coined here is the German *Weltanshauung*. There are several possible ways to translate this word. In the text quoted above, as you can see, it's translated as 'theory of the universe'. It could also be translated as 'theory of things' or 'world conception'. Most English speakers use the simpler and more elegant sounding phrase 'worldview'. Here's how Schweitzer himself defined it:

> The greatest of the spirit's tasks is to produce a theory of the universe. What is meant by a theory of the universe? It is the content of the thoughts of society and the individuals which compose it about the nature and object of the world in which they live, and the position and the destiny of mankind and of individual men within it. What significance has the society in which I live and I myself in the world? What do we want to do in the world? What do we hope to get from it? What is our duty to it? The answer given by the majority to these fundamental questions about existence decides what the spirit is in which they and their age live.[4]

Schweitzer's idea is that a worldview is more than a group of beliefs about the nature of the world. It is also a bridge between those scientific or metaphysical beliefs, and the ethical beliefs about what people can and should do in the world. It is the intellectual narrative in terms of which the actions, choices, and purposes of individuals and groups make sense. It therefore has indispensable practical utility: It is the

justification for a way of life, for individuals and for whole societies. In this sense, a worldview is not just something you 'have'; it is also something that you 'live with'. And we cannot live without one. For individuals as for the community, Schweitzer said, 'life without a theory of things is a pathological disturbance of the higher capacity for self-direction' (Schweitzer, ibid, p. 86).

Let's define a worldview as follows: A worldview is the sum of a set of related answers to the most important questions in life. Your own worldview, whatever it is, will be the sum of your own answers to your philosophical questions, whatever you take those questions to be, and whether you have thought about them consciously or not. Thus, your worldview is intimately tied to your sense of who you are, how you want to live, how you see your place in your world and the things that are important to you. Not only your answers to the big questions, but also your choice of which questions you take to be the big questions, will form part of your worldview. And this is a big part of why people don't like hearing criticism. A negative judgment of a worldview is often taken to be a judgment of one's self and identity. But it doesn't have to be that way.

Some worldviews are so widely accepted by many people, perhaps millions of people, and are so historically influential, perhaps over thousands of years, that they have been given names. Here are a few examples:

MODERNISM: A set of values associated with contemporary Western civilization, including democracy, capitalism, industrial production, scientific reasoning, human rights, individualism, etc.

HELIOCENTRISM: The idea that the sun is at the centre of our solar system, and that all the planets (and hundreds of asteroids, comets, minor planets, etc.) orbit around the sun.

DEMOCRACY: The legitimacy of the government comes from the will of the people, as expressed in free and fair elections, parliamentary debate, and other institutions designed to bring this will into effect.

CHRISTIANITY: The God described in certain Near Eastern texts exists; humankind incurred an 'original

---

4 Schweitzer, The Decay and Restoration of Civilization, pp. 80-1.

sin' due to events that took place in the Garden of Eden, and this God became a man in the person of Jesus in order to redeem humanity from its original sin.

ISLAM: This same God exists; Mohammed was the last of God's prophets; and we attain blessedness when we live by the five pillars of submission. These are daily prayer, charity, fasting during Ramadan, pilgrimage to Mecca, and personal struggle.

MARXISM: All political and economic corruption stems from the private ownership of the means of production, and a more fair and just society is one in which working class people collectively own the means of production.

DEEP ECOLOGY: There is an important metaphysical correlation between the self and the earth; or to phrase it another way, the earth forms a kind of expanded or extended self. Therefore, protecting the environment is as much of an ethical requirement as protecting oneself.

THE AGE OF AQUARIUS / THE NEW AGE: An era of peace, prosperity, spiritual enlightenment, and complete happiness is about to dawn upon humankind. The signs of this coming era of peace can be found in astrology, psychic visions, Tarot cards, spirit communications, and so on.

You might notice from these examples that some worldviews are more comprehensive than others. Modernism, for instance, covers a wide range of practices and problems in politics, economics, society, and culture. Heliocentrism, by contrast, covers a comparatively narrower range of scientific discoveries and their implications for other worldviews.

It may be helpful to think of a worldview as a continuity of thoughts, feelings, and actions, bequeathed to us from past people and widely shared in the present. We have already seen how philosopher Alisdair MacIntyre regarded traditions as continuities of conflict, and not (or not always) continuities of thought. So, some of these worldviews have other, sub-views bundled inside them, and the people who are committed to one of those sub-views may regard themselves as competing with people committed to

other sub-views for control over the larger worldview. For example, within the worldview of Democracy there are liberals, conservatives, and social democrats, and within the worldview of Buddhism there are practitioners of Mahayana, Theravada, and Zen.

Clearly, not all worldviews are the same. Some have different beliefs, different assumptions, different explanations for things, and different plans for how people should live. Not only do they produce different answers to these great questions, but they often start out with different foundational questions. Some are so radically different from each other that the people who subscribe to different worldviews at times can find it very difficult to understand each other.

In summary, your worldview and the intellectual environment in which you live, when taken together, form the background of your thinking. They are the source of most of our ideas about nearly everything. If you are like most people, your worldview and your intellectual environment overlap each other: They both support most of the same ideas. Sometimes there will be slight differences between them; sometimes you may find differences so large that it can lead you to feel that one of them must be seriously wrong, in whole or in part. Differing worldviews and differing intellectual environments often lead to social and personal conflict. It can be very important, therefore, to consciously and deliberately know what your own worldview really is, and to know how to peacefully sort out the problems that may arise when you encounter people who have different worldviews.

2.3. Framing Languages

One of the ways that your intellectual environment and your worldview expresses itself, or reveals itself, is in the use of framing language. These are the words, phrases, metaphors, symbols, definitions, grammatical structures, questions, and so on which we use to think and speak of things in certain set ways. These are also the contexts, narratives, and intangible structures of meaning which surround our worldviews and at the same time inform them. We frame things by choosing certain words and not others, by placing emphasis on certain words and not on others, and by selectively interpreting and responding to things said by other people. Journalists, reporters, and PR professionals sometimes refer to this as putting a 'spin' on a story; their critics might say that amounts to 'slanting' the story. The frame that surrounds discussions lends a sense to the meaning of words. There are always power relations in play here: For example, when one person or social group controls the framing of a discussion, or prevents another person or group from controlling the frame.

As another example, think of some of the ways that people speak about their friendships and relationships. We say things like 'We connected', 'Let's hook up', 'They're attached to each other', and 'They separated'. These phrases borrow from the vocabulary of machine functions, so to use them is to place human relations within the frame of machine functions. Now this might be a very useful way to talk about relationships, and if so, it is not so bad. But if for some reason you need to think or speak of a relationship differently, you may need to invent a new framing language with which to talk about it. And if this is the only framing language you've ever used to talk about relationships, it might be extremely difficult for you to think about relationships any other way. As a thought experiment, see if you can invent a framing language for your friendships and relationships based on something other than the language of machinery. Try using a framing language based on cooking, or travel, or music, or house building, as examples. What kind of framing language gives us expressions like 'henpecked', 'rules the roost', 'pecking order', 'queen bee', 'top dog', and the like?

The fact that it is possible to frame the discussion of events in different ways, does not mean that all those different frames are 'equal', *even if the facts described by different frames are accurate and empirically verifiable*. The reason for this is that different frames will be more or less helpful; they will tend to emphasize different facts, or they will tend to presuppose different moral or religious or philosophical worldviews. They can also prompt different moral choices, different moral interpretations of events, and different ways of

taking political action. Consider the following pairs of statements:

1a. The man was killed.
1b. The man was murdered.

2a. She has ongoing mental health issues.
2b. She was diagnosed with clinical depression.

3a. His parenting style was firm and consistent.
3b. His parenting style kept his children in constant fear of punishment.

Suppose that each of these pairs of statements describes exactly the same circumstances, and suppose that there are no falsehoods here. These different frames would still give you a very different impression of what happened, how to interpret it, and what—if anything—to do about it.

News reports, especially headlines, are almost always framed in one particular way. Most journalists, of course, try to be impartial and objective; nonetheless their choices of words and phrases (or their editor's choices) reveal what they think of the events they describe, as well as what they would like the reader to think. The use of a frame to describe the event can have economic or political consequences. Consider, as an example, the case of a woman who drove a car for Lyft (a ride-sharing company) while pregnant and close to birth. She began contractions while on the job, a week earlier than she expected. So, she drove to the hospital, but she picked up a passenger on the way. The company described the event as 'an exciting Lyft story' about entrepreneurship and dedication. Critics, however, described the story as being about 'an unprotected worker in precarious circumstances' and about 'the essentially cannibalistic nature of the gig economy'.[5] Your decision about which description best fits the facts will usually depend on which framing language you have accepted. The consequences of accepting one of these frames might be praise for the story's hero, or a boycott of the company.

For another example, consider the national debate that took place in the United States over the

---

5 Jia Tolentino, "The Gig Economy Celebrates Working Yourself To Death" The New Yorker, 22 March 2017.

Affordable Health Care Act of 2009. The very name of the legislation framed the discussion in terms of market economics: The word 'affordable' tells us that the issue has to do with money. And most people who participated in that national debate—including supporters, opponents, and everyone in between—spoke of health care as a kind of market commodity that can be bought or sold for a price. The debate thus became primarily a matter of questions such as who will pay for it (the state? individuals? insurance companies?) and whether the price is fair. But there are other ways to talk about health care outside the language of economics. Some people frame heath care as a human right. Some frame it as a form of organized human compassion. Some frame as a religious duty.[6] But once the debate had been framed in the language of market economics, these other ways of thinking about health care were mostly excluded from the discussion.

Here are a few more examples, some of which are inspired by events that were prominent in the news as I was working on this textbook. For each pair of statements, consider what you are likely to think or feel about the event described if you heard only one of them, or if you used one of them to search the internet for more information about the event.

4a. Following the appearance of anti-Islam graffiti on a mosque, Prime Minister Justin Trudeau visited the mosque to show his solidarity with Muslim Canadians.
4b. Following the appearance of anti-Islam graffiti on a mosque, Justin Trudeau, a man who calls himself a feminist, attended a gender-segregated event at the mosque.

5a. In August 2017, a group of American patriots in Charlottesville, Virginia gathered around a statue of a civil war hero to publicly defend their right to freedom of speech.
5b. In August 2017, a group of white supremacists in Charlottesville, Virginia gathered around a statue of a slave-owning Confederate general and chanted anti-Semitic slogans.

6a. In the year 1605, Guy Fawkes attempted to start a people's revolution against corruption, inherited

privilege, and social injustice in the British government.
6b. In the year 1605, Guy Fawkes planned a terrorist attack against a group of Protestant politicians, in an attempt to install a Catholic theocracy in Britain.

7a. Sir John A. Macdonald, first Prime Minister of Canada, helped to unify a deeply divided nation and completed Canada's first trans-continental railway.
7b. Sir John A. Macdonald, first Prime Minster of Canada, was forced to resign his office when his party accepted bribes from a railway company.
7c. Sir John A. Macdonald was an alcoholic, who once vomited in his seat in Parliament.
7d. Sir John A. Macdonald instituted the *Indian Act* and the residential school system, an act which the Truth And Reconciliation Commission of 2015 described as 'cultural genocide'.

8a. The purpose of education is to assist people in preserving and advancing the possibilities for human flourishing, in our social, cultural, intellectual, and political fields of life.
8b. The purpose of education is to prepare human resources to meet the needs of the workforce.

Words configure reality by telling people how to think about things and events. Words draw out the significance of events, while at the same time also imposing significance. They can empower or harm people. They can open various paths for thinking, while closing others. Becoming aware of how people use framing languages is the easiest way to see how this work of configuration happens. As noted earlier, it's probably not possible to speak about anything without framing it in one way or another—but the use of a framing language can limit or restrict the way things can be thought of and spoken about. Strictly imposed frames can effectively prevent certain ways of thinking and speaking. And when two or more people frame their topic differently in a conversation, misunderstandings or conflicts can result. Therefore, it can be important to be aware of what frame you are using, and whether that frame is assisting or limiting your ability to think and speak critically about a par-

---

6 See, for example, Isaiah 58:7, Matthew 25:35-6.

Words configure reality by telling people how to think about things and events. Words draw out the significance of events, while at the same time also imposing significance. They can empower or harm people. They can open various paths for thinking, while closing others.

ticular issue. It can also be important to listen carefully to the framing language used by others, especially if a difference between their framing language and yours is creating problems. (Mind you, if someone's framing language casts a group of murderous racists as 'patriots' or as 'very fine people', then our problems are not merely a matter of rhetoric.)

By learning the framing languages used by others, you can make yourself better understood; by inviting others to enter your framing language, you can be more persuasive and influential; by imposing your language upon them, you can be more domineering. Each of these strategies for dialogue is also a moral choice, undergirded by different levels of respect for the autonomy of others, as I'm sure the alert reader can readily see.

This leads us to the next topic: Problems.

2.4. Problems and Limit Situations

Usually, logic and critical thinking skills are invoked in response to a need. And often, this need takes the form of a problem which can't be solved until you gather some kind of information. Sometimes the problem is practical: That is, it has to do with a specific situation in your everyday world. For example:

- Perhaps you have an unexpected or unusual illness and you want to recover as soon as possible.
- Perhaps you are an engineer and your client wants you to build something you've never built before.
- Perhaps you just want to keep cool on a very hot day and your house doesn't have an air conditioner.

The problem could also be theoretical: In that case, it has to do with a more general issue that affects your life as a whole, though perhaps not any single separate part of it in particular. Religious and philosophical questions tend to be theoretical in this sense. Here are some examples:

- You might have a decision to make which will change the direction of your life irreversibly.
- You might want to make up your mind about whether

God exists.

- You might be mourning the death of a beloved friend.
- You might be considering whether to ask your intimate partner to marry you.
- You might have lost something in which you had invested a lot of time and preparation: A job, a sports competition, your health, or the like.
- You might be contemplating whether there is special meaning in an unusual dream you had recently.
- You might be a parent considering the best way to raise your children.

The philosopher Karl Jaspers described a special kind of problem, which he thought was the origin of philosophical thinking. He called this kind of problem a *Grenzsituation*, or limit situation.

> Limit situations are moments, usually accompanied by experiences of dread, guilt or acute anxiety, in which the human mind confronts the restrictions and pathological narrowness of its existing forms, and allows itself to abandon the securities of its limitedness, and so to enter new realm of self-consciousness.[7]

In other words, a limit situation is a situation in which you meet something in the world that is unexpected and surprising. More than that, it is a situation that forces you to acknowledge that your way of thinking about the world so far has been very limited, and that you have to find new ways to think about things in order to solve your problems and move forward with your life. This acknowledgement, according to Jaspers, produces anxiety and dread. But it also opens the way to new and (hopefully!) better ways of thinking about things.

As an exercise, ask yourself: What has been the most significant limit-situation that you have encountered in your life so far? What did you believe before you met that situation? What do you believe now?

In general, a limit situation appears when something happens to you in your life that you have never experienced before, or which you have experienced very rarely. It might be a situation in which you realized a long-standing belief you have held until

now seems to have no supporting evidence, or that the consequences of acting upon it turn out very differently than expected. You may encounter a person from a faraway culture whose beliefs are very different from yours, but whom you must regularly work with at your job, or see them around your neighbourhood. You may experience a crisis event in which you are at risk of death. A limit situation doesn't have to be the sort of experience that provokes a nervous breakdown or a crisis of faith, nor does it have to be a matter of life and death. But it does tend to be the type of situation in which your usual and regular habits of thinking cannot help you. It can also be a situation in which you have to make a decision of some kind, which doesn't necessarily require you to change your beliefs, but which you know will change your life in a non-trivial way.

2.5. Observation and Objectivity

Thus far, we have noted the kinds problems that tend to get thinking started, and the background in which thinking takes place. Now we can get on to studying thinking itself. In the general introduction, I wrote that clear critical thinking involves a process. The first stage of that process is the stage of *observing and questioning.*

When observing your problem, and the situation in which it appears, try to be as objective as possible. Being **objective**, here, means leaving aside influences from personal feelings, interests, biases, or expectations, as much as possible. It means observing the situation as an uninvolved and disinterested third-person observer would see it. (By 'disinterested' here, I mean a person who is curious about the situation but who has no personal stake in what is happening; someone who is neither benefitted nor harmed as the situation develops.)

When you are having a debate with someone whose argument you don't like or whose ideas are merely different from yours, it is often very easy, and tempting, to accuse that person of being biased, and to conclude that his or her argument is therefore flawed, or should be ignored. This is a kind of one-size-fits-all

---

7 <u>Stanford Encyclopedia of Philosophy</u>, online edition, entry on Karl Jaspers, 15th November 2017. https://plato.stanford.edu/entries/jaspers/

accusation, because it is probably impossible to find someone who is completely and purely objective in every way. Now, under most circumstances, someone's bias can be a basis for having reasonable doubt concerning whether to believe what that person says. But having a worldview is not the same as having a bias. Identifying someone's beliefs or opinions as belonging to a certain worldview is not the same as evidence that his or her beliefs and opinions are wrong. Let us define a **bias** here as the holding of a belief or a judgment about something even after evidence of the weakness or the faultiness of that judgment has been presented. We will see more about this when we discuss value programs. For now, note that having a bias is not the same thing as having a worldview.

Given the meanings of the terms '**objective**' and '**bias**', you might think it's impossible for anyone to be totally, completely, and absolutely objective. (That includes you!) It may also be impossible to come up with a framing language that is completely objective. Still it certainly is possible to be objective *enough* to understand a situation as clearly and as completely as needed in order to make good decisions about what to believe or what to do. And it certainly is possibly to compare and evaluate different beliefs (and different framing languages) to see which ones are more objective, and which are less so. Here are some ways in which we can increase the objectivity, and reduce the bias, from our observations as much as possible:

- Take stock of how clearly you can see or hear what is going on. Is something obstructing your vision? Is it too bright, or too dark? Are there other noises nearby which make it hard for you to hear what someone is saying?
- Describe your situation in words, and as much as possible use value-neutral words in your description. Make no statement in your description about whether what is happening is good or bad, for you or for anyone else. Simply state as clearly as possible what is happening. If you cannot put your situation into words, then you will almost certainly have a much harder time understanding it objectively, and reasoning about it.
- Describe, also, how your situation makes you feel. Is the circumstance making you feel angry, sad, elated, fearful,

disgusted, indignant, or worried? Has someone said something that challenges your worldview? Your own emotional responses to the situation is part of what is 'happening'. And these too can be described in words so that we can reason about them later.
- Also, observe your instincts and intuitions. Are you feeling a 'pull', so to speak, to do something or not do something in response to the situation? Are you already calculating or predicting what is likely to happen next? Describe these impulses as well.
- Using numbers can often help make the judgment more objective. Take note of anything in the situation that can be counted, or measured mathematically: Times, dates, distances, heights, shapes, angles, sizes, monetary values, computer bytes (kilobytes, megabytes, etc.), and so on.
- Take note of where your attention seems to be going. Is anything striking you as especially interesting or unusual or unexpected?
- If your problem is related to some practical purpose, take note of everything you need to know in order to fulfil that purpose. For instance, if your intention is to operate some heavy machinery, and your problem is that you've never used that machine before, take note of the condition of the safety equipment, and the signs of wear and tear on the machine itself, who will be acting as your 'spotter', and so on.

If other people are also observing the situation with you, consult with them. Share your description of the situation with them, and ask them to share their descriptions with you. Find out if you can see what they are seeing, and show them what you are seeing. Also, try to look for the things that they might be missing.

Separating your observations from your opinions can often be difficult. Your framing language can also make it difficult to improve your degree of objectivity about something, especially when your framing language requires you to think of things a certain way even when there are more objective ways to describe the observable facts.

The more serious the problem you are considering, the more important it can be to strive for objectivity

---

2 See the Parable of the Divided Line, in Plato, The Republic, book 6, 509d-511e

3 Krathwohl, D.R. "A revision of Bloom's Taxonomy: An Overview." Theory Into Practice, 41(4), 2002, pp. 212-218.

Perhaps more than the problems, good questions get the process of reasoning up and running. Questions express doubts, identify problems, call for solutions and demand answers. Indeed, we might not fully understand the nature of a given problem until we have asked a decent question about it.

before coming to a decision. With that in mind, here's a short exercise: which of the following are objective observations, and which are opinions? Or, are some of them a bit of both?

- That city bus has too many people on it.
- The letter was delivered to my door by the postman at 10:30 AM.
- The two of them were standing so close to each other that they must be lovers.
- The clothes she wore suggested she probably came from a very rich family.
- The kitchen counter looked like it had been recently cleaned.
- He was swearing like a sailor.
- The old television was too heavy for him to carry.
- There's too much noise coming from your room, and it's driving me crazy!
- The latest James Bond film was a lot of fun.
- The latest James Bond film earned more than $80 million in its first week.
- I hate computers!
- The guy who delivered the pizza pissed me off because he was late.

2.6. Questions

Perhaps more than the problems, good questions get the process of reasoning up and running. Questions express doubts, identify problems, call for solutions and demand answers. Indeed, we might not fully understand the nature of a given problem until we have asked a decent question about it. Moreover, the best answers to one's questions tend to become ideas, beliefs, propositions, theories, arguments, and worldviews. These, in turn, guide our lives and our choices in numerous ways. But some kinds of questions are better than others, and it can be important to discern the differences between them.

Good questions are:

- Tenacious. We cannot easily put them away or ignore them.

- DIRECT. They address the actual problem that you are facing, and not a tangential or unrelated issue.
- SEARCHING. When you pose a good question, you don't already know the answer. You might have a rough or vague idea of what the answer might be, but you don't know for sure yet, and you are committed to finding out. Or, you might have several possible answers, and you want to find out whether any of them are good answers, or which one is the best.
- SYSTEMATIC. Although you don't have a clear answer to your question, still your question is associated with a method or a plan, even if only a loose one, which you can use in your search for an answer. In other words: Even when you don't know the answer, you still know what you're doing, and you're not scrambling in the dark. You have an idea where to look for an answer. And you are covering every place where a useful answer could be found, leaving nothing out.
- USEFUL. The process of answering a good question actually helps you solve your problem.
- OPEN. There might be more than one possible correct answer. (There can also be more than one possible wrong answer.) With several good answers to your question, you may have to do a lot more work to find which of them is the best one, especially if your circumstance requires you to pick just one answer. But that work is ultimately very useful, and almost always leads us to better quality answers.
- FERTILE. Some of the better answers to the question prompt more good questions. In this way, good questions can keep the mind active.
- CONTROVERSIAL. A good question is often one which addresses itself to beliefs, ideas, ways of living, etc., that people normally take for granted. It may even be a question that no one else or very few others are asking. This does not necessarily mean that the questioner is being aggressive or confrontational. It should still be a searching question, and a direct question, and so on. But with a controversial question, the questioner often places herself at odds, in some way, with those who are committed to the beliefs being questioned, or who might not want the question asked at all. Indeed, a controversial question can sometimes place the questioner in some danger by the very act of asking it. That danger

might be social: By asking the question, she might risk being cold-shouldered or ostracized by her friends. Or it might be physical: By asking the question, she might place herself at odds against politically or economically powerful people and institutions, such as the law or an employer.

A good question need not have all eight of these qualities to be a good question. In general, the more of these qualities that a question has, the better it is. However, there are also several kinds of bad questions. Let's take a look at a few examples:

- RHETORICAL QUESTIONS: This is a question to which the questioner already knows the answer, and is trying to prompt that same answer from his or her listeners. Rhetorical questions can be interesting and perfectly appropriate in poems or storytelling, and sometimes useful in education as a technique for introducing a topic. But in a nonfiction text or in a more 'straight talk' conversation they are stylistically weak. Often, rhetorical questions are plain statements of belief or of fact merely phrased in the form of a question: A good example of this is the line from Robert Browning's poem *Andrea Del Sarto:* 'A man's reach should exceed his grasp, or what's a heaven for?' But it is generally better to express the belief or fact directly as a proposition. This is because rhetorical questions can sometimes be used as a form of verbal aggression: They position the questioner as the controller of the debate, and put others on the defensive, which makes it harder for them to contribute to the debate as equals. It is also possible that someone will answer the rhetorical question in an unexpected way and thus throw the speaker off balance.
- LEADING QUESTIONS: These are questions designed to manipulate someone into believing something that they may or may not otherwise believe. Normally, leading questions come in a series, and the series is designed to make the person answering respond to the last question in the series in a particular way. Leading questions are often used in a form of political campaigning called 'push polling' (to be discussed in the chapter on 'Reasonable Doubt'). For instance, a pollster might ask a series of questions like these: 'Do you think young

people today need good role models? Do you think young people need more discipline in their lives? Do you think they need well-paid jobs with on-the-job training?' Someone who answers 'Yes' to those questions is more likely to answer 'Yes' to this one: 'Would you support national mandatory military service?'

- LOADED OR COMPLEX QUESTIONS: A loaded question is one that cannot be addressed with a straight answer unless the person answering it accepts a proposition that he or she may not want to accept. (More discussion of this type of question appears in the chapter on 'Fallacies'.) Like rhetorical questions, loaded questions can also be used aggressively, to control a debate and to subordinate the other contributors. For example: 'I heard a disturbance in my back yard last night. So did you climb the fence to get in, or pick the lock on the gate?'

- OBSTRUCTIONIST QUESTIONS: This is the kind of question that someone asks in order to interrupt someone else's train of thought. Obstructionist questions often look like good questions, and in a different context they may be perfectly reasonable. But the obstructionist question is designed to steer a discussion away from the original topic, and prevent the discussion from reaching a new discovery or a clear decision. Typically, the obstructionist question asks about definitions, or pushes the discussion into a very abstract realm. It may also engage ins needlessly hair-splitting the meanings of certain words. In this sense an obstructionist question is much like the fallacy of 'red herring'. As an example, someone might obstruct a discussion of whether same-sex couples should be allowed to marry by saying: 'Well, that all depends on what you mean by 'marriage'. What is marriage, anyway?'

- FRAMING QUESTIONS: The framing question uses specific words, terms, and phrases to limit the way a certain topic can be discussed. There's probably no such thing as a question that doesn't frame the answers that flow from it, even if only in a small way. But it is possible to 'cook' or 'rig' a question so that the only direct answers are ones which remain within a certain limited field of assumptions, or within a certain limited worldview. Framing questions may even share some of the qualities of good questions: They might allow more

than one answer, or they might open the way to further questions. But they are also like loaded questions in that they presuppose a certain way of thinking or talking about the topic, and you can't give a straight answer unless you reply within the bounds of that way of thinking and talking. For example: someone might ask, 'How can women best serve God's will?' This question assumes all the listeners are religious, and that God's will for women is clear. But that might not be the case.

- EMPTY QUESTIONS: A question is empty when it has no answer. Sometimes people will declare a question to be empty when in fact it is 'open', but a question with more than one possible good answer is not an empty question, and it is important to understand the difference between the two. A question is empty when all its answers lead to dead ends: When, for instance, the best answers are neither true nor false, or when different answers are nothing more than different descriptions of the same situation, or when the question cannot be given a direct answer at all. Such questions might be interesting for artistic or religious or similar purposes, and they can be the basis for some beautiful poems and meditations, or some very enjoyable comedy. But reasoning about such questions in a logical or systematic way doesn't produce any new discoveries. An empty question is a question for which none of the answers tell you anything you don't already know. For instance, suppose someone started a new philosophy student club at a university. Suppose after a few years membership lapsed, the club stopped meeting, and the club was de-listed from the university's register. But a year later some of the original members re-registered the club and held meetings again. Is it the same club as before? Any answer to that question would not produce any new information. It would only be a different description of facts that are already well understood.[8] Depending on your worldview, some philosophical questions might be empty. Most atheists would regard the question 'Is there a God?' as empty. Those who are reductionist about personal identity might regard the question 'What is the self?" as empty.

When you are trying to observe a situation as objectively as possible before making a decision about it,

---

8 For a deeper discussion of empty questions, see Parfit, <u>Reasons and Persons</u> (Clarendon Press / OUP, 1984) pg. 213-4

you may also be able to observe the way other people are talking about it. What kind of questions are they asking? What kind of framing language are they using in their descriptions? This, too, is part of the first stage in the process of reasoning.

As we will explore in more detail in the part of the book dedicated to propositions, there are certain features you should look for in a good answer to a good question. One of these is that a good answer can be expressed in the form of a proposition, but more on that later…

2.7. Differing Worldviews

Perhaps the most difficult things to observe and question are your own beliefs. So, let's look at how to do exactly that.

Once in a while, you are going to encounter differences between your own worldview and the intellectual environment in which you live. But much more frequently, you are also likely to encounter differences between your worldview and other people's worldviews, as well as differences in the intellectual environments of different religions, political arrangements, and cultures. In some of those situations, you will not be able to just stand back and 'live and let live'. A judgment may have to be made, for instance about which worldview you are personally prepared to live by, or which one you will support with your money or your votes or your actions in your community. Sometimes you may find it necessary to oppose the actions of people who have different worldviews; for instance, when people are doing something that you are sure is harmful or oppressive to yourself or others. And finally, you are also going to occasionally discover places where your worldview doesn't 'work'; that is, places where it clearly does not help you understand the world, nor accomplish any goals you have decided to pursue.

Many people may not be aware that they have a worldview. But we probably wouldn't be able to think about much of anything without having at least one worldview. Furthermore, it is quite likely that you subscribe to several worldviews at the same time, which

may be religious, political, cultural, philosophical, or scientific.

But not all worldviews have equal merits. Some are problematic, whether in great or small ways. Some worldviews that are generally acceptable may still contain some unexamined and rarely enacted prejudices about race, class, sex, or some other characteristic. Some are seriously faulty, because those prejudices dwell in their core beliefs. If some part of your worldview is faulty, this can muddle your thinking, and create conflict between you and other people. It is therefore very important to learn to tell the difference between a faulty worldview and an acceptable one.

Some worldviews are faulty because their ideas concerning the nature of the world have been proven wrong through scientific discoveries, such as the Ptolemaic model of the solar system, the 'four elements' theory of matter, or the 'four humours' theory of medicine. Others are faulty because their political and moral consequences have turned out to be very destructive. Mediaeval feudalism, Soviet communism, and Nazism are the best-known examples of morally faulty worldviews. And some worldviews that are deeply faulty may have one or two features that seem very appealing and plausible. The way the sun rises in the east and sets in the west certainly makes it look as if the earth is standing still and the sun is traveling around it, as the Ptolemaic worldview suggests. The 'four humours' theory of medicine seems to correspond elegantly to the 'four elements' theory of matter. Under Soviet communism, people were entitled to a full month of holidays every year, at their full salary. And in Nazi Germany, productive and high-achieving workers could receive free holiday trips, paid for by the government. But these apparent benefits should not blind you to the moral and empirical failures of a faulty worldview.

Albert Schweitzer described three properties that he thought an acceptable worldview must have. In his view, an acceptable worldview had to be: Rational, ethical, and optimistic. Let's see how Schweitzer explains each of these points in turn.

First, an acceptable worldview is *rational* when it is the product of a lot of careful thinking about the way things really are.

> Only what has been well turned over in the thought
> of the many, and thus recognised as truth, possesses a
> natural power of conviction which will work on other
> minds and will continue to be effective. Only where
> there is a constant appeal to the need of a reflective view
> of things are all man's spiritual capacities called into
> activity (Schweitzer, ibid, pp. 86-7).

This is stipulated in order that the worldview
may help people come to an understanding of the
world and of one another. A worldview derived from
unreflective instincts and impulses, in his view, cannot
properly reflect reality, nor will it have sufficient power
to motivate people to take action when they should.

Now, Schweitzer's words in that quotation might
seem very circular. It may look as if he's saying 'a
worldview is rational when it's rational'. But what I
suspect Schweitzer had in mind is something like this.
A worldview is rational when lots of people examine it
carefully and critically, and in so doing, they together
determine whether or not its logic is internally consistent, and whether or not it corresponds appropriately
and usefully to the world as people actually experience
it.

Second, an acceptable worldview is *ethical* when
it can tell us something about the difference between
right and wrong, and when it can help us become
better human beings.

> Ethics is the activity of man directed to secure the inner
> perfection of his own personality…From the ethical
> comes ability to develop the purposive state of mind
> necessary to produce action on the world and society,
> and to cause the co-operation of all our achievements
> to secure the spiritual and moral perfection of the
> individual which is the final end of civilization (ibid pp.
> 94-5).

It's important to note here that when Schweitzer
speaks of a worldview as 'ethical', he is not saying that
an acceptable worldview has to include certain specific
moral statements. He is not saying, for example, that an

ethically acceptable worldview must be Christian, or
that it must be liberal, or whatever. And in that sense,
he is not speaking of any particular civilization; In his
day, the word was used to mean all humanity. Rather,
he is saying that it has to have *something* to say about
what is right or wrong, and *something* to say about how
we can become better human beings. One worldview
might say that it is always wrong to harm animals, for
instance. Another might say it can be right to harm
animals under certain conditions, such as to kill them
for food. Schweitzer's proposition here is that one (or
both) of these might be acceptable if, and to the extent
that, following them leads you to be a better person.

Schweitzer's third criterion for an acceptable
worldview may help clarify what he means by 'a
better person'. He says an acceptable worldview must
be *optimistic*: it must presuppose that life on earth is
valuable and good.

> That theory of the universe is optimistic which gives
> existence the preference as against non-existence and
> thus affirms life as something possessing value in itself.
> From this attitude to the universe and to life results the
> impulse to raise existence, in so far as our influence can
> affect it, to its highest level of value. Thence originates
> activity directed to the improvement of the living condi-
> tions of individuals, of society, of nations and of human-
> ity.' (ibid, pp. 93-4)

Overall, according to Schweitzer, a worldview that
is not rational, not optimistic, and not ethical, whether
in whole or in part, is (to that extent) a problematic or
faulty worldview. To continue the exercise from earlier
in this chapter: Take another look at what you thought
was the most significant limit situation of your life so
far and how it changed your worldview. Did it make
you more rational, optimistic, and ethical?

2.8. Value Programs

One important type of faulty worldview is the kind
that the Canadian philosopher John McMurtry called
a value program. Value programs are worldviews
which have the following two qualities:

- There's at least one proposition about values that cannot be questioned under any circumstances or for any reason, even when there is evidence available which shows that the proposition is weak, open to reasonable doubt, or even clearly false.
- Acting on the unquestionable proposition, and behaving and making choices as if that proposition is true, tends to cause a lot of preventable harm to people, or to their environments.

Here are McMurtry's own words, to describe what value programs are like:

> In the pure-type case, which will be our definition of a value program, all people enact its prescriptions and functions as presupposed norms of what they all ought to do. All assume its value designations and value exclusions as givens. They seek only to climb its ladder of available positions to achieve their deserved reward as their due. Lives are valued, or not valued, in terms of the system's differentials and measurements. All fulfil its specified roles without question and accept its costs, however widespread, as unavoidable manifestations of reality. In the strange incoherence of the programmed mind, the commands of the system are seen as both freely chosen and as laws of nature, or God…Those who are harmed by the value program are ignored, or else blamed for falling on its wrong side, because its rule is good and right. Its victims must, it is believed, be at fault. A value program's ideology is in great part devoted to justifying the inevitability of the condition of the oppressed.[9]

McMurtry added to his discussion that worldviews become value programs not due to a fault in human nature, but rather due to a kind of social or psychological conditioning: '…it is not "human nature" that is the problem. The problem is not in how we are constructed, but in the inert repetition of the mind, a condition that does not question socially conditioned value programs.' (*ibid.*)

It's usually easy to identify value programs from history: Mediaeval feudalism, for instance. But perhaps the more important questions are:

- What are the value programs of our time?
- Are you, or the people around you, unknowingly subscribing to a value program?
- Are there propositions in your intellectual environment which cannot be questioned, or which can be questioned but only at great personal risk?
- Is anyone harmed through the ways you live your life in accordance with the teachings of your worldview? How are those harms explained? And are those explanations justifiable? Why or why not?
- In what ways, if at all, does your worldview meet, or fail to meet, Schweitzer's three criteria for acceptability?

As an exercise, have a look at this short list of worldviews of our time, and think about whether any of them are value programs, and why (or why not):

Representative parliamentary democracy
Free-market capitalism
Human rights
The right to bear arms
The pro-choice movement
The pro-life movement
the pro-gun movement
The gun control movement
American exceptionalism and Manifest Destiny
The fandom of any professional sports team
The fandom of any popular television show, film franchise, or musical group
The culture and the official platform of any major political party
The teachings, doctrines, and creeds of any religion, or any form of atheism or humanism.

---

9 McMurtry, Unequal Freedoms: The Global Market as an Ethical System (Garamond, 1998) p. 6.

Chapter Three:
Informal Logic—Habits of Thinking

WE HAVE seen some of the problems that can arise when different worldviews and different intellectual environments come into conflict with each other. Now let us look at some of the problems that can arise when a given worldview comes into conflict with *itself*. There are various ways that people think, and various ways people pull their worldviews together that actually make it harder for them to find the truth about anything, communicate with each other effectively, and solve their problems. And there are other ways people think which make it easier to communicate, solve problems, and discover truths. I shall call these 'good and bad thinking habits'.

Note that I call these principles of thinking 'habits' rather than rules, because there are exceptions to some of them. There can occasionally be situations in which a good thinking habit might be inappropriate, or in which a bad thinking habit might turn out to be useful. But such exceptions tend to be very rare. Your thinking will almost always be rational and clear when it follows the good habits and avoids the bad ones.

The bad habits tend to arise in two ways. They can arise because of *how* we think: These bad habits are mostly based in psychological factors such as fears, motivations, and attitudes. Bad habits also arise because of *what* we think: These habits arise when our thinking involves problematic beliefs. Again, thinking in terms of such bad habits are not signs that one's thinking is necessarily or inevitably wrong. (In this way, they are different from the fallacies, which we will discuss later on.) They do, however, tend to make one's thinking very weak, and therefore vulnerable to criticism and

objection. They also render one's views and beliefs easily manipulated by other people. When they form a prominent part of one's intellectual environment, they tend to introduce faults into one's worldview.

3.1. Self-Interest

On its own, self-interest need not be a bad thing. Most people make decisions at least in part on the basis of what they think will benefit them. However, self-interest can be a problem when you advance some argument or defend some worldview only because you personally stand to benefit if it's true, and for no other reason.

The notion of self-interest has an important place in some specialized forms of reasoning, such as game theory and economics. We find it in sources as ancient as Aristotle: His claim that everyone by nature desires happiness was the starting place for his theory of ethics. We find it in the work of John Stuart Mill, who made the pursuit of 'utility', meaning pleasure or personal benefit, the basis of his theory of ethics, called Utilitarianism. Adam Smith, widely regarded as 'the father of modern economics', also placed self-interest at the centre of his work. To Smith, self-interest was a normal part of rational human behaviour, and often a very self-defeating kind of behaviour. But in a properly functioning economy, Smith reasoned, businesspeople and investors would direct their self-interest toward public goods.

Self-interest also plays an important part in a branch of mathematics called game theory. Without going into a lot of detail about each of these writers and others who were like them, let it suffice to say that self-interest is a very powerful psychological force that motivates people. All the writers mentioned here are very careful to specify the ways in which self-interest is rational and useful, and the ways in which it is irrational and even damaging. For this reason, some logicians prefer to separate 'intelligent self-interest' from ordinary selfishness and egotism. Intelligent self-interest looks for the 'bigger picture', sees the ways in which one's own interests can align with others' interests, is willing to sacrifice short-term benefits for the sake of longer-term benefits, and recognizes that some kinds of benefits or advantages for the self are not really worth pursuing.

Self-interest tends to get in the way of good reasoning when people have a strong emotional or economic stake in something that looks like it might be under threat by others. In such situations, people tend to get passionate and emotional, and this almost always clouds their judgments. If you secretly want something to be true, and you stand to benefit from it being true (for instance, if you might make money from it), but there's little or no reason for it to be true, you may inadvertently misinterpret the evidence, discount contradictory evidence, or invent rationalizations that have little or no logical strength. This can lead you to a faulty understanding of your situation, and as a result you are more likely to make bad decisions.

Another way that self-interest can lead to bad-quality thinking is by leading people to believe that they must dominate every conversation and win every argument, even when there's no emotional or economic stake in it for anyone. Especially in societies where competitiveness is afforded a good deal of social prestige, it can be tempting to treat discussions and debates (online, in classrooms, at parties, anywhere that people talk to each other about significant questions) as if they are another arena where people may fight each other and defeat opponents. But this tends to worsen the overall quality of debate, such as when a speaker finds he can 'win' by interrupting others when they speak, introducing obstructionist questions, nit-picking and hair-splitting the meaning of another

speaker's statements, insulting people, or even physically dominating a space with aggressive gestures and a loud voice.

It is unproductive and usually unfair when arguments turn into shouting matches. And when used properly, systematic critical reason is not a weapon. If we are engaging with others in a rational search for the answers to significant questions, the engagement is collaborative and not competitive. The point is not to dominate or to win a match—it is to learn and progress. In that sense, a win for one speaker is a win for everyone. At the end of this chapter, we will suggest some informal rules for how to conduct a debate with that aim in mind. But before we get that far, there's a special version of self-interest which deserves its own heading.

3.2. Saving Face

Among the various ways that people are self-interested, most people are also interested in having a good reputation and being liked or even admired by others around them. No one, or almost no one, enjoys having their faults, weaknesses, harmful actions, or foolish choices pointed out to them. And nobody, or almost nobody, likes to be proven wrong. This in itself is fairly standard and unobjectionable, but sometimes it leads people to cover up their mistakes. Or, if they have been shown that some of their ideas or beliefs are unworkable or absurd, they still may continue arguing in favour of them anyway, in order to avoid admitting that their opponent could be right. This is what is meant by 'saving face'.

The habit of saving face is in some ways related to a condition called **cognitive dissonance** by psychologists. This is what happens when someone is confronted with, or contemplates, two or more beliefs that cannot both be true at the same time. For instance, the thoughts: 'I am a good person' and 'I caused someone harm' might induce deep discomfort in someone who wants the first statement to be true, but cannot ignore evidence that the second statement might also be true. Most people are strongly psychologically disposed to avoid having contradictions like that in their thoughts.

And most people don't like to have muddled thoughts like that pointed out to them by others: It makes them look foolish. They therefore tend to invent self-interested reasons to reject one or other of the contradicting beliefs, with the real purpose of restoring their sense of self-worth. But it is a bad tactic, and doing it may blind us to the truth, or make it difficult or impossible to discover what the truth really is.

Examples:

> 'Only six people came to the company picnic. I was on the organizing team. But it wasn't my job to send out the invitations.'

> 'I got an "F" on that essay. But I'm getting an "A" in all my other classes. Clearly, the professor doesn't know what he's doing.'

> 'Jim has been my best friend for ten years and he's always been nice to me, so I just can't believe he is the one who stole the old man's wallet. You must be mistaken.'

> 'Sally has been my best friend for ten years. But tonight she stole my wallet. I guess she was a bad person all along, and she just tricked me into thinking she was a good person.'

3.3. Peer Pressure

All of us are members of various communities and social groups, as was discussed in the section on worldviews and intellectual environments. And each of those groups tends to have a few prevalent ideas, practices, and beliefs, that form part of the group's identity. Here let us add that most of these groups also exert a bit of psychological pressure on the members to accept the group's prevalent ideas, practices, and beliefs. Sometimes that pressure can be very subtle, and very limited. You might get nothing more than an odd look or a cold shoulder if you do or say something that doesn't fit with the group's main beliefs. Other times, it might be very overt and unambiguous, and perhaps connected to threats of punishment

The habit of saving face is in some ways related to a condition called cognitive dissonance by psychologists. This is what happens when someone is confronted with, or contemplates, two or more beliefs that cannot both be true at the same time.

for non-conformity. You might be shut out of the group's decision-making process, or not invited to the group's events anymore, or (if one's non-conformity is persistent) even targeted with malicious gossip or threats of violence. Sometimes the peer pressure might be a constant barrage of messages, statements, and reinforcements. Propagandists sometimes create multiple fake user accounts on social media ('sock puppet' or 'troll' accounts), to make the community which supports the message appear larger than it really is, thus increasing the influence the message. The online campaign to damage the reputation of the film *Star Wars: The Last Jedi* (2017) was conducted that way.[1] Any of these techniques tend to make people keep their dissenting views to themselves, or else change their views to better fit in with the group.

Now, the ideas shared by the group might be right, they might be wrong, or they could be somewhere in between. But the number of people who believe these ideas has nothing to do with whether those ideas are any good. Problems almost always arise when someone accepts an idea or a worldview *only* because it is an idea or a worldview favoured by the group he or she belongs to, and for no other reason.

3.4. Stereotyping and Prejudice

Since we are speaking of peer pressure: a community or social group may also have a few beliefs about those who belong to other groups. The group might look up to other groups, or down upon them, or attribute certain qualities or behavioural traits to all of them. This becomes a bad habit when there is little or no real evidence that all members of that other group actually do share that quality. We might build stereotypes of people based on how they are characterised in entertainment media, or on experiences meeting one or two members of that group. But in terms of actual evidence to support the stereotype, the 'sample size' from these personal encounters is always too small. It's usually based on only a handful of cases, and then generalized to a massively larger group. In this way it is a case of the fallacy of hasty generalization. In fact, the sample size can be as small as zero: Some people de-

velop stereotypes without any evidence at all. They've just been taught to think that way by their intellectual environment. Stereotyping almost always treats people as representatives of a type, and almost never as individuals with their own distinct qualities. In this way, it prevents us from knowing (or caring about) the truth about individuals, and can even prevent us from knowing (or caring about) the truth about the various groups that another person might belong to.

While stereotyping is the assumption that all members of a given social group are somehow essentially the same, prejudice is hostile or harmful judgment about the merit or worth of people in that group, assigned on the basis of stereotypical assumptions. One of the ideas that a group might pressure its members to believe is the idea that this group is better than other groups. This almost always leads people to see the ideas and worldviews of rival groups in the very worst possible light. And it leads people to treat members of the rival group badly: To harm them with racist, sexist, classist, able-ist, religiously hateful behaviour. Prejudice is also hurtful when the qualities it assigns are qualities that subordinate people, attribute negative traits, or even deny them full membership in the human race. There might be a spectrum of intensity, which at one end attributes only a few relatively minor bad qualities such as foolishness or uncleanliness, and which at the other might incite strong feelings of hate or fear. There may be anxiety that the others are emotionally unstable, have criminal tendencies, animalistic physical features, disease, or even a secret conspiratorial agenda. But in any case, stereotyping and prejudice almost always prevents people from seeing things and people as they truly are.

Why do prejudiced beliefs persist? The main reason is that those beliefs are supported by peer pressure. When among prejudiced people, uttering a disparaging remark about the target group might be actually encouraged and rewarded in various ways: Smiles, happy laughter, welcoming gestures, and approving words. In this way, prejudice persist when people do not think for themselves, and instead allow other (prejudiced) people to do their thinking for them.

1 Bay, Morten (Research Fellow, Center for the Digital Future, USC Annenberg School for Communication and Journalism) "Weaponizing the haters: The Last Jedi and the strategic politicization of pop culture through social media manipulation." Research Gate [online edition], October 2018. See also: Pulver, Andrew. "Star Wars: The Last Jedi abuse blamed on Russian trolls and 'political agendas'" The Guardian, 2nd October 2018; Watercutter, Angela. "Star Wars: The Last Jedi, Russian Trolls, and the Disintegration of Discourse" Wired, 2nd October 2018.

3.5. Excessive Skepticism

It is usually healthy to be at least a little bit skeptical, and not take everything at face value all the time. Some people, however, believe that we cannot truly know anything unless we can be absolutely certain of it, and that we are beyond any possible doubt about it. That level of skepticism is almost always too much. (Unless you are Socrates.)

Excessive skepticism tends to arise when people try to estimate the riskiness of some activity. The excessively skeptical person tends to make a 'big deal' of the potential risks, and might be unwilling to do anything until he is satisfied that everything is absolutely safe and certain. Or he might be unwilling to do something because 'it's never been tried before'. But it's often the case that we have to act even in situations where success is very uncertain, and there is no way to absolutely guarantee safety. The moon landings from 1969-72 are good examples here. No one really knew whether the missions would succeed, or fail, or even end in total disaster. (At one time, astronomers thought that the dark 'seas' on the moon were made of sand, and they worried that the landing craft would sink!) The excessively skeptical person weighs the risks too heavily, and often ends up unable to act because of that skepticism. He may even try to prevent others from acting, because of his own doubts.

Excessive skepticism can also appear in matters that are almost purely theoretical. For instance, some people might doubt the reality of the world outside their own minds. It can be fun to speculate on whether or not we are being deceived by Descartes' 'evil genius', or whether we are all living inside a computer-generated virtual reality or holographic projection. Sometimes it can be fun to ask 'How do you know?' in an infinite regress, the way small children do. There are also some branches of postmodern philosophy which hold that no one can know all there is to know about complex situations in politics, economics, and culture. Or that all truths are subject to interpretations and contextual situations, which makes certainty impossible—or, more radically, that there are no truths of any kind; there are only interpretations. There are

interesting reasons for why some philosophers argue for those positions. But most of the time, we don't need to have such high standards for certainty. As an aside, the creators of **disinformation** often count upon people's radical skepticism about the truth, in order to make fascist or otherwise repugnant **value programs** appear no better or worse than any other worldview. But I digress.

It is enough that one's beliefs are beyond *reasonable* doubt; they do not have to be beyond *all possible* doubt. As a rule of thumb, remember that doubt based on speculation without evidence is not reasonable doubt. It's not enough to say that something is doubtful because some alternative explanation might be valid. It's also important to say something about how probable the alternative explanation really is. If an alternative explanation is possible but very unlikely, and there isn't much evidence for it, it doesn't serve as a good basis for skepticism. Therefore, if you dreamed last night that you ran away to a foreign country and married your worst enemy, that 'might' be because in some parallel universe that's exactly what you did. But since there is absolutely no evidence to support that possibility, it's best to discount it as a reasonable explanation for your dream.

We shall see more about healthy scepticism in the discussion of good thinking habits, as well as in the discussion of reasonable doubt.

3.6. Intellectual Laziness

This is the habit of 'giving up too soon', or deliberately avoiding the big questions. This is the habit we indulge when we say things like: 'Thinking that way is too confusing', or 'your questions drive me crazy', or 'these questions cannot be answered, you just have to accept it'. Laziness also appears when you answer a philosophical question with a witty quotation from a movie or a popular song, as if that's all that needs to be said about the topic. Some people actually go to great efforts to defend their laziness, with complex arguments for why intellectually enquiring or scientifically minded people 'can't handle the mystery of things', or why they want to 'take away the beauty and the magic of the world.'

A variation of intellectual laziness is willed ignorance. This is the habit of deliberately preventing oneself from answering hard questions or acknowledging relevant facts. Some people prefer to live in a kind of bubble, where serious challenges to their worldviews never appear. While it can be a sign of integrity to preserve the core values of one's worldview, it is also the case that deliberately shutting out facts or realities that challenge this worldview can lead one to make poor decisions. Your worldview might hold that some questions are unanswerable, or that some questions are not allowed to be asked. Similarly, you might prevent yourself from acknowledging facts or realities that could serve as evidence of the wrongness of some part of your worldview. Willed ignorance actually takes some effort, and perhaps isn't precisely the same as laziness. But it has the same effect: It prevents people from learning things that they may need to know, and makes it more likely that they will make bad decisions or turn their worldviews into value programs. In this respect, willed ignorance is similar to **cognitive dissonance**: the intellectually lazy person suspects there is an inconvenient truth out there and she takes steps to avoid being confronted by it.

Some people might even argue that there is no such thing as 'Truth', with a big capital T, referring to statements about the ultimate things like God, or justice, or knowledge, or reality. They might believe that it is pointless to claim that any given idea or belief or explanation of such things is true, no matter how well supported it might be by the facts or by logic. There may be an appeal to some kind of relativism as the reason for why there's no such thing as an ultimate truth. This line of thinking is not truly lazy: it goes to some effort to seriously defend the claim that no one can make a serious claim about such things. But the real function of such assertions is to justify a refusal to think deeply and carefully about the things that matter. It may be the case that there are, or that there are not, ultimate truths about such things. But the intellectually lazy or wilfully ignorant person does none of the work needed to find out. They actually do

Laziness is the habit of 'giving up too soon', or deliberately avoiding the big questions. This is the habit we indulge when we say things like: 'Thinking that way is too confusing,' or 'your questions drive me crazy', or 'these questions cannot be answered, you just have to accept it'.

not know, and they have made their ignorance into a kind of rule for their thinking.

It might not be polite or kind to name this habit 'laziness', or not completely accurate given the effort that sometimes goes into remaining lazy. But just as one can be lazy at practical tasks like cleaning your house, you can be lazy in your thinking about pressing problems or important questions. And just as laziness in your practical affairs can hurt you eventually, there are times when lazy thinking can cause you great trouble later on, too. Lazy thinking can make it easier for others to manipulate and deceive you, for instance. And it can also paralyze you into doing nothing in situations where decisions must be made.

3.7. Using 'Deepities'

A **deepity** is a statement that appears to be very wise and inspirational, but which actually has little or no meaning. It is the sort of quick and ready-to-hand statement that people might use when they want to sound intelligent, or they want to be consoling or compassionate, or to signal to listeners that they are in agreement about something. Yet at the same time they want to do as little independent thinking as possible. In that sense it is like a form of intellectual laziness.

The term 'deepity' was first used by American philosopher Daniel Dennett, though he attributed its coining to the daughter of one of his friends. Here's his definition.

> A deepity is a proposition that seems both important and true—and profound—but that achieves this effect by being ambiguous. On one reading it is manifestly false, but it would be earth-shaking if it were true; on the other reading it is true but trivial.[2]

You're probably familiar with some popular examples:

'Children are the future.'
TRUE BUT TRIVIAL READING: Children eventually grow up and become adults.
FALSE BUT IMPRESSIVE READING: When today's children grow up and become adults, they and only

they will create all the important progress in human society.

'It is what it is.'
TRUE BUT TRIVIAL READING: An event or a state of affairs, referred to in a given discussion, exists, that that both speaker and audience understand the situation in the same way.
FALSE BUT IMPRESSIVE READING: The situation referred to in a given discussion is absolutely beyond anyone's ability to do anything about it.

'Love is a word.'
TRUE BUT TRIVIAL READING: The four letters L-O-V-E, spell out the word 'love'.
FALSE BUT IMPRESSIVE MEANING: Love (the human phenomenon) is no more or less important than other phenomena which can also be represented with words: 'Friendship', 'cruelty', 'traffic ticket', 'fnord'.

'Beauty is in the eye of the beholder.'
TRUE BUT TRIVIAL READING: Beauty is an experience of the physical senses.
FALSE BUT IMPRESSIVE READING: Beauty is only a matter of personal-belief relativism, and so cannot be discussed or reasoned about with others.

There can be expressions of profound thoughts that are not deepities: Poetic symbols, for example. We can also treat some paradoxical statements as exercises in handling complex and difficult problems. The deepity, however, is the kind of statement in which the true-but-trivial reading lends to the false reading a glamour of wisdom. In so doing, it becomes a form of intellectual laziness.

3.8. Bullshit

It may surprise some of you to learn that in the study of logic, the term 'bullshit' has a specific technical meaning. It comes from the American philosopher Harry Frankfurt, who published an essay about it in 1986 and then gave it a book-length treatment which enjoyed a brief but noteworthy popularity.

---

2 Daniel Dennett, Intuition Pumps and Other Tools for Thinking (New York: W.W. Norton &co., 2014), p. 56.

Every graduate student in philosophy knows—and one of my professors once told me in the following words—that in order to be a career academic it's helpful to know how to speak intelligently about a paper you've never read. Of course, she did not recommend doing this this all the time. But this throwaway comment tells us something about what bullshit is. It's not merely lying: It's blustering, pontificating, or gabbing on some topic which you know nothing about, with the result that your talk is only a lot of hokum and hot air—even if some of what you are saying is true. As Frankfurt says, 'What is wrong with a counterfeit is not what it is like, but how it was made.'[3]

Bullshit is like lies, but the person who utters it—the bullshitter, the bullshit artist—is not necessarily deceiving someone about facts. The ordinary liar hides some truth from others in order to achieve an aim, such as the truth about some state of affairs in the world, or the truth about his intentions. The ordinary liar therefore crafts his statements in some relationship to what he believes to be true. The bullshit artist, however, is playing a different game:

> Since bullshit need not be false, it differs from lies in its misrepresentational intent…The fact about himself that the bullshitter hides, on the other hand, is that the truth-values of his statements are of no central interest to him.[4]

In other words, bullshit is that which spews forth from the mouth of someone who neither knows, *nor cares*, what the truth might be. Bullshit appears when people feel obliged or required to talk about things they know nothing about. In a society where everyone has the right to their own opinions, some people may feel obliged to have opinions about everything. It may also appear in situations where relativism and excessive skepticism are widely accepted: Situations, that is, where people believe no one can be sure of anything, so you may as well say whatever you want. And, of course, the bullshit artist can also be someone who just tells lies for the fun of it; someone who enjoys keeping people on edge, or keeping himself at the centre of attention.

I concede that uttering bullshit can be fun. But it's ultimately not very enlightening, for speakers or for listeners. Indeed, Frankfurt's notion of bullshit looks to me like the opposite of Socratic Wisdom: it's the utterance of a person who is unable, or unwilling, to utter the words 'I don't know.'

3.9. Relativism

Philosophical arguments are often presented in the form of debates. Sometimes there are two positions that are opposed to each other, and each side presents arguments that support their position while showing the problems with the opposing position. Consider, as an example, a debate about the moral permissibility of the death penalty. The speakers might take these two positions:

> 1: The death penalty is morally permissible (for reasons x, y, z).
> 2: The death penalty is not morally permissible (for reasons a, b, c).

When assessing the evidence for these claims, philosophers try to establish whether it is true or false that the death penalty is morally permissible. In this case the moral permissibility of the death penalty is being treated like a fact. Often beginning philosophers are not comfortable with treating moral, epistemic, or aesthetic claims as either right or wrong. Philosophical claims are not scientific claims for which we can provide empirical evidence, and often both sides provide very compelling arguments. This can make it seem as if both sides are right. Sometimes it makes sense to search for a middle ground, but that is not always possible or desirable. It is, furthermore, a contradiction to say that the death penalty both is and is not morally permissible. When is it morally permissible? What makes the death penalty morally permissible in some cases but not others? More needs to be said.

Relativism is the view that a claim is only true or false relative to some other condition. There are many varieties of relativism, but the two most common are:

3 Harry Frankfurt, "On Bullshit", Raritan Quarterly Review, Vol. 6, No.2, Fall 1986.
4 ibid.

Subjective relativism, also known as **personal belief relativism**, is the claim that the truth about anything depends on what someone believes. It is the view that all truth is in the 'eye of the beholder'; or that something is true *if (and only if) someone believes it to be true*, and then it is true *for that person*, and perhaps only for that person. In ethics, subjective relativism is the idea that an action is morally right if the person doing that action believes it to be morally right. In other words, nothing makes an action right or wrong except the judgment of the person doing it.

Cultural relativism is the idea that something is true, or right, etc., because it is generally believed to be so by some culture or society. Further, it is true, or right, etc., for *that* society.

Here we will examine relativism about truth as it pertains to philosophical claims about ethics and knowledge that you are likely to encounter in an introductory class. As relativism is very appealing to beginning philosophers, it is important to look at some different kinds of relativistic arguments, the problems with them, and some of the typical reasons for adopting a relativistic position.

One reason to adopt relativism is that philosophical claims, particularly ethical claims, can seem very subjective. With so much debate it can seem as if there are no correct answers, and that what is right or wrong can be different for different individuals. Alice believes the death penalty is acceptable and Barbara believes it is not, and who are we to tell them what to believe?

The problem with accepting this kind of relativism is that it makes a claim true or false relative to someone's beliefs—and takes beliefs to be above any justification. While it may seem arrogant to challenge other people's beliefs, examining what we take to be true and why is one of the most fundamental practices in philosophy. It isn't enough to say 'Alice believes that X is okay, so X is right for her,' because it's possible that Alice has never examined her beliefs, or came to hold them because she was given false information. Investigating what we believe and why can help us to have consistent beliefs, and also to be confident and conscientious in our ethical choices.

While it is respectful to consider others' points of view, the presence of differences in perspective does not mean that philosophical questions are entirely subjective. Learning how to carefully consider and assess reasons and justifications is part of studying philosophy. And there are ways to be culturally sensitive while challenging the practices of our own and other cultures. Something to look out for is when disagreement between conclusions can sometimes mask similarities in underlying beliefs. For instance, two people can agree that murder is unjustified killing but disagree about which deaths should be counted as murder. Alice might believe that the death penalty is state-sanctioned murder, and thus oppose it. Barbara might believe that a death that has been sanctioned by the state is always justified. Their disagreement over the death penalty is thus not only about whether it is right or wrong, but also over acceptable justifications for taking a person's life.

Someone else might note that some cultures accept action X while some do not, and argue that X is morally permissible relative to culture. This is known as cultural relativism. We can use our understanding of how other cultures' concepts work to question or critique practices in our own. As it turns out, some of the concepts that seem natural or objectively true are non-universal and contingent. Thus, if a culture has three rather than two concepts of gender we might reconsider why we think about gender as we have done for so long. Often students accept cultural relativism because they want to be sensitive to cultural differences. Different cultures have different practices, but can we say that if a given culture uses the death penalty that it is sometimes morally permissible? There are two problems with this approach. One is that it does not allow people within a culture to disagree with the practice. If someone from culture A wants to argue against the death penalty they could not do so on moral grounds—their culture permitting it has already made it a morally acceptable act by this logic. Another problem is changes in cultural practices. We want to say that slavery was abolished because people realized that it was wrong to treat people as property, not that it became immoral once the practice stopped.

There is also a difference between issues that are moral and those that are social norms or matters of etiquette. In some cases, it makes sense to accept cultural relativism about social practices, but in others it might seem as if some other factor—such as human rights—trumps concerns for cultural variation. It can be difficult to determine when we should and when we should not challenge the practices or beliefs of other cultures. And such considerations require rational inquiry and a sensitive analysis of the arguments that demands more than knee-jerk relativism.

The problems with relativism do not mean that we have to accept the view that ethical or epistemic truths are universal and absolute. There is a great deal of conceptual space between individual relativism and accepting a general moral principle. Being open to other cultures' beliefs and attitudes can be very important for learning to see things in a different light, but it does not mean that we have to accept them without good reasons.

3.10. The Consequences of Bad Habits

The consequences of living with and falling into the bad thinking habits described above can be very serious. For instance, they can:

- Make you more vulnerable to being intimidated, bullied, or manipulated by others;
- Make you less able to stand up for yourself, or for others in need;
- Make it harder to tell the difference between truth and lies;
- Make you more dogmatic and closed-minded;
- Make you less flexible, less creative, and less prepared to handle unpredictable changes in your situation.
- Lead you to justify moral decisions that needlessly harm people, including yourself;
- Lead you to suppress or ignore evidence that goes contrary to your beliefs, even if that evidence is very reliable or important;
- Provoke confusion or anger when presented with reasons why certain beliefs might be problematic or faulty;

- Prevent serious philosophical thinking about the most important problems in our lives;
- Prevent personal growth, maturity, and self-awareness.

With these observations in mind, let's look at some good habits.

3.11. Curiosity

As an intellectual habit, curiosity is the desire for knowledge. The usual explanations of things are not enough to satisfy an intellectually curious person: She is the one who always wants to find out more about whatever is new, strange, or interesting in the world. When something different, unusual, unexpected, or even weird and scary appears, the curious person doesn't hide from them or pretend they are other than what they are. She faces them directly, and makes an honest attempt to investigate them, not satisfied to let them remain mysterious. For philosophers, just like scientists, try to understand things as completely as possible, and render them less mysterious.

It is precisely by being intellectually curious that good reasoning helps prevent closed-minded dogmatism. Curiosity leads to discovery, invention, expanded awareness of the world, and of the self. Sometimes it leads to beauty; sometimes it leads to power. Most of all, it leads to, just as it depends on, a sense of wonder. Those who think that rationality is a set of rules for thinking which limit or constrain your experiences, or who think that rationality kills the sense of creativity and imagination, are simply wrong—and there's no polite way to say it. It's probable that such people have actually limited their own experiences by excluding from their minds the most powerful, most inquisitive, and most successful way of knowing the world ever devised. (It is also possible that those who say rationality kills the sense of wonder are trying to control you, by discouraging you from asking your own questions. But I digress.)

It is precisely by being intellectually curious that good reasoning helps prevent closed-minded dogmatism. Curiosity leads to discovery, invention, expanded awareness of the world, and of the self. Sometimes it leads to beauty; sometimes it leads to power. Most of all, it leads to, just as it depends on, a sense of wonder.

3.12. Self-Awareness, and Socratic Wisdom

Above the entrance to the famous Oracle of Delphi, the religious centre of the classical Greek world, was written the phrase γνωθι σεατον. In English, this means 'know yourself'. The idea was that those who wanted to enter the temple should have done a sustained exercise in personal soul-searching, in order to be fully honest about their own individual character and habits, and they should also be honest about a few basic and unavoidable facts about human life (especially human mortality).

Self-awareness involves knowing your own presuppositions, desires, biases, worldviews, and so on, as well as your habits, faults, desires, powers, and talents. It also means knowing something about what it means to be a thinking human being. This is a more difficult prospect than it may appear. Some people do not find out what their own worldview is until someone else says or does something that challenges it. But it is an essential quality: Those who do not know themselves tend to make poor decisions, and they are easily manipulated by others.

In the chapter on the history of logic, we briefly mentioned a principle called **Socratic wisdom**: The willingness to acknowledge what you do not know. Here we can add that practicing Socratic wisdom can also be a helpful exercise in cultivating mature self-awareness. Knowing something of the limits of your knowledge is a large part of knowing who you are. It requires courage, too, since admitting one's ignorance is often embarrassing. Yet a healthy sense of the extent of one's own ignorance, coupled with curiosity, can lead to a life of very enjoyable intellectual discovery.

3.13. Physical Health

As unrelated as it may seem, taking care of your physical health is actually a good thinking habit. If you are feeling unwell, or sleep-deprived, or under stress, or for whatever reason you are physically uncomfortable, it becomes harder for you to observe and understand your situation, and harder to reason about it clearly.

Maintaining good health, for the sake of good thinking, involves getting enough exercise, eating healthy real food and avoiding junk food, bathing regularly, and getting enough sleep. It also means taking care of your mental health—and one of the simplest ways to do that is to take time every day for leisure activities that are restful.

A study conducted by psychologists in Japan found that people who gazed on forest scenery for twenty minutes produced 13.4% less salivary cortisol, a stress hormone. Walking in forests and natural settings also helped reduce high blood pressure, and it reduced heart rate fluctuations. As these effects became more known, some municipalities in Japan created 'forest therapy' programs for stressed-out factory workers.[5] High-stimulation activities like playing video games, watching action films, participating in intensely athletic sports, and doing other activities that get adrenaline rushing can be a lot of fun, but they are not restful. I'm not saying you should avoid doing these things altogether, but being ready to do good critical thinking requires some calm, and peace, and quiet. To be better able to calm yourself when you need to think, give around twenty minutes or more, every day, to doing something genuinely relaxing, such as walking in a forest, meditating, reading, or cooking and eating a proper meal. And don't try to multitask while you are doing the restful activity. If you are experiencing a lot of frustration dealing with a certain problem, you will probably have an easier time with it after a shower, a healthy dinner, a walk in the park with a friend and a dog, or a good night's sleep.

3.14. Courage

Sometimes your process of thinking about things will lead you to possibilities or conclusions that you won't like, or which your friends or associates won't like. Sometimes, you might reach a conclusion about something that might land you in trouble with your boss at work, or your teacher, your priest, your family members, your government, or anyone who has some kind of power, authority, or influence in your life. Expressing that conclusion or that thought might even

put you in some degree of danger: For example, you might risk being fired from your job, or ostracized from your community. Depending on the situation, and the idea you are expressing, you could find yourself excluded, angrily criticized, ignored, arrested, imprisoned, or even killed. Even in countries where the freedom of speech and expression, and the freedom of the press are guaranteed by constitutional law, people can still run great risks by speaking their minds, even when their words are true.

Courageous thinking means thinking and expressing the dangerous thought anyway. It means thinking and speaking without fear. It means committing yourself to what you rationally judge to be the best conclusion, whether you like it or not, and whether your friends or your 'betters' like it or not—which is a lot harder to do than it sounds. Strong social forces like the desire to be welcomed and included and loved, or strong institutional forces like laws or corporate policies, can lead people to keep quiet about ideas that might be controversial.

Questions and arguments can require personal courage when they challenge a very important part of one's worldview. Consider the following examples:

- What if there are no gods? What if the god I've been told about from an early age doesn't exist?
- What if there is no objective moral right or wrong?
- What if a very popular or charismatic person is telling half-truths or lies?
- At my workplace, am I participating in or benefitting from something unjust, or evil?
- What if life has no purpose or meaning?

People who take such questions seriously, and who consider answers that are radically different from the answers provided by their worldviews, may experience a lot of self-doubt or even despair. They may find that they have to change their lives. Even the mere act of posing the questions, aside from the attempt to answer them, can land people in trouble with their friends and families. Strong social forces might pressure the questioner to not ask certain questions, or to answer them only in acceptable ways. In such situations, it

5 Akemi Nakamura, "'Forest Therapy' Taking Root" The Japan Times Online, 2 May 2008.

can take great courage to ask such questions, and to do one's own thinking in search of a decent answer.

Questions and arguments can require public or political courage when they challenge some arrangement in your social world. It could something as simple as choosing to support a different professional sports team than the one based in your home city, or the one supported by all your friends and family. Or, it could be something as complex and dangerous as opposing a policy of a large corporation that you work for, or which has a significant presence in the area where you live. It can also take a lot of courage to criticize the actions of some entity with political power, especially when that entity can threaten people who disagree with it. If you criticize your employer, you might lose your job. If you criticize your government, you might be arrested. If you criticize your church leaders, you might be shamed, denounced, or dismissed from the church. As the philosopher Voltaire wrote, 'It is dangerous to be right in matters on which the established authority is wrong.'

The classical Greek language gives us a word for statements that require this kind of courage: *Parrhesia*, which roughly translates as 'bold speech'. The person who makes such a bold statement is called a *parrhesiastes*. Two qualities are necessary for a proposition to count as parrhesia. One is that the speaker incurs some personal risk from social or political forces. The second is that the speaker's words must be true. (Thus, a person who creates controversy for the sake of creating controversy is not a parrhesiates.) Today we might call such people '**whistle-blowers**': Individuals who act like referees in a game who stop a player who breaks the rules. Whistle-blowers are people who draw public attention to some act or policy of moral wrongdoing in their workplaces, their governments, or in any other social group to which they belong. Whistle-blowers often face all kinds of problems: Harassment, defamation of their reputations, job losses, lawsuits, vandalism of their homes and vehicles, and in some cases death threats. But no public cause has ever succeeded 'by itself' without courageous people willing to speak out in favour of it. To be a courageous thinker means to care more for the truth than for personal interests (and

sometimes, more than for one's own safety). But it also means to be an agent for necessary changes.

3.15. Healthy Skepticism

Earlier, we characterized 'excessive skepticism' as a bad habit, but there is also a very healthy kind of skepticism. Healthy skepticism is the general unwillingness to accept that things are what they appear to be. It is the unwillingness to take things for granted, or to accept that things are as you have been told they are by anyone else, no matter who they are.

This does not mean we have to doubt absolutely everything, nor does it mean we cannot trust anyone. It does, however, mean that we do not jump to conclusions. The healthy skeptic is slow in accepting popular explanations for things—instead, he prefers to investigate many possibilities before settling on the best available explanation.

Unhealthy skepticism, as we saw earlier, involves doubting everything and trusting no one, often without good reasons for doubting. Healthy skepticism is willing to trust, but it needs a good **prima facie** reason to trust, or a prima facie reason to doubt. A 'prima facie' reason is evidence which appears to show that things are a certain way 'on the face' or 'at first glance', that is, before you investigate the evidence very deeply. Reasoning about things with prima facie evidence is like taking a kind of quick look.

Sometimes you may feel skeptical about something because of what your 'gut instincts' are telling you. Of course, it's not really your gut that is doing the thinking here. What is actually happening is that your unconscious mind is looking for patterns, comparing the present patterns of things to events in the past when the pattern of things was similar, remembering what followed next on those previous occasions, and reporting its findings to your conscious mind in the form of a feeling or a hunch, or even an apparently 'psychic' experience. I like to call this process **perceptual intelligence**.[6] It is an entirely intellectual exercise, although it may not feel like one. Your prima facie reasons for believing or disbelieving something tend to emerge from this work of perceptual intel-

---

6 C.f. Brendan Myers, <u>Circles of Meaning, Labyrinths of Fear</u> (Moon Books, 2012) pp. 75-83. See also the discussion of 'pattern

To think autonomously simply means to think for yourself, and not let other people do your thinking for you. Autonomous thinkers do not blindly accept what they have been told by parents, friends, role models of every kind, governments, newspaper columnists, or anyone who could influence their thinking.

ligence. It is not a completely perfect process: On closer inspection, some prima facie conclusions might turn out to be misleading or wrong. Even so, it can still serve as a good starting place for investigations.

Healthy skepticism is also known as **reasonable doubt**. We'll see more of that in a later chapter. But before we get there:

3.16. Autonomy

To think autonomously simply means to think for yourself, and not let other people do your thinking for you. Autonomous thinkers do not blindly accept what they have been told by parents, friends, role models of every kind, governments, newspaper columnists, or anyone who could influence their thinking.

However, you are under no obligation to follow anybody's party line. Your only obligation for thinking, if it is an 'obligation' at all, is to think clearly, consistently, rationally, and, where necessary, courageously.

At the end of some curious, courageous, and skeptical soul-searching, you may decide that your worldview should be more or less the same as that which is held by your family, friends, role models, and other influences. That is okay—the point is that the worldview is now *yours*, and it was not simply transferred to you by others.

3.17. Simplicity

Sometimes you may find that things are more complex or more elaborate than they appear to be at first. And it is often the job of reason to uncover layers of complexity behind appearances. Still, if you have two or more explanations for something, all of which are about of equal worth, the explanation you should prefer is the simplest one.

This principle of simplicity in good reasoning is sometimes called **Ockham's Razor**. It was first articulated by a Franciscan monk named Brother William of Ockham, who lived from 1288 to 1348. His actual words were '*Entia non sunt multiplicanda sine necessitate*.'[7] In English, this means 'No unnecessary repetition of identicals'. This is a fancy way of saying,

---

7 William of Ockam, <u>Sentences of Peter Lombard,</u> (ed. Lugd., 1495), i, dist. 27, qu. 2, K.

'Well it's possible that there are twenty-three absolutely identical tables occupying exactly the same position in space and time, but it's much simpler to believe that there's just one table here. So, let's go with the simpler explanation.' Ockham's original point was theological: He wanted to explain why monotheism is better than polytheism. It's simpler to assume there's one infinite God, than it is to assume there are a dozen or more.

Ockham's idea has also been applied to numerous other matters, from devising scientific theories to interpreting poetry, film, and literature. Other ways to express this idea go like this: "All other things being equal, the simplest explanation tends to be the truth", and "The best explanation is the one which makes the fewest assumptions."

3.18. Patience

Good philosophical thinking takes time. Progress in good critical thinking is often very slow. The process of critical thinking can't be called successful if it efficiently maximizes its inputs and outputs in the shortest measure of time: We do not produce thoughts in the mind like widgets in a factory.

The reason for this is because good critical thinking often needs to uncover that which subtle, hard to discern at first, and easy to overlook. I define subtlety as 'a small difference or a delicate detail which takes on greater importance the more it is contemplated.' As a demonstration, think of how many ways you can utter the word 'Yes', and mean something different every time. This also underlines the importance of precision, as a good thinking habit. As another example: Think of how the colour planes in a painting by Piet Mondrian, such as his 'Composition with Yellow, Blue, and Red' have squares of white framed by black lines, but none of the white squares are exactly the same shade of white. You won't notice this if you look at the painting for only a few seconds, or if you view a photo of the painting on your computer screen, and your monitor's resolution isn't precise enough to render the subtle differences. But it is the job of reason to uncover those subtleties and lay them out to be examined directly. And the search for those subtleties cannot be rushed.

3.19. Consistency

When we looked at what a worldview is, we defined it as 'the sum of a set of related answers to the most important questions in life'. It is important that one's worldview be consistent: That its answers to the big questions generally cohere well together, and do not obviously contradict each other. Inconsistent thinking usually leads to mistakes, and it can produce the uncomfortable feeling of cognitive dissonance. And it can be embarrassing, too. If you are more consistent, you might still make mistakes in your thinking, but it will be a lot easier for you to identify those mistakes and fix them.

Consistency also means staying on topic, sticking to the facts, and following an argument to its conclusion. Obviously, it can be fun to explore ideas in a random, wandering fashion. But as one's problems grow more serious, it becomes more important to stay the course. Moreover, digressing too far from the topic can also lead you to commit logical fallacies such as Straw Man and Red Herring.

3.20. Open-ness and Open-mindedness

Being open-minded means listening to others, taking their views seriously, and treating their ideas with respect even while critically examining them (a difficult thing to do, but not impossible). It also means not resorting to fear and force when promoting one's own views, but rather presenting them in a way that leaves them open to the critical scrutiny of others. In philosophy this is sometimes called the **principle of charity**. The principle of charity requires speakers and listeners to interpret and understand each other's ideas in the very best possible light. Listeners must assume that other speakers are rational (unless there are good reasons to assume otherwise), and that what they say is rational, even if that rationality is not immediately obvious. Philosophers do this partially as a kind of professional courtesy to one another. Open-ness and open-mindedness do not, however, mean that we have to accept everyone's ideas as equally valid. Open mindedness is not the same as assuming that all

---

8 For a deeper discussion of empty questions, see Parfit, <u>Reasons and Persons</u> (Clarendon Press / OUP, 1984) pg. 213-4

things are true; it is also not the same as relativism. Rather, the open-minded person looks for the best explanation for things, whether he or she personally likes that explanation or not, and whether it fits with his or her worldview or not. She is open to the idea that she might be wrong about something, or that her worldview might be partially faulty, or that her thinking about something that matters to her may have to change. But she does not change her thinking for no reason. She is interested in the truth, whatever it might be.

An open-minded person may still find that some ideas, arguments, and explanations are better than others. But if we are open-minded, we can be more confident that we have understood other people's views properly: We will not fall into the logical trap of the straw man (see the chapter on Fallacies). It is also much easier to find common ground with others, which is an essential step in quelling conflict. And if we reject some idea, we will have rejected it for the right reasons. Open-mindedness also helps prevent intellectual or ideological differences from descending into personal grudges.

Open-mindedness is also helpful in other ways. Suppose that some of my friends and I went for a picnic to the park, but soon after we got to our picnic site it started to rain. One member of the party might say the rain was caused by ghosts or supernatural creatures who live in the park and don't want us picnicking there. Another might say that the rain was caused by air pressure changes in the upper atmosphere. Now, the open-minded person is not necessarily the one who accepts that both explanations are equally possible and leaves it at that. The open-minded person is the one who goes looking for the evidence for each explanation. If he doesn't find the evidence for one of those explanations, he rejects it and goes in search of the evidence for another one. The closed-minded person, by contrast, is the one who picks the explanation he likes best, whether or not there's any evidence for it, and then refuses to consider any alternative explanation. Closed-mindedness is one of the signs that someone's mind is occupied by a value program.

As a general rule, the closed-minded person is usually the one who is quickest to accuse other people of being closed-minded, especially when his own ideas are criticized.

The point of this example is to show how open-mindedness helps people arrive at good explanations for things that happen. It does not mean that all explanations for things are equally 'valid'. We do not have to put unlikely or weird explanations on the same footing as those with verifiable evidence or a consistent logical structure. But it can mean that every explanation or idea which appears to be sound, at least at first glance, is given a fair examination, no matter where that explanation came from, or who thought of it first.

3.21. Asking for Help

So far, I have been stressing good thinking habits that one can practice on one's own. Good thinking tends to require independence and autonomy. And problems often arise when we allow other people to have too much influence over our own thinking, such as when we allow ourselves to be influenced by peer pressure. However, it can be helpful to ask others who you respect and admire, or who you believe may have relevant knowledge, to help. And while it is important to make your own decisions about your own life, there's nothing wrong with asking others who you trust to offer you advice and guidance. Even if you do not ask anyone to offer suggestions, it can sometimes be helpful to hear a different point of view, or just to talk things over with someone who can be both critical and appreciative. The shared wisdom and experience of one's friends, elders, and associates can often lead to different perspectives and better decisions. Others people, for instance, can offer possibilities that you might not have thought of. Or they might know things that you didn't know, and thus point you in new directions. Or they might have faced a similar problem or situation in the past, and their description of their experience might help clarify something about your own situation. As an example, here's the

Roman philosopher Seneca describing how some kind of social interaction is important for one's personal intellectual growth:

> Skilled wrestlers are kept up to the mark by practice; a musician is stirred to action by one of equal proficiency. The wise man also needs to have his virtues kept in action; and as he prompts himself to do things, so he is prompted by another wise man.[8]

A lot may depend on who you choose to ask for advice, how much you trust them, and how often you go to them. But the overall point here is that knotty and complicated problems need not always be handled alone. A habit of asking elders, peers, colleagues, and friends for help can often help clarify one's thinking, and lead to better solutions.

3.22. Summary Remarks

None of the bad habits of thinking *necessarily* or *inevitably* lead to unsound arguments, false beliefs, or faulty worldviews. They are not the same as fallacies (which are be discussed in a later chapter.) An argument can be strong and sound even if its conclusion coincides with the speaker's personal interests, or with the presuppositions of the speaker's culture, worldview, etc. The bad habits are, however, signs that one's thinking is probably not fully clear, critical, and rational. It may even mean that one has given up the search for the truth of the matter too soon.

Similarly, the good habits, by themselves, do not guarantee that one's thinking will always be perfectly rational, but they do make one's thinking *very much more likely* to be rational.

"Skilled wrestlers are kept up to the mark by practice; a musician is stirred to action by one of equal proficiency. The wise man also needs to have his virtues kept in action; and as he prompts himself to do things, so he is prompted by another wise man."
- *Seneca*

8 Seneca, Letters to Lucilius, 109, 2; trans. R. M. Grummere: Loeb Classical Library.

Ingsoc
English Socialist Party
War is Peace
Freedom is Slavery
Plusgood, Minipax, Facecrime, Miniluv, Goodthink.

Chapter Four:
Basics of Formal Logic

THE PREVIOUS chapters were about informal reasoning: General 'rules of thumb' that are meant to help with everyday reasoning, which aren't intended to be applied strictly to every case. In this chapter, we move on to formal logic: The kind of reasoning in which the rules are very strict. The purpose here is less focused on helping people get on with their lives, and more on learning to draw correct conclusions.

Let's define argumentation as the process of seriously debating the worth and merits of propositions. The word '**argument**' here does not refer to an angry shouting match. Rather, it indicates any two (or more) statements in which one is the reason for the other, one is supported by the other(s), or one follows from the other(s). We 'build' arguments by assembling basic statements into particular kinds of structures. Then, having put them together that way, we can more easily test to see whether the ideas being discussed are worth our time.

4.1. A Few Words About Words

You might have noticed that in the preceding chapters we paid close attention to the ways people use words.

The ability to reason is very closely related to the ability to express oneself. There are, obviously, many ways that people can express their thoughts and feelings, and not all of them require words: We also sing, make art, move our bodies, and so on. You may also have encountered feelings or experiences that seem deeply personal and primal, and sometimes putting them into words is astonishingly difficult.

Some philosophical and religious traditions hold that words 'get in the way', or teach that by talking about things, and especially by naming things, we diminish their reality. Some Asian philosophical traditions are famous for holding positions like this: Taoism is an example I mentioned in Chapter 1. Yet the idea appears in European philosophy as well.

However, the kind of **formal logic** this chapter discusses, which is the foundation of the Western philosophical tradition, is most closely related to *verbal* self-expression; that is, to speaking and to writing. Without intending to diminish the importance of non-verbal knowledge and non-verbal expression, this chapter is about how to use words, spoken and written, to reason about anything you may want to.

Words are surprisingly powerful: They configure how we think about and understand nearly everything in the world. As we saw in the discussion of framing languages, some of the things configured by words include the ways we think about people and about issues, and they also shape our moral judgments, our plans of action, and even our perceptions. Words can single out things or events, making them stand out as significant. They also pass over other things and events, which causes them to fade into the background. In that respect, what is left unsaid can be equally as significant as what is said. Words also tend to confer a kind of certainty about the identity and the meaning of the things and events that they refer to. Or to put it another way, to name a thing or an event is a powerful way to know—and tell others—what it is. All this is not to say that words *create* reality: That would be taking it too far. Yet it seems undeniable that words *configure* reality; they are the instruments we use for the individual and communal production of meaning.

It is, of course, precisely this point which leads some people to believe that words are dangerous. They would therefore like to leave some areas of life, such as religious experience, or one's first-person sense of self, 'out of bounds', and not allowed to be described or analysed with words. In reply to this point of view about words, let us note that while words configure our understanding of reality, they also open up spaces for sharing reality, as well as playing with it, experimenting with it, manipulating it, and revealing its many sides and natures. Of course, words can also configure our understanding of reality by attempting to control it, or to control who can speak about it, and how it is to be spoken of. (This was the entire point of 'newspeak', the fictitious language invented by George Orwell for his novel *1984*.) This is only to say that the use of words is complicated, and they are comparable to other things we use that are both useful and at the same time potentially dangerous: Kitchen knives, for instance, or bricks, or chain saws, or paint brushes. There may also be forms of thinking that do not require words. But as it is rather difficult to do many kinds of cooking without using a kitchen knife, logic is rather difficult, or actually impossible, without using words. If you cannot express your beliefs with words, it is possible to doubt that you understand your beliefs. If you cannot explain your choices and actions with words, it is possible to doubt that you had reasons for your choices and actions. Part of the purpose of logic is to help us express ourselves with greater clarity and honesty, so that we can understand and examine our worldviews, beliefs, and choices.

It is part of the job of reason and logic to teach us how to use our words as well as we possibly can, in order to get as near to the truth of things as we are able. At any rate, the very highest and deepest things in the world—the real, the true, the good, and the beautiful—always retain their immensity. For however much we speak of them, there is always more to say.

4.2. Definitions

In formal logic, the first moves in the crafting of an argument are about clarifying the meaning of our words, as precisely as we can.

In every language, there are many words that have more than one meaning. This is good inasmuch as it allows us more flexibility of expression: It is part of what makes poetry possible, and also comedy, irony, and so on. But for the purpose of reasoning as clearly and as systematically as possible, it is important to use our words very carefully. This usually means avoiding metaphors, symbols, rhetorical questions, weasel words, euphemisms, tangents, equivocations, and 'double speak'. When building a case for why something is true, or something else is not true, etc., it is important to say exactly what you mean, and eliminate ambiguities as much as possible.

The simplest way to do this is to craft good definitions. But a definition can be imprecise in several ways, as seen in the following examples.

TOO BROAD: The definition covers more things than it should. Example: 'All dogs are four-legged animals.' (Does that mean that all four-legged animals are dogs?)

TOO NARROW: It covers too few things. Example: 'All tables are furniture pieces placed in the dining rooms of houses and used for serving meals.' (Does that mean that tables in other rooms used for other purposes are not 'true' tables?)

CIRCULAR: The word being defined, or one of its closest synonyms, appears in the definition itself. Example: 'Beauty is that which a given individual finds beautiful.' (This actually tells us nothing about what beauty is.)

TOO VAGUE: The definition doesn't really say much at all about what is being defined, even though it looks like it does. Example: 'Yellowism is not art or anti-art. Examples of Yellowism can look like works of art but are not works of art. We believe that the context for works of art is already art.'[1] (And I don't know what this means at all!)

---

1 Marcin Lodyga and Vladimir Umanets, 'Manifesto of Yellowism', retrieved from www.thisisyellowism.com, 8 July 2010 / 17

4.3. Sense and Reference

Having clarified the exact meaning of words, the next thing to do is clarify the exact meaning of sentences. It's possible to have a sentence that is a proposition which cannot be used in an argument because of some vagueness or ambiguity in its words or its grammar. Consider these examples:

> Women are stronger than men.
> People who get good marks in school are very intelligent.
> Beer is better than wine.
> Art is good for the soul.
> Little John is all grown up now.

Each of these sentences are propositions: It's clear that they all could be either true or false. But some of the words here have more than one meaning. We would have to figure out exactly which meaning is used here, before we can try to draw any conclusions about them (or, for that matter, find out whether the proposition is true or false). In the first example, 'Women are stronger than men', what is meant by the word 'stronger' here? Does it mean that women have more willpower than men? Does it mean that women have thicker and tougher bones than men? Does this statement generalize about the 'average man' and the 'average woman'?

Most of the time, the meaning of our words will be mostly obvious because of the context in which we say them. This was the point raised by Gottlob Frege in his discussion of the sense and the reference of proper names.[2] Here's a simple version of what he described.

> The *Reference* of a word or a proposition (also sometimes called the Denotation) is that object or event in the world which the word stands for. A word *designates* a reference; the word-as-reference is the proper name for the object or event.
> The *Sense* of a word or a proposition is its cognitive significance, the thought being expressed; this being shown by its mode of presentation and by its context.

> A word or a sign designates a reference but also *expresses* a sense.
> The *meaning* of a word, or of an entire proposition, comes from the combination of its reference and its sense.

Distinguishing the sense of a word is not the same as determining its truth-value. The meaning of the proposition 'People who get good marks in school are very intelligent' looks fairly straightforward, but you need to clarify the sense of the word 'intelligent' before finding out whether the reference of the whole proposition is true or false. The problem here isn't just that some intelligent people get bad marks in school, or that some stupid people get good marks. Those kinds of issues can come up when the argumentation is underway. But before we get that far, we have to know what sense the speaker wishes to express with the use of the word 'intelligent'. Is it the ability to perform well on school tests? Is it the ability to speak clearly and sound like you know what you're talking about? Is it the ability to solve problems quickly? What kind of intelligence are we talking about—literary, mathematical, emotional, kinaesthetic, or some other type? Similarly, in the proposition 'Beer is better than wine', we would need to know the sense of the word 'better'. Is beer considered better here because it is cheaper? Or because it has less alcohol per unit of volume? Or because it's easier for people to make their own beer at home? Or, is this person merely expressing a personal preference? Also, given that there are thousands of recipes for beer, and thousands of recipes for wine, it might not be clear what kind of beer and what kind of wine are being compared.

The context contributing to the sense of a word can include the speaker's social situation, the gestures or facial expressions made by the speaker, the speaker's tone of voice, recent events in the speaker's world, the framing language that the speaker is using, and so on. If we do not have the context of the words we say, we may not get the sense of them, and therefore also may not know what is meant. For example, if a man who looks like he is 40 years old or more were to say, 'I'm

2 'Über Begriff und Gegenstand', in Vierteljahresschrift für wissenschaftliche Philosophie, 16: 192–205. Translated as 'Concept and Object' by P. Geach in Translations from the Philosophical Writings of Gottlob Frege, P. Geach and M. Black (eds. and trans.), Oxford: Blackwell, third edition, 1980.

only seventeen!' in the context of attempting to get a student discount on a bus ticket, we would judge that he is lying, or maybe in denial about himself. The reference of his words is *incorrect*. But if he were to say those exact same words as a line in a theatrical performance in which he was playing a seventeen-year-old character, we would judge the sense of his words differently. The reference of his words points to the dramatic character he is playing, as everyone in the audience would understand.

It's obvious that words with a certain reference can have more than one sense. Frege also observed that different words sometimes have the same reference. To use his example: The names 'morning star' and 'evening star' have different senses, but they refer to exactly the same object: The planet Venus. He also showed how there can be words which have a sense but not a reference: Again, to follow his example, the phrase 'the furthest distant object from the Earth' has a sense, because we grasp the thought that is expressed here, but it might not have a reference, because we might not know exactly what object is the furthest distant object from the Earth. (For instance: Are we speaking in the context of our own solar system? Or the universe as a whole?) Another philosopher working in this area, Bertrand Russell, showed that words can be meaningful even if they refer to nothing at all. For example, an utterance like 'The present King of France' (that's Russell's own example), can be understood by anyone and found to be meaningful, yet France is presently a republic and therefore has no king.

4.4. Implicature

British philosopher Paul Grice created a theory of conversational implicature, whose purpose is to help people get their meanings across to others with greater clarity and precision. His theory consists of four principles, which are now called Grice's Maxims:

> The maxim of quantity:
> Make your contribution as informative as is required (for the current purposes of the exchange).
> Do not make your contribution more informative than

is required.

> The maxim of quality:
> Do not say what you believe to be false.
> Do not say that for which you lack adequate evidence.

> The maxim of relation:
> Be relevant.

> The maxim of manner:
> Avoid obscurity of expression.
> Avoid ambiguity.
> Be brief (avoid unnecessary prolixity).
> Be orderly.[3]

There can be occasions when you may want to deliberately break one or more of these rules. For example, you may be speaking ironically, or you may want to leave unsaid that which does not need to be said because it's already understood. This is called 'flouting a maxim', and it is part of what makes language fun. For instance, if one of my friends accompanied me to a used car dealership and found a car there that was rusty and dented, and I said 'That's definitely a top-end model', I will have broken the maxim of quality. But the context of the condition of the car, and my tone of voice, and so on, would provide the *sense* of the words, so my friend would immediately understand exactly what I mean: 'The car is certainly *not* a top-end model.'

4.5. Propositions

By following the guidelines noted above (precise definitions, necessary and sufficient conditions, sense, reference, and implicature), we can craft the kinds of sentences that can be used to build arguments. Such sentences are called propositions; or they are also sometimes called statements and claims. A proposition is a simple sentence that has just one meaning, for it expresses one thought according to the rules of grammar in the language in which it is expressed. Also, a proposition asserts that something is the case, or is not the case. When a proposition asserts that something

---

3 Grice, Paul. <u>Studies in the Way of Words</u> (London: Harvard University Press, 1989) pp. 26-7.

is the case, it is also called an affirmation; when a proposition asserts that something *is not* the case, it is also called a negation or a denial.

Not all sentences are propositions. Some sentences are questions, some are commands, some are emotional exclamations, and some are poetic devices, such as metaphors. (Did you notice that every sentence in this paragraph so far is a proposition?) One way to recognize a statement is to look for sentences that could be given as a direct answer to a straightforward question. Another is to look for sentences that could be either true or false; a sentence that one could either agree or disagree with.

It is additionally possible for a single sentence to contain more than one proposition.

- It's raining today, and I'm feeling blue. (Two propositions.)
- The book on my table is well-thumbed, but boring. (Two propositions.)
- This new kitchen gadget can slice any vegetable, as well as any fruit, but it can't handle meat. (Three propositions.)

And finally, it is also possible to have a paragraph of dialogue in which only one or two sentences are propositions, and the rest of the paragraph is made of expressions that, while they might help communicate the speaker's feelings, are not expressions that can be used to build an argument. Consider this example:

'I'm really pissed off. I ordered this new computer from the internet. And it took three weeks to get here, which was bad enough. Then when it arrived I got so mad again! Because the one I ordered was silver, but the one they sent me was black! Somebody in that company is asleep at the wheel.'

Clearly, the speaker here is angry about this situation. But if the speaker wanted to draw any logical conclusions from this discussion, for instance about what to do, or about whether to trust the company again, the only relevant sentences here are the ones

A proposition is a simple sentence that has just one meaning, for it expresses one thought according to the rules of grammar in the language in which it is expressed. A proposition also asserts that something is the case, or is not the case. When a proposition asserts that something *is* the case, it is called an affirmation; when a proposition asserts that something *is not* the case, it is called a negation or a denial.

3 MacIntyre, <u>After Virtue</u>, 2nd Edition (London: Duckworth, 1985) p. 222.

which stick to the facts. Here's the same discussion again, with the irrelevant expressions crossed out:

> ~~'I'm really pissed off.~~ I ordered this new computer from the internet. And it took three weeks to get here, ~~which was bad enough. Then when it arrived I got so mad again! Because~~ the one I ordered was silver, but the one they sent me was black! ~~Somebody in that company is really asleep at the wheel.'~~

As you can see (I hope!), it's usually easy to tell the difference between useful propositions, and other expressions that do not serve this purpose. Logic starts to look complicated when there are lots of propositions with lots of relations to each other. But even the argument with thousands of lines is still made up of simple, straightforward true-or-false sentences like these. The other parts of the argument have to do with the way that propositions are used, or the way they are positioned in relation to other propositions in the general structure of the argument. If you can figure out this part of the textbook, you can figure out everything else!

4.6. Truth

We haven't yet said anything about how we know a given proposition is true or false. To cover that topic, we need to ask: What is truth? The origin of the English word *truth* is in Anglo-Saxon words like *getriewe*, *treow*, and *troth*, words relating to faithfulness, fidelity, honesty, promise keeping, and loyalty, especially in relation to an important undertaking.[4] Truth, in the kind of logic we've been discussing here, is a property of propositions. As we've already seen, arguments must be made of propositions and can't be made from other kinds of sentences. Let's now examine some ways to find out whether a given proposition is true.

One (perhaps obvious) kind of truth is the kind where the proposition corresponds to the observable facts. This is called the **correspondence** theory of truth. Here, a proposition is true if you can test it with the empirical evidence: Looking around, confirming it with your own eyes and ears, or perhaps confirming it

with a scientific experiment. It may happen that after conducting a scientific experiment, two observers still disagree about what was observed. In such a case, the two observers would have to conduct more experiments. This theory of truth is closely related to a school of thought called **Empiricism**, and it is the way most people make their ordinary, everyday decisions about what to believe.

Yet most people also believe many things about the world which are not seen in our ordinary, everyday lives. This is where the **coherence** theory of truth can help you. With this model, the truth of a proposition depends on your worldview, your beliefs about the sort of world that we all live in. Before you dismiss this as a kind of relativism, consider how many beliefs you hold which are not based on empirical evidence that you personally have access to. For instance, you probably believe that the earth orbits the sun, that matter is made of tiny particles called molecules and atoms, and that radiation is real and that it can harm you. But if you're like most people, you acquired these beliefs not from your own observations, but instead from your intellectual environment. A teacher, parent, or scientist taught you these beliefs; you soon found that just about everyone around you also believes them, so you adopted them yourself.

There's also a third kind of truth, called the **pragmatic** theory. With this one, a proposition is true if it is a useful thing to believe. It may be easier to explain this theory with an example. If you are in a city with a subway system and you would like to travel from one side of the city to the other, you would consult the subway map. The map almost certainly won't correspond to the actual positions of the subway stations: They will be closer or further distant in the city than the map lines suggest. And the tracks might not follow the exact lines on the map: They won't be perfectly horizontal or vertical, or they won't turn on perfect 90-degree angles. Nevertheless, the map tells you everything you need to know about how to get to where you want to go. Thus, although the map doesn't correspond to observable facts and has nothing to do with anyone's worldview, it nonetheless it tells the truth according to the pragmatic theory.

---

4 J. Shipley, Dictionary of Word Origins (New York USA: Philosophical Library, 1945), pg. 278; The Shorter Oxford English Dictionary On Historical Principles (Oxford UK: Oxford University Press / Clarendon Press, 1973) Vol.II, pg. 2370.

Not only because it's fun, but also because it is part of the intellectual environment of our time, an honourable mention should go to the concept of **truthiness**. Coined by the American comedian Stephen Colbert in 2007, truthiness is the property of sentences that feel intuitively correct, regardless of facts, evidence, or logic; it is the property of sentences claimed to be true on the basis of the audience's gut feelings, which means they were designed to **appeal to emotion**. The word was quickly adopted by dictionaries and newspapers: It was named Miriam-Webster's Word of the Year for 2008. In our discussion of **prima facie** reasons, we saw that intuitions or 'gut feelings' do have a place in the process of reason. But unlike prima facie reasoning, truthiness has nothing to do with one's perceptual intelligence. Rather, it is more closely related to **deepities**. More seriously, it is a technique of social and political manipulation: It weakens the possibility that an audience will be ready to receive certain knowledge about things, and instead makes them more receptive to **propaganda** and **disinformation**. In this respect, Colbert may have anticipated the contemporary phenomena of **fake news**, **alternative facts**, and **post-truth** by at least seven years. But we will see more of than in a later chapter.

A final comment about truth. In the chapter on the history of logic, we mentioned that in some branches of the **Continental tradition**, truth is sometimes treated as a kind of **aletheia**, a revealing of the being of things. Alas, it's a bit beyond the purpose of this textbook to discuss that model of truth. We mention it here just to let you know if you think the idea 'truth is a property of sentences' is a rather boring way to think of truth, there are other ways to think about it.

4.7. Categorical Propositions

As discussed earlier, an argument is a set of statements from which we can infer another statement (the argument's conclusion). In formal logic there are several common forms of statements that will be useful to know when we discuss argument forms.

Aristotle, who is usually regarded as the father of philosophical logic, proposed that all ideas can be analysed using a type of statement called a **categorical proposition**. This kind of statement is the basic building-block of **categorical logic**, a way of inferring true statements from other true statements by showing that some or all things of one category also belong to another category. For instance, the statement 'All cats are blue' tells us that there is a category of cats, and a category of blue things, and that everything that is a cat is also blue. In categorical logic, we can divide a statement into parts, each part describing a category. This is something we cannot do if we are only evaluating statements as a whole. For instance, if I claim 'All cats are blue' and 'Benny is a cat', then the logical inference we can make is 'Benny is blue'. But if we're looking at the propositions as a whole, we can't see the relation between the two statements. That is, if we symbolized 'All cats are blue' as 'A, and 'Benny is a cat' as 'B', then we have lost the relation between the two claims that allows us to infer that 'Benny is blue'.

There are four main types of categorical proposition. We will use 'S' to indicate the subject of the proposition, and 'P' to indicate the predicate we are attributing to the subject.

Universal Affirmative: All S are P.
Example: 'All cats are fuzzy.' (S: cats. P: fuzzy things.)

Universal Negative: No S are P.
Example: 'No dogs are ten feet tall.'
(S: dogs. P: things that are ten feet tall.)

Particular Affirmative: Some S are P.
Example: 'Some skyscrapers are beautiful.'
(S: skyscrapers. P: beautiful things.)

Particular Negative: Some S are not P.
Example: 'Some books are not meant for children.'
(S: books. P: things meant for children.)

There have been various attempts to represent Aristotle's logic using math-like symbols, but most have resulted in horribly complicated systems that have frustrated logicians all over the world for millennia.

Gottlob Frege made the most successful attempt so far, which he called 'predicate logic'. One of the differences between Aristotle's logic and Frege's predicate logic is that while predicate logic would symbolize Aristotle's universal statements as conditionals (see below), Aristotle did not use conditionals in his logic, as he believed that a conditional statement did not properly express the relation between the antecedent and the consequent. The proper relation, Aristotle thought, is that of belonging to a category. This is why you might see 'All S are P' reinterpreted by modern logicians as something like, 'If X is an S, then X is a P' (where X is some random noun: A person, place, or thing). Predicate logic also assumes that when we make a statement about a particular thing, that particular thing exists, but when we make a universal statement, the subject of that statement doesn't necessarily exist. Thus, particular statements are said to have 'existential import' that universal statements do not.

CONTRADICTORIES

In categorical logic, two statements are said to be **contradictories** if it is impossible for both of them to be true, and also impossible that both of them should be false. For instance, 'I'm wearing white shoes' and 'I'm not wearing white shoes' are contradictory statements.

Of the kinds of statements given above, the universal affirmative is contradictory to the particular negative, and the universal negative is contradictory to the particular affirmative. This is best illustrated by example. Let's say that 'S' stands for 'cats' and 'P' stands for 'fuzzy'. The statements will then look like this:

Universal affirmative: All cats are fuzzy.
Universal negative: No cats are fuzzy.
Particular affirmative: Some cat is fuzzy.
Particular negative: Some cat is not fuzzy.

The universal affirmative and particular negative statements are contradictory because *it is impossible* that all cats are fuzzy and that at the same time some cat is not fuzzy. It is also impossible that both statements are false. That would mean that 'All cats are not

fuzzy' and 'Some cat is fuzzy' would both have to be true.

Likewise, the universal negative and the particular affirmative statements are contradictory. Again, this is because *it is impossible* that 'No cats are fuzzy' and 'Some cat is fuzzy' are both true statements. Likewise, they cannot both be false. This would mean that 'No cat is not fuzzy' and 'Some cat is not fuzzy' would both have to be true.

CONTRARIES

Two statements are said to be **contraries** if it is impossible for them both to be true, but possible for them both to be false. Carrying on with our fuzzy cats, the Universal Affirmative and Universal Negative statements are contraries. 'All cats are fuzzy' and 'No cats are fuzzy' cannot be true at the same time. However, they could both be false. When they are both false is when both of their contradictory statements are true: When some cats are fuzzy and some are not.

SUBCONTRARIES

Two statements are said to be **subcontraries** if it is possible for them both to be true, but impossible for them both to be false. The particular affirmative and particular negative statements are subcontraries, as it is possible for 'Some cats are fuzzy' and 'Some cats are not fuzzy' to be true at the same time. But both statements cannot be false at the same time. In that case, both of their contradictories would have to be true: 'All cats are fuzzy' and 'No cats are fuzzy' (even though of course this is impossible!)

SUBALTERNS

Since categorical logic did not distinguish between statements having existential import and those that did not, it is also possible to make inferences from universal statements to particular statements. That is, categorical logic assumes that if 'All cats are fuzzy' (All S are P) then it must be true that 'My cat Neelix is fuzzy' (Some S are P). Similarly, if 'No cats are fuzzy' (No S is P), then it follows that 'My cat Mister Bigglesworth is not fuzzy' (Some S is not P).

The Square of Opposition

The above conclusions can be (and often are) summarized in a diagram, like this one:[5]

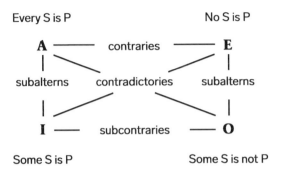

Every S is P   No S is P

For each of the four types of propositions, the diagram shows which other type of proposition can be inferred. A proposition cannot infer a contrary or a contradictory, but it can infer a subcontrary. The relation of **subalterns** goes only one way: The two universal propositions (the two on the top) can infer their relative subalterns, but the two particular propositions (the two on the bottom) cannot infer their relative subalterns. So, for example, you can use the diagram to show that a proposition like:

> All concrete bricks are heavy (All S are P)

can imply the proposition:

> Some concrete bricks (like the ones in this pile) are heavy

but cannot imply the propositions

> No concrete bricks are heavy
> Some concrete bricks are not heavy.

Similarly, the proposition:

> Some carnivorous plants, like the Venus Flytrap, make good houseplants (Some S are P)

can imply the proposition

> Some carnivorous plants do not make good houseplants

But cannot imply the propositions

> All carnivorous plants make good houseplants
> No carnivorous plants make good houseplants

By the way: Did you notice the letters in the corner of the diagram? They refer to a symbol system that was used as a shorthand by Latin-speaking philosophers in the Middle Ages, and is sometimes still used today:

All S are P:	Universal Affirmo
No S are P:	Universal nEgo
Some S are P:	Particular affIrmo
Some S are not P:	Particular negO

Some carnivorous plants, like the Venus Flytrap, make good houseplants. (Some S are P)

5 Diagram taken from Parsons, Terence, 'The Traditional Square of Opposition', The Stanford Encyclopedia of Philosophy (Fall 2012 Edition), Edward N. Zalta (ed.), online edition at http://plato.stanford.edu.

4.8. More Kinds of Propositions

NEGATIVE STATEMENTS

A negative statement is true when the corresponding positive statement is false. For instance, if we were to take the positive statement 'I can clone this pig', a negation of that statement could be expressed by any of the following examples:

> I can *not* clone this pig.
> *It is not the case that* I can clone this pig.
> *It is false that* I can clone this pig.
> *It is untrue that* I can clone this pig.

If we symbolize 'I can clone this pig' with the letter 'A', and its negation as '~A', then we can represent the truth values for 'A' and '~A' in a table. The first row of this table says that if A is true, then ~A is false, and the second row says that if A is false, ~A is true.

A	~A
T	F
F	T

CONJUNCTIONS

When a statement affirms or denies more than one thing, that statement is a **conjunction**. In essence, a conjunction claims that all of the statements composing it are true. The individual statements of a conjunction, which could be either negative or positive, are called its conjuncts. However, if even one of the statements of which a conjunction is composed is false, the whole conjunction is therefore also false. For instance, the conjunction 'My house is red, and I like to eat buttons' is only true if both of the individual statements are true; that is, if my house is red *and* I like to eat buttons. If I don't like to eat buttons, then the conjunction, 'My house is red, and I like to eat buttons' is false. But conjunctions don't necessarily use the word 'and', so it is useful to recognize some other indicator words that tell us we are dealing with a conjunction. Consider the following examples, all of which could be reduced to the conjunction 'I childproofed the house, and children get in the house':

> I've childproofed the house, *and* they still get in.
> I've childproofed the house, *but* they still get in.
> I've childproofed the house, *yet* they still get in.
> *Although* I've childproofed the house, they still get in.
> *Even though* I've childproofed the house, they still get in.
> I've childproofed the house; *however*, they still get in.

If we symbolize 'I've childproofed the house' as 'A' and 'Children get in the house' as 'B', and the conjunction as 'A&B', the truth table for the conjunction appears as follows:

A	B	A&B
T	T	T
T	F	F
F	T	F
F	F	F

From this we can see that the only case where the conjunction 'A&B' is true is when both of the individual statements are true.

Conjunctions are used when we need to put two or more statements together and treat them both/all as if they are one single statement. This can make it easier to analyse an argument as a whole.

DISJUNCTIONS

Disjunctions, like conjunctions, are composed of two or more statements that can be positive or negative. Creating a disjunction is another way to put two statements together and treat them as if they are one statement. We do this when we know that only one of them is true, but we are not sure which one. The statements disjoined in a disjunction are called its disjuncts, and only one of those statements needs to be true in order to make the disjunction as a whole true. For instance, the statement 'Either I'll save this money, or I'll spend it on candy' is true in two possible cases: if I save the money, or if I spend it on candy. The statement would be false, however, if I bought a motorcycle instead of candy with the money. All of the following examples are cases of disjunctions:

> The hoarder will clean the house *or* be evicted.
> *Either* the hoarder will clean the house, or he'll be evicted.
> *Unless* the hoarder cleans the house, he will be evicted.

If we symbolize 'The hoarder will clean the house' as 'A', and 'The hoarder will be evicted' as 'B', then the disjunction as a whole would be represented as 'A∨B'. We can summarize the truth of the disjunction in the table below. In it, we can see that a disjunction is true in all of the cases where A is true or B is true, and where both A and B are true. The only case where the disjunction is false is if both of the statements are false.

A	B	A∨B
T	T	T
T	F	T
F	T	T
F	F	F

CONDITIONAL STATEMENTS

Conditional statements are intended to express a one-way relation between the statements of which it is composed, such that the truth of one implies the truth of the other. In general, a conditional statement takes the form, 'If P, then Q'. For instance, a conditional statement 'If Stacey is going to the party, then I'm not going' implies that my decision about whether to go to the party is dependent on whether Stacey is going (because I hate Stacey).

When we have a conditional statement composed of two statements, we call one the antecedent, and the other the consequent. In the statement, 'If P, then, Q', 'P' is the antecedent (what goes before), and 'Q' is the consequent (what follows).

Conditional statements can also be used to express sufficient and necessary conditions. A sufficient condition is something that is *enough* to bring about an expected result; for instance, 'If I get 85% of the questions right, I will get an A on the exam.' A necessary condition is something that might not be enough, but is necessary; for instance, 'If I'm going to write the exam at all, I'll need to bring a pencil.'

Conditional statements can be symbolized with an arrow telling us which way the relation goes. For instance, if 'P' symbolizes 'You will give me that pony' and 'C' symbolizes, 'I will cry', all of the following statements would be symbolized '~P→C'. Note that '~P' is the negation of 'P'.

> *If* you don't give me that pony, *then* I'll cry.
> *If* you don't give me that pony, I'll cry.
> I'll cry *only if* you don't give me that pony.
> You not giving me that pony *is a sufficient condition* to make me cry.
> My crying is *necessary*, given that I haven't gotten my pony.
> *Unless* you give me that pony, I'll cry.
> *When* I don't get that pony, I cry.
> I cry *only when* I don't get that pony.

A conditional statement is true if both of the statements of which it is composed are true, or if the consequent is true. It is only false if the antecedent is true and the consequent is false. This is the only case where we can be sure that the relationship does not hold. For instance, if Stacey goes to the party and I go too (and, if I knew in advance that Stacey would be there), the statement 'If Stacey is going to the party, then I'm not going' is false, because in fact we have shown that my hatred of Stacey is not strong enough to prevent me from going. However, if I don't go to the party, it might be because Stacey is going, or it might be for another reason. Thus, in any case where I don't go to the party, we say that the conditional statement is true.

The truth of the conditional statement A→B can be summarized in the following table:

A	B	A→B
T	T	T
T	F	F
F	T	T
F	F	T

BICONDITIONAL STATEMENTS

A **biconditional statement** describes a two-way relationship between two statements, such that either one implies the other. For instance, if my decision to go to the party depends on my being able to bring my cat—and if I don't get to bring my cat, then I won't go—then there are two possible results: Either I get to bring my cat, and therefore go to the party, or they won't let me bring my cat, so I won't go. This means that the two-way relation holds if the truth of the statements is the same. Either both are true, or both are false.

All of the following statements describe a biconditional relation, for the case in which if you eat your vegetables you will get dessert, and if you don't eat your vegetables, you won't. However awkwardly phrased some of them appear, they are all simple enough to be understood (and disliked) by any small child who won't eat his vegetables.

You can have dessert *if and only if* you eat your vegetables.
You can have dessert *exactly if* you eat your vegetables.
You can have dessert *precisely if* you eat your vegetables.
You eating your vegetables is a *necessary and sufficient*

condition for you to get dessert.
You can have your dessert *if* you eat your vegetables, *but only if* you eat them.
You can have your dessert *only in the case that* you eat your vegetables.

We can summarize the truth of a biconditional statement in a table:

A	B	A↔B
T	T	T
T	F	F
F	T	F
F	F	T

4.9. Parts of Arguments

Once we have figured out which propositions we want to study, and whether they are true, we can reason more deeply about them. We do this by building **arguments**: That is, by arranging propositions into particular relationships with other propositions, in the hope of discovering what new information might pop out of the arrangement. (Remember, an argument needs at least two propositions; a true proposition by itself is not an argument.)

The first type of proposition that an argument needs is a **premise**. This is a statement given in support of another statement, and it is the *reason* that the other statement should be accepted as true. Most arguments have more than one premise, and most arguments state their premises first.

The other type of proposition that an argument needs is a **conclusion**. This is the 'point' of an argument; it is that which is supported by the premises; it is that which the speaker is trying to persuade another person to believe is the case. Rather than coming from your experience or your worldview or some other source, the conclusion follows from the premises of the argument.

The difference between the premises of an argument and its conclusion are not differences in the statements themselves. Rather, to identify the premise(s) and the conclusion, you have to rely on where they are in the argument, and what function they serve in the argument as a whole. What is being used as a reason, and what is supposed to follow from those reasons? Sometimes a conclusion that follows from a number of premises is put into service as a premise for another conclusion. Consider the following argument:

> 'I don't believe he's telling the truth. You see how his eyebrow twitches, and he's sweating a little more than normal. If he is lying, you shouldn't give him your money.'

In this example there are two arguments. The speaker intends to support the conclusion that 'he is not telling the truth/he is lying' with the premises that 'his eyebrow twitches' and 'he's sweating more than normal'. And then, the conclusion of 'he is lying' is used again as a premise, to support the new conclusion that 'you shouldn't give him your money', which is the *overall conclusion* of the argument.

Stories, poems, explanations, speeches, and so on, can sometimes look like arguments, and they might even be made up of statements. But if they do not have premises giving you *reasons* for accepting conclusions, they are not arguments. This, in case I haven't mentioned it yet, is why thinking logically about something is often called 'reasoning' about it.

The other parts of arguments have to do with the way premises and conclusions are put together.

An **inference** is the name for the relationship between statements in an argument. It is a line of logic between propositions that lead you from the premises to the conclusion. Inferences are often embodied in certain indicator words, which show you which way the direction of the argument is flowing. Here are a few examples of indicator words:

Because

Since

Given that

Which means that

We can conclude that

Hence

It follows that

Therefore

Consequently

So

This implies

…and so on. I've mentioned that an argument needs at least two propositions—but two propositions placed side by side do not make an argument. There must be a relationship between them, showing that one leads you to the other, one supports the other, and one follows from the other. That form of relationship is called an inference, and an argument must have inferences between its propositions too, or else it is not an argument. The indicator words 'because', 'since', 'given that' (etc.) indicate that whatever follows the indicator word is being used as a premise or reason to support a conclusion. Indicator words that indicate the conclusion are 'which means that', 'we can conclude that', 'hence', 'therefore', 'consequently', etc.

As truth is a property of sentences, so **validity** is a property of inferences. We say that an argument is valid if its inferences lead you properly from premises to conclusions. Validity is determined by looking at the form, or the structure of the argument, and *not* the content - those are two separate issues.

And finally, **soundness** is a property of arguments as a whole. An argument is sound if it has true premises and valid inferences. Both of these conditions must be met

Arguments themselves also come in two main types: **Deduction** and **induction**. A deduction, or a **deductive** argument, is a type of argument that, if it begins with true premises, logically guarantees that the conclusion is also true. Deduction works because in a deductive argument, nothing appears in the conclusion that was not already present in at least one of the premises. You can think of a deductive argument as a kind of 'unpacking' or 'synthesizing' of the premises.

An induction, or an **inductive** argument, is a type

"Most films in the DC Cinematic Universe franchise aren't very good."

"Did you get enough sleep last night?"

"No one expects a Spanish inquisition!"

"There's still some good in this world, Mr. Frodo, and it's worth fighting for."

"Commander Sheppard will save the galaxy from the Reapers, or die trying." *

* Exercises pg. 93

of argument that asserts the likelihood of the conclusion. In an inductive argument, if the premises are true, then the conclusion is probably true as well. However, by contrast with deductions, inductions can go beyond what is asserted in their premises and the conclusion can say more than what the premises say. For example, you can use an induction to make a prediction about the future, but an induction cannot guarantee the truth of a conclusion the way a deduction can. It can only assert probability.

Some Exercises

With that in mind, which of the following sentences are propositions, and which are not?

1. The lamp on my table is switched on.
2. Good morning, everyone!
3. My sweater is green.
4. How many cars are parked outside right now?
5. Smoking is bad for your health.
6. Smoking is good for your health.
7. Stop driving on the wrong side of the road.
8. The revolution will not be televised.
9. My love is like a red, red rose.
10. WTF?
11. Tea time is at 2 p.m.
12. Why don't you love me anymore?
13. Please keep off the grass.
14. There's something wrong with kids today.
15. Thou shalt not kill.
16. Those six swans are looking at me funny.
17. Some people have trouble with propositions.
18. Can you pass the salt?
19. There's a hole in my bucket.
20. Could you be any more ridiculous?
21. 67% of statistics are made up on the spot.
22. Don't you dare kick that puppy.
23. Puppy kickers are evil.
24. This cat is my white whale.
25. My feet hurt.
26. There will be a sea battle tomorrow.
27. Parades are stupid.
28. You should probably not kidnap children.

- Kidnapping is illegal.
- Don't go into that barn.
- Fa la la la la, la la la la.

Which of the following statements are categorical propositions? Positive statements? Negative statements? Conjunctions? Disjunctions? Conditional statements? Biconditionals? Not any kind of proposition? Which are more than one type of proposition at the same time?

1 • Most films in the *DC Cinematic Universe* franchise aren't very good.

2 • The capital city of Egypt is Cairo.

3 • Did you get enough sleep last night?

4 • If the groundhog sees his shadow on the morning of February 2nd, we will have six more weeks of winter.

5 • The International Space Station is either a magnificent achievement of technology and science, or it's a giant waste of money.

6 • Black lives matter.

7 • By itself, a cup of coffee isn't a complete breakfast.

8 • *The Iliad* is a very old Greek epic poem, and it's still popular today.

9 • No one expects a Spanish inquisition!

10 • *An Mhorrigan* is the name of Ireland's ancient goddess of sovereignty.

11 • There's still some good in this world, Mr. Frodo, and it's worth fighting for.

12 • If you will not be turned, then you will be destroyed.

13 • Darmok and Jalad, at Tanagra.

14 • If you take the red pill, you will see how far down the rabbit hole goes.

15 • One does not simply walk into Mordor.

16 • The Flat Earth society has members all around the globe.

17 • I used to be an adventurer like you; then I took an arrow in the knee.

18 • Commander Sheppard will save the galaxy from the Reapers, or die trying.

19 • Some men just want to watch the world burn.

20 • Lois is awesome.

21 • If you don't eat your meat, you can't have any pudding.

22 • You can go to the party if and only if your homework is done.

23 • You said you would give me a pony, but you didn't.

24 • Either you're going to the dentist, or I'll rip that tooth out myself.

25 • 'Hoser' is not an acceptable Scrabble word.

26 • Your professor is dreamy—and so smart, too!

27 • If he kisses the puppy, he'll get the votes; and if he doesn't, he won't.

28 • Having a computer is necessary if you want to Skype with your grandmother.

29 • Happy faces are so 1990s.

30 • Either you're going to eat this candy, or I will.

31 • I keyed your car, and I boil bunnies.

32 • You're not special.

33 • He didn't know what he was doing.

34 • If you hear sirens, you're supposed to pull over.

35 • You're going to work today, or you're not getting paid.

• I have a test tomorrow, and my paper is due.

Did you know?
67% of statistics are
made up on the spot.

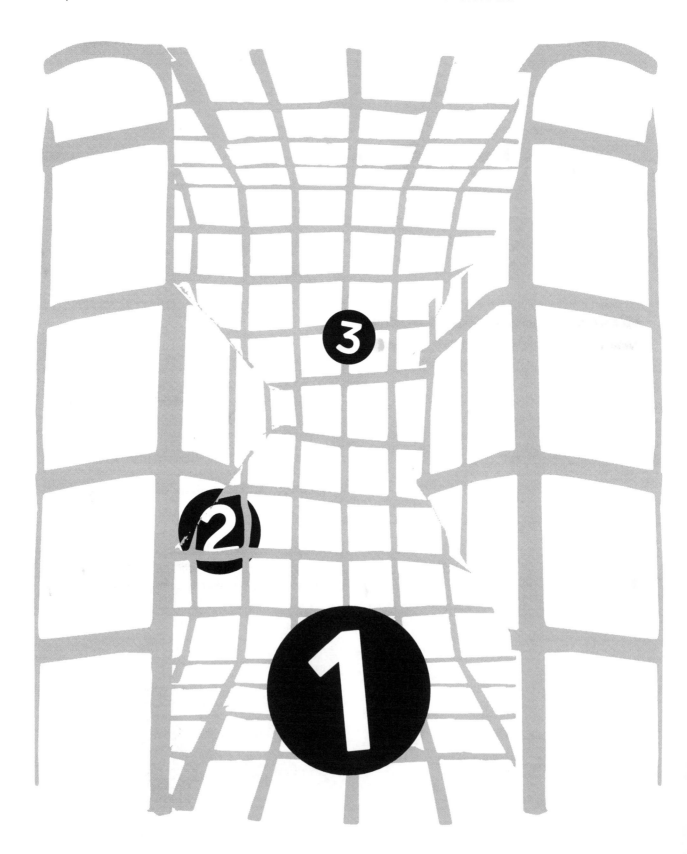

Chapter Five: Arguments

THE DEFINITION of an **argument** from the previous chapter is 'any two (or more) statements in which one is the reason for the other'. Here we may add that arguments come in two flavours: **deductions**, and **inductions**. This chapter will introduce some common forms of both kinds of arguments.

5.1. Deductions

In **deductive** argumentation, we take some number of premises as given, and from these we are able to make other claims according to certain logical rules of **inference**. If the conclusion derived has come out of the given premises as a result of applying the accepted rules of inference, we can say that the conclusion follows necessarily from the premises, or that the argument is 'valid'.

The **validity** of an argument is determined not by what it says, but by its *form*. This means that when we assess the validity of an argument, we assume that the **premises** are true. To put it another way: When we test for an argument's validity, we ignore all questions about whether the propositions are true or false. Instead, we only look at the way the propositions are arranged in relation to each other, and whether they conform to a correct logical structure. When we question the truth of the premises, we are not evaluating an argument's validity; we're evaluating its *soundness*. Consider the following argument:

All pigs can fly.
Babe is a pig.

Therefore, Babe can fly.

This argument is valid. That is, assuming that the premises are true, the conclusion necessarily follows. The validity of an argument is like the correct-ness of a mathematical equation: 'Two apples plus two apples equals four apples' is *valid* whether or not you know what apples are, or whether or not you happen to have any apples to count at all.

Of course, we can also question the *soundness* of the argument. If we can disprove the premise 'All pigs can fly', the argument must be unsound. We might also question whether we want to consider Babe a pig, rather than a fictional character resembling a pig. In either case, if either one of the premises is not true, the argument is not sound—but that does not mean it is not valid, because an argument can be valid without being sound. Let's look at an example of the same *form*:

All humans are mortal.
Brendan is a human.
Therefore, Brendan is mortal.

This argument is both valid and sound. In fact, both arguments are examples of a categorical syllogism of the form AII (Modus Darii), which is a shorthand for 'Universal Affirmative / Particular Affirmative / Particular Affirmative'. But that will come later.

5.2. Categorical Syllogisms

The four standard types of propositions in categorical

logic can be combined into twenty-four possible valid logical argument forms called Categorical Syllogisms. Look again at the sample argument that was used above:

> All humans are mortal.
> Brendan is a human.
> Therefore, Brendan is mortal.

Most people can tell that it's valid just by looking at it. That's because most people know, as a general rule, that if an entire class of things has some quality, and if something is a member of that class, that something will have the named quality. What makes this kind of argument valid is it obeys a few basic rules that are derived from straightforward facts about how classes of things can be fitted together. However, there are some other rules that are more specific:

- A categorical syllogism has exactly three terms: A subject, a predicate, and a middle term.
- Each of those three terms appears in the argument twice.
- The subject of the conclusion statement (not the first premise) is the subject for the whole argument; the predicate for the conclusion is the predicate for the whole argument.
- The middle term appears in both of the two premises, but not in the conclusion.
- Categorical syllogisms cannot have two negative premises.
- A categorical syllogism with one negative premise must also have a negative conclusion.

In the example above, the three terms are 'humans', 'Brendan', and 'mortals'. The subject is 'Brendan' and the predicate is 'mortal'; these being the subject and the predicate of the *conclusion* statement. 'All humans' is the middle premise. If we removed the content of the argument and replaced it with symbols, it will be easier to see the form:

> All M are P.
> All S are M.
> Therefore, all S are P.

Where:
S = the *subject*; a class of things that the argument is examining.
P = the *predicate*; a property or an attribute that belongs to members of a class.
M = the '*middle premise*'; another class of things under examination in the argument.

We can also generalize further. If an entire class of things has some quality, and all of the things that have that quality also have some other quality, we can make a valid inference that the entire class also has that other quality. For example:

> All farm animals are cannibalistic. (All M are P.)
> All cows are farm animals. (All S are M.)
> Therefore, all cows are cannibalistic. (All S are P.)
> Where:
> S = cows, P = cannibalistic things, and M = farm animals.

If you accept the validity of the previous argument, you must also accept the validity of this argument. This makes sense, because if every individual cow is a farm animal and therefore cannibalistic, then the whole cow species is cannibalistic.

Validity, remember, is a property of inferences and not propositions. So, it is possible for an argument to be valid even if one of its propositions is false. In this chapter it will be extremely important to remember that distinction, so that false propositions in the examples don't distract from the structure of the argument. (Some examples in this chapter have false propositions precisely for that reason. In the above example, the second premise is false: There are some sub-species of cattle which are not farm animals, such as the aurochs (*Bos taurus primigenius*). But the presence of a false proposition does not make an argument invalid: It makes the argument *unsound*.

Now let's try some negative statements.

> No human is immortal. (No M are P.)
> Brendan is a human. (All S are M.)
> Therefore, Brendan is not immortal. (All S are not P.)

What this argument says is that if none of the

members of the class of humans is immortal, then neither is a specific individual of that class. Again, we can generalize: If no specific member of the class is immortal, the whole class is excluded from immortality.

No human is immortal.
All philosophy professors are humans.
Therefore, no philosophy professor is immortal.

These are only some of the possible combinations of categorical statements that result in valid syllogisms. If you can keep track of what thing or what kind of thing belongs to what class, you'll be in pretty good shape for evaluating the validity of categorical syllogisms.

5.3. Enthymemes

more.

An **enthymeme** is a categorical syllogism in which one of the premises is missing. People use them all the time—often without realizing it—when they want to get a certain point across quickly or when they can assume that listeners know what they are talking about. It is very easy to commit a fallacy called the '**undistributed middle**' when making an enthymeme, because we aren't always keeping close track of where the premises are. So, to analyse an enthymeme, one must lay out all the propositions in the places where they would stand in a categorical syllogism, fill in the missing proposition, and then determine whether the inferences are valid or invalid. I've done it for the first two; you try the next ones.

'Many songs by Justin Timberlake are popular, so this new song will be popular too.'
> P1. Some Justin Timberlake songs are popular.
> P2. *This new song is a Justin Timberlake song.*
> C. Therefore, this new song will be popular.

'Yond Cassius has a lean and hungry look. He thinks too much. Such men are dangerous.' (Shakespeare, *Julius Caesar*, III.2)
> P1. Cassius has a lean and hungry look and thinks too much.
> P2. Men who have lean and hungry looks and who think too much are dangerous.
> C. *Therefore, Cassius is dangerous.*

'He's a country boy. And as everyone knows, country boys are big and strong.'

'All good investigative journalists keep their sources confidential. Therefore, Jane is a good investigative journalist.'

'All good investigative journalists keep their sources confidential. Therefore, Jane keeps her sources confidential.'

'All good things must come to an end. *Star Trek: The Next Generation* was a good thing.'

'Beowulf was bold. Fortune favoured him.'

(By the way: Which of these enthymemes are sound, and which are not?)

'All good things must come to an end. Star Trek: The Next Generation was a good thing'

5.4. Using Venn Diagrams to Find the Validity of a Categorical Syllogism

Venn Diagrams are graphic representations of propositions, which look like two or more overlapping circles. Each circle stands for a term in a categorical proposition: One represents the subject (usually placed on the left side), the other represents the predicate (usually placed on the right). The overlapping area represents the relationship between the terms. For example, here's a Venn diagram for the proposition: 'Some of the furniture in my apartment is made of wood'.

Each circle is like a field of objects belonging to a class. The circle on the left is the field of 'all the furniture in my apartment', and the circle on the right is 'all things that are made of wood'. The overlapping field between them thus represents 'all things that are

both items of furniture in my apartment *and* made of wood'. Since the two circles don't overlap completely, the diagram above is also telling us that there are some pieces of furniture that are not made of wood (that's the area of the circle on the left which does not overlap with the circle on the right), and that there are things made of wood which are not items of furniture in my apartment (the area of the circle on the right that doesn't overlap with the circle on the left).

If I wanted to say, 'All the furniture in my apartment is made of wood' (all S are P), then I could draw a diagram with the S circle entirely enclosed inside the P circle. Or, if I wanted to say 'None of the furniture in my place is made of wood' (No S are P), I could draw two circles standing apart from each other and not touching at all.

But if your purpose is to use these diagrams to find out whether a given categorical syllogism has valid inferences, we need to use the diagram in a particular way:

- We always draw the circles as partially overlapping one another;
- We place an X in the area when there is at least one thing that's a member of that class;
- And we shade in the area where nothing is a member of that class.

This gives us a diagram for all four of the categorical propositions, as follows:

(A) All S are P.

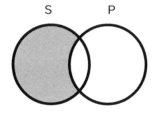

(E) No S are P.

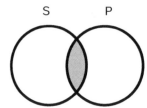

(I) Some S are P.

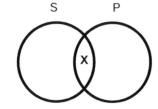

(O) Some S are not P.

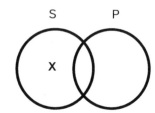

To diagram an entire categorical syllogism, including its middle premise, we draw three overlapping circles arranged in a triangle with the middle premise on top, like this:

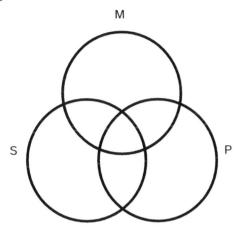

Having drawn the three circles for the argument, you can fill in the diagram for the argument that you are examining. Let's suppose we are checking this one:

(P1): Every tree in this forest belongs to a native British species. (All M are P.)

(P2): The 'Major Oak' is a tree in this forest.
(All S are M.)

(C): The 'Major Oak' belongs to a native British species.
(All S are P.)

The first part of the process is to fill in the diagram for the first premise. This uses only the M and P circles in the diagram; we pretend for the moment that the S circle isn't there.

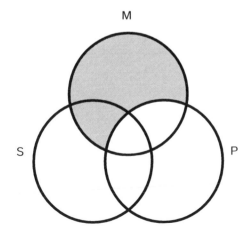

Next, we fill in the diagram for the second premise, using the circles for S and M. This time, we ignore the P circle, and now the diagram looks like this:

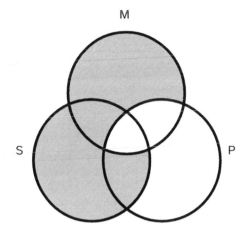

Finally, we stop drawing, and look at the circles for S and P which represent the conclusion statement; this time ignoring the circle for M. If the argument was structured properly, the diagram for the conclusion should already be drawn. In our example, the conclusion statement is an A-form proposition. So, if the circles representing the conclusion show the diagram of an A-form proposition, the diagram tells us that the argument's inferences are valid. The example above does show the correct diagram: The circle for S is fully shaded in except for an area that overlaps with P. (Remember: The shaded-out zones means there's nothing in them.) It's like saying the only place where you will find any S is inside an area that overlaps with P.

Let's suppose we are checking an *invalid* argument. In that case, once we've filled in the diagram for the first and second premise, we should see that the diagram representing the conclusion is the wrong diagram for its kind of proposition. Here's an example:

(P1): Some of the stray dogs in this city have fleas.
(Some M are P.)

(P2): No animals our shelter are stray dogs from the city.
(No S are M.)

(C): Therefore, no animals in our shelter have fleas.
(No S are P.)

To make a diagram for this argument: First we place the X in the space shared by M and P. There are two sub-zones here: One that's also shared with S, and one that's not. We place the X on the line between those two sub-zones, to show that the X belongs to both of them. Next, we shade in the area that overlaps S and M. The diagram thus looks like this:

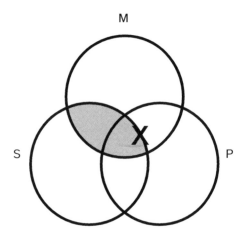

When we read the diagram for S and P, ignoring the circle for M, we find that the diagram for 'No S are P' is not already drawn—there's still an area of overlap between S and P that is not shaded out as it should be. Furthermore, we find a contradiction: There's an X in a shaded area! It's like saying there is at least one thing in an area where there's supposed to be nothing. Thus, we instantly see that the argument is invalid. (After all, even if this shelter didn't pick up any stray dogs with fleas, it might have picked up other animals that have fleas.)

5.5. Modus Ponens or Affirming the Antecedent

Modus ponens is a valid argument form taking a conditional statement as one premise, and the affirmation of its antecedent as another premise. So, if I claim 'If something, then another thing' and then I affirm 'something', I can logically deduce that 'other thing'. If the conditional statement and the affirmation of its antecedent are both true, the truth of the conclusion is guaranteed.

Let's take an example.

> (P1) If the dog is barking, there's an intruder in the house.
> (P2) The dog is barking!
> (C) Therefore, there's an intruder in the house!

Of course, there might be other reasons why the dog might bark. But according to Premise 1, the fact that the dog is barking implies that there is definitely an intruder in the house. And we are assuming that P1 is true.

This argument takes the general form:

> (P1) If P, then Q
> (P2) P
> (C) Q

Rendered symbolically:

> (P1) P→Q
> (P2) P
> (C) Q

The validity of this form is pretty intuitive. But if we are ever unsure, we can refer back to our truth table for conditionals and prove it beyond a doubt.

P	Q	P→Q
T	T	T
T	F	F
F	T	T
F	F	T

Premise 1 gives us a conditional statement. Considered alone, we can see that there are three possible cases where it could be true: Where the antecedent (P) is true and the consequent (Q) is true; where the antecedent (P) is false and the consequent (Q) true; and where the antecedent (P) and consequent (Q) are both false. We can therefore eliminate the fourth possibility that the antecedent (P) is true and the consequent (Q) false, because this would make Premise 1 false (and we are assuming that it's true). So, let's cross it off.

P	Q	P→Q
T	T	T
~~T~~	~~F~~	~~F~~
F	T	T
F	F	T

Now, taking into account Premise 2, which tells us that our antecedent is true, we can eliminate the possibilities in the table where P is false.

P	Q	P→Q
T	T	T
~~T~~	~~F~~	~~F~~
~~F~~	~~T~~	~~T~~
~~F~~	~~F~~	~~T~~

It seems now that the truth of the consequent is guaranteed, for based on what we know from Premise 1 and Premise 2, there is no other possible conclusion.

Let's look at another example:

(P1) If it is raining, I will need my umbrella.
(P2) It is raining.
(C) Therefore, I will need my umbrella.

There might be other reasons why you might need your umbrella. Perhaps it's to be used as a prop in a theatrical performance. But nothing in this argument tells you that. And besides, whether or not that's the case, the first premise still tells you that you need it when it rains.

PRACTICAL USES OF MODUS PONENS: Every circuit in your computer uses this pattern of argument to make calculations. In effect, the diodes and transistors in your computer CPU are like 'switches', which operate as if they are reasoning like this:

(P1) If a signal comes in from direction X, send it out again in direction Y.
(P2) A signal just came in from direction X.
(C) Therefore, the thing to do is send it out in direction Y.

5.6. Affirming the Consequent: Modus Ponens' Invalid Half-Brother

There's a sneaky invalid argument out there that looks a lot like modus ponens. What would happen if we affirmed the consequent, instead of the antecedent? We would have an argument like this:

(P1) If it is raining, I will need my umbrella.
(P2) I will need my umbrella.
(C) Therefore, it is raining.

We tend to make this logical leap and equate the fact that we need our umbrella with the fact that it's raining. It's not likely that we would need the umbrella for some other reason, such as the aforementioned theatrical performance, but it's still a possibility. The fact that I need my umbrella does not *absolutely guarantee* that it's raining. This argument form is therefore invalid.

Since the invalidity of Affirming The Consequent is hard to spot, it is sometimes used as a technique for manipulating or 'gaslighting' others (see Chapter 8.14). Consider, as an example, an argument like this:

(P1) If you are crazy, you are going to see things that aren't there.
(P2) You are seeing things that aren't there.
(C) You're therefore crazy.

But as you can surely see, the logical structure

of this argument is exactly the same as the example with the umbrella. It does not logically guarantee that you're crazy.

5.7. Modus Tollens, or Denying the Consequent

Modus tollens is a valid argument form taking a conditional statement as one premise, and the denial of its consequent as another premise. So, if I claim 'If something, then another thing' and then deny 'another thing', I can logically deduce 'not something'. Here, I'm recognizing that if the relation between 'something' and 'another thing' holds, and if 'another thing' failed to happen, or is false (depending on what that thing is), then 'something' must not have happened, or must not be true.

Let's take an example.

> (P1) If you gave me a diamond tiara, I'd be the happiest girl in the world!
> (P2) I am not the happiest girl in the world.
> (C) Therefore, you did not give me a diamond tiara.

This argument takes the general form:

> (P1) If P, then Q.
> (P2) Not Q.
> (C) Not P.

Rendered symbolically:

> (P1) P→Q
> (P2) ~Q
> (C) ~P

Again, the validity of this form is rather intuitive. But, we can still go through the truth table proof, just for fun.

Again, Premise 1 tells us that the conditional statement is true. Therefore, we can again eliminate the possibility that it is false by referring to our table.

P	Q	P→Q
T	T	T
~~T~~	~~F~~	~~F~~
F	T	T
F	F	T

Then, Premise 2 tells us that the consequent (Q) is false. We can therefore also eliminate all of the possibilities where Q is true from our table.

P	Q	P→Q
T	T	T
~~T~~	~~F~~	~~F~~
~~F~~	~~T~~	~~T~~
~~F~~	~~F~~	~~T~~

Now we're left with just what we expect. If P→Q is true, and Q is false, then P must also be false.

Like modus ponens' evil half-brother, there's another bad argument out there attempting at every turn to pass itself off as valid.

5.8. Denying the Antecedent: Fallacy!

Again, when we see a conditional statement and a negation, we're immediately tempted to think 'modus tollens'. But what happens if we deny the antecedent instead of the consequent? We get an argument like this:

> (P1) If you gave me a diamond tiara, I'd be the happiest girl in the world!
> (P2) You did not give me a diamond tiara.
> (C) Therefore, I am not the happiest girl in the world.

Again, the truth of these premises does not

absolutely guarantee the truth of the conclusion. Even if you did not give me a diamond tiara, I might still be the happiest girl in the world for some other reason. I might have been the happiest girl in the world all along, and there's quite possibly nothing you could do to change that. This argument form is invalid.

5.9. Hypothetical Syllogism

A hypothetical syllogism is a valid argument form that takes two conditional statements as premises and then concludes a third, where the consequent of the first premise is identical to the antecedent of the second.

For instance, if I make this claim:
(P1) If it gets below freezing outside, I can make ice out there.

And I additionally claim:
(P2) If I can make ice out there, my soft drinks will be deliciously refreshing.

I will be able to conclude that
(C) If it gets below freezing outside, my soft drinks will be deliciously refreshing.

Essentially, we are demonstrating the transitive property of conditional statements. That is, if we have two conditional statements where the consequent of one is identical to the antecedent of another, we can eliminate them and mash the rest of the two premises together to get a conclusion that is definitely true.

This argument takes the general form

(P1) If P, then Q.
(P2) If Q, then R.
(C) If P, then R.

Rendered symbolically:

(P1) P→Q
(P2) Q→R
(C) P→R

The truth table proof of this argument now has to take into account three terms. Therefore, when we make the table, we must account for all of the possible truth values of P, Q, and R, for a total of 8 combinations. Then we can fill in the truth values for the conditional statements acting as our premises:

P	Q	R	P→Q	Q→R
T	T	T	T	T
T	T	F	T	F
T	F	T	F	T
T	F	F	F	T
F	T	T	T	T
F	T	F	T	F
F	F	T	T	T
F	F	F	T	T

If we assume that both P→Q and Q→R are true, we can eliminate all of the possibilities where either one of them is false.

P	Q	R	P→Q	Q→R
T	T	T	T	T
~~T~~	~~T~~	~~F~~	~~T~~	~~F~~
~~T~~	~~F~~	~~T~~	~~F~~	~~T~~
~~T~~	~~F~~	~~F~~	~~F~~	~~T~~
F	T	T	T	T
~~F~~	~~T~~	~~F~~	~~T~~	~~F~~
F	F	T	T	T
F	F	F	T	T

Now let's take the values for P and R that are left over and see what the values for P→R look like. There are four possible combinations of P and R left, after we have taken into account the truth of our premises:

P	R	P→R
T	T	T
F	T	T
F	T	T
F	F	T

Now it looks like no matter what leftover values of P and R we might choose, if P→Q and Q→R are true, P→R is definitely going to be true.

But this could all be made clearer by taking a few examples. We can apply the hypothetical syllogism to categorical thinking:

(P1) If Socrates is a man, Socrates is an animal.
(P2) If Socrates is an animal, Socrates is a substance.
(C) If Socrates is a man; Socrates is a substance.

We could also apply the hypothetical syllogism to causal relations:

(P1) If I set the house on fire, it will burn down.
(P2) If the house burns down, I'll collect insurance money.
(C) If I set the house on fire, I'll collect insurance money.

In any case, the *transitive property* of the implication relation that constitutes a conditional statement guarantees that the hypothetical syllogism is valid. That is, the hypothetical syllogism can be proven valid just by the definition of conditional statements.

5.10. Disjunctive Syllogism

This argument establishes the truth of some proposition by ruling out all other possibilities until there's just one left standing.

Form:
Either P is true, or Q is true.
P is false.

Therefore, Q is true.

Either P is true, or Q is true.
Q is false.
Therefore, P is true.

Examples:
(P1) This tree is either coniferous or it is deciduous.
(P2) I see by its flat leaves that it is not coniferous.
(C) Therefore, this tree is deciduous.

(P1) One of us is going to die here, Mister Bond. It's either you or me.
(P2) And it isn't going to be me.
(C) So, it will have to be you!

This is a valid argument form:

(P1) PvQ
(P2) ~P
(C) Q

Truth table proof:
If we take our truth table for disjunction and assume Premise 1 is true, we are left with three possible interpretations: Both P and Q are true, P is true and Q is false, or P is false and Q is true.

P	Q	PvQ
T	T	T
T	F	T
F	T	T
~~F~~	~~F~~	~~F~~

But Premise 2 tells us that P is false. Therefore, we can eliminate some more possibilities and guarantee that Q is true:

P	Q	PvQ
T	T	T
T	F	T
F	T	T
F	F	F

Actually, you can have as many propositions as you like in the first premise, and then rule them out one by one in the middle premises until you arrive at the last one standing. So, the argument could also look like this:

(P1) Either P, or Q, or R, or S, or T.
(P2) P is false.
(P3) Q is false.
(P4) R is false.
(P5) S is false.
(C) Therefore, T is true.

This is basically what I mean when I make the argument:

(P1) You talkin' to me?
(P2-?) I'm the only one here. (That is, nobody else *is* here—John isn't here, Mary isn't here, Neil isn't here, Bob isn't here, Sheila isn't here—and you must be talking to *someone here*.)
(C) I guess you're talkin' to me.

PRACTICAL USES: The game of 'Clue' (first published as 'Cluedo' in England in 1949) operates entirely on the basis of the disjunctive syllogism. In this game players try to figure out who killed 'Mr. Body' by locating suspects, murder weapons, and crime scenes offered in a list of possibilities. The first player to figure out which suspect, weapon, and location cannot be accounted for can make an accusation, and perhaps win the game.

5.11. Adjunction

The rule of adjunction allows us to form a conjunction from any two true statements. It is also known as 'conjunction introduction'. This is one of the most intuitively obvious rules of inference in the world of logic. It simply states that if two statements are true independently, then their conjunction is also true.

For example, from the premises:
(P1) I'm a little man.
(P2) I'm also evil.
(P3) I'm also into cats.

I can conclude:
(C) I'm a little man, and I'm also evil, and also into cats.

Generally, this is done by adding one premise to another individually, such that a logical proof would look like this:

(P1) P
(P2) Q
(P3) R
(C1) P&Q
(C2) (P&Q)&R

The result is the same.

'Why would we do this?' you might ask. It all seems so obvious. Well, there are some cases where you might need a conjunction and don't have one. For instance, say you know that everything that looks like a duck *and* quacks like a duck is a duck, and you want to prove that your mystery pet Billy is a duck. We would construct an argument like this:

(P1) Everything that looks like a duck and quacks like a duck is a duck.
(P2) Billy looks like a duck.
(P3) Billy quacks like a duck.
(C1) *Therefore, Billy looks like a duck and quacks like a duck.*
(C2) Therefore, Billy is a duck.

This rule is valid by the definition of conjunction, whereby we stated that a conjunction is true if and only if all of its conjuncts are true.

5.11. Dilemmas

A dilemma, stemming from the Greek 'δίλημμα', refers to an 'ambiguous proposition'. In logic, a dilemma occurs when we have two possibilities somewhere in the argument. Often a dilemma is associated with an undesirable consequence. Consider, for instance, this simple dilemma:

'You're damned if you do, and damned if you don't.'

We can separate this dilemma into two conditional statements.

(P1) If you do, you're damned.
(P2) If you don't, you're damned.

Then we can take these premises together with the logical truth that either you do or you don't:

(P3) You do or you don't.

And then make the obvious conclusion:

(C) You're damned.

But sometimes our dilemmas are not simple. This section will introduce two complex dilemmas, where our *conclusions* turn out to be ambiguous statements. That is, while we can infer that *either this one or that one* of our possible conclusions is true, we don't know which one. We can, however, confidently state the conclusion that *either 'this' or 'that'*.

5.13. Constructive Dilemma

The constructive dilemma gives us two conditional statements and a disjunctive statement. For example:

(P1) If I go to the movies tonight, I'll have to stand in line.
(P2) If I go to that party tonight, I'll have to do laundry.

(P3) I'm either going to the movies or going to the party.

From these statements we can validly conclude:

(C) I'm either going to have to stand in line, or I'll have to do laundry.

We don't know which one. But one of them is going to happen.

Notice how similar this argument is to modus ponens. Where in modus ponens we had a conditional statement and a true antecedent, now we have two conditional statements and another one saying that *one* of the antecedents is going to be true. If we knew which one, we could make a valid modus ponens argument, but we don't. Still, though, we can conclude that depending on my choice of what to do this evening, I'll also have to do something unpleasant.

The argument form looks like this:

(P1) If P, then Q.
(P2) If R, then S.
(P3) P or R.
(C) Q or S.

Rendered symbolically:

(P1) P→Q
(P2) R→S
(P3) PvR
(C) QvS

Let's look at another example:

(P1) If your mother loves you, she will pack you a bagged lunch.
(P2) If your father loves you, he will knit you some mittens.
(P3) Either your father or your mother loves you.

Our conclusion is:

(C) Your mother will pack you a bagged lunch or your father will knit you some mittens.

Note that in this example, it is completely possible that you'll end up with both a bagged lunch and some mittens. This is as a result of the *inclusive* nature of disjunction. That is, while it is safe to say that only one of your parents loves you, it's also possible that both do.

5.14. Destructive Dilemma

While the constructive dilemma allows us to infer a disjunction using the same kind of reasoning that makes modus ponens valid, a destructive dilemma mirrors closely the same kind of reasoning as modus tollens. In a destructive dilemma, we are again provided with two conditional statements and told that one of their consequents is false. However, we do not know which one it is. The only thing we can say for sure is that if *at least one* of their consequents is false, *at least one* of their antecedents will be as well.

(P1) If the people value free puppies for all, Jim will win the election.
(P2) If the people value extended library hours, George will win the election.
(P3) Either Jim will *not* win the election, or George will *not* win the election.
(C) Either the people *don't* value free puppies for all, or the people *don't* value extended library hours.

While we might be able to guess at which one of these possibilities is true, neither one of them is assured by the rules of deductive logic. All we know is that *at least one* of the disjuncts in our conclusion will be true.

The argument form looks like this:

(P1) If P, then Q
(P2) If R, then S
(P3) Not Q or Not S
(C) Not P or Not R

Rendered symbolically:

(P1) P→Q
(P2) R→S
(P3) ~Q∨~S
(C) ~P∨~R

Let's take a look at another example.

(P1) If your mother loved you, she would pack you a bagged lunch.
(P2) If your father loved you, he would knit you some mittens.
(P3) Since your care package looks rather small, you infer that it either does not contain a bagged lunch, or it does not contain mittens.
(C) Either your mother doesn't love you, or your father doesn't love you.

Again, it's possible that neither of your parents love you, and that they sent an empty box just to taunt you. It's cruel, but logically valid.

5.15. Induction

All of the argument forms we have looked at so far have been deductively valid. That meant, we said, that the conclusion follows from necessity if the premises are true. But to what extent can we ever be sure of the truth of those premises? **Inductive** argumentation is a less certain, more realistic, more familiar way of reasoning that we all do, all the time. Inductive argumentation recognizes, for instance, that a premise like 'All horses have four legs' comes from our previous experience of horses. If one day we were to encounter a three-legged horse, deductive logic would tell us that 'All horses have four legs' is false, at which point the premise becomes rather useless for a deducer. In fact, deductive logic tells us that if the premise 'All horses have four legs' is false, even if we know there are many, many four-legged horses in the world, when we go

Chapter Five   5.16. Inductive Generalization

to the track and see hordes of four-legged horses, all we can really be certain of is that 'There is at least *one* four-legged horse.'

Inductive logic allows for the more realistic premise 'The vast majority of horses have four legs'. And inductive logic can use this premise to infer other useful information, like 'If I'm going to buy Chestnut some booties for Christmas, I should probably get four of them.' The trick is to recognize a certain amount of uncertainty in the truth of the conclusion, something for which deductive logic does not allow. In real life, however, inductive logic is used much more frequently and (hopefully) with some success.

The following are some of the uses of inductive reasoning.

PREDICTING THE FUTURE. We constantly use inductive reasoning to predict the future. We do this by compiling evidence based on past observations, and by assuming that the future will play out in a similar way to the past. For instance, I make the observation that every other time I have gone to sleep at night, I have woken up in the morning. There is actually no certainty that this will happen, but I make the inference because this is what has happened every other time. In fact, it is not the case that 'All people who go to sleep at night wake up in the morning'—but I'm not going to lose any sleep over that. We also do the same thing when our experience has been less consistent. For instance, I might make the assumption that if there's someone at the door, the dog will bark. But it's not outside the realm of possibility that the dog would be asleep, has gone out for a walk, or has been persuaded not to bark by a clever intruder with sedative-laced bacon. I make the assumption that if there's someone at the door the dog will bark, because that is what *usually* happens.

EXPLAINING COMMON OCCURRENCES. We also use inductive reasoning to explain things that commonly happen. For instance, if I'm about to start an exam and notice that Bill is not here, I might tell myself that Bill is stuck in traffic. I might base this on the reasoning that being stuck in traffic is a common

excuse for being late, or because I know that Bill never accounts for traffic when he's estimating how long it will take him to get somewhere. Again, whether Bill is actually stuck in traffic is not certain, but I have some good reasons to think it's probable. We use this kind of reasoning to explain past events as well. For instance, if I read somewhere that 1986 was a particularly good year for tomatoes, I assume that 1986 probably had some ideal combination of rainfall, sun, and consistently warm temperatures. Although it's possible that back in 1986 there was a scientific madman who circled the globe planting tomatoes wherever he could, inductive reasoning would tell me that the former, environmental explanation is more likely. (But I could be wrong.)

GENERALIZING. Often, we are tempted to make general claims, but it can be very difficult to prove such claims with certainty. The only way to do so would be to observe *every single case* of something about which we wanted to make an observation. This would be the only way to truly prove such assertions as 'All swans are white'. Without being able to observe every single swan on Earth, I can never make that claim with certainty. Inductive logic, on the other hand, allows us to make the claim with a certain degree of modesty.

5.16. Inductive Generalization

Inductive generalization allows us to make general claims, despite being unable to actually observe every single member of a class of something or other in order to make a reliably true general statement. We see this in scientific studies, in population surveys, and in our own everyday reasoning. Take, for example, a drug study. A doctor would like to know how many people will go blind if they take a certain amount of some drug for so many years. If they have determined that 5% of people in the study went blind, they will then assume that 5% of all people who take the drug for that many years will go blind. Likewise, if I survey a group of people and ask them what their favourite colour is, and 75% of them say 'purple', I will assume that purple is the favourite colour of 75% of people. However, we have to be careful when we make an inductive generalization. If I claim that 75% of people really like purple, you will likely want to know whether I gave that survey at a Justin Bieber concert!

Let's look at how we set up a formal argument. If I asked a class of 400 students whether they think logic is a valuable course and 90% of them answered 'yes', I could make an inductive argument like this:

> (P1) 90% of the 400 students I surveyed believe that logic is a valuable course.
> (C) Therefore 90% of all students believe that logic is a valuable course.

However, there are certain things I need to take into account in judging the quality of this argument. For instance, did I ask this in a logic course? Did the respondents have to raise their hands so that the professor could see them, or was the survey taken anonymously? Are there enough students in the course to justify using them as a representative group for students in general? Or is this professor so awesome, his students would enjoy listening to him read from a dictionary?

If I did, in fact, make a class of 400 *logic* students raise their hands in response to the question of whether logic is valuable course, we can identify several problems with this argument. The first is **bias**. We can assume that anyone enrolled in a logic course is more likely to see it as valuable than other students selected at random. I have therefore skewed the argument in favour of logic courses. I can also question whether the students were answering the question honestly. Perhaps if they are trying to save the professor's feelings, or if they hope it will get them a better grade, they will be more likely to raise their hands and assure her that the logic course is a valuable one.

Now let's say I've avoided those problems. I have ensured that the 400 students I have asked are randomly selected, say, by soliciting email responses from randomly selected students from the university's entire student population. The argument now looks stronger.

Another problem we might have with the argument is whether I have asked *enough* students to adequately represent the whole student body. If the entire population consists of 400 students, my argument is very strong. But if the student body numbers in the tens of thousands, I might want to ask a few more before assuming that the opinions of a few mirror those of the many. This would be a problem with my **sample size**.

Let's take another example. Now I'm going to run a scientific study, in which I will pay someone $50 to take a drug with unknown effects and see if it makes them blind. In order to control for other variables, I open the study only to white males between the ages of 18 and 25.

A bad inductive argument would say:
> (P1) 40% of 1000 test subjects who took the drug went blind.
> (C) Therefore, 40% of all people who take the drug will go blind.

A better inductive argument would make a more modest claim:
> (P1) 40% of the 1000 test subjects who took the drug went blind.
> (C) Therefore, 40% of white males between the ages of 18 and 25 who take the drug will go blind.

The point behind this example is to show how inductive reasoning imposes an important limitation on the possible conclusions a study or a survey can make. In order to make good generalizations, we need to ensure that our sample is *representative*, *non-biased*, and *sufficiently sized*.

5.17. Statistical Syllogism

With the inductive generalization example above, we saw a statement expressing a statistic applied to a more general group, but it is also possible use statistics to move from the general to the particular. For instance, if I know that most computer science majors are male, and that some randomly-chosen individual with the androgynous name Cameron is a computer science major, we can be reasonably certain that Cameron is a male. The uncertainty of this conclusion can be represented by qualifying it with expressions like 'probably'. If, on the other hand, we want to say that something is unlikely, such as Cameron being female, we can use 'probably not'. Besides 'probably', it is also possible to hedge conclusions with other similar qualifying words or phrases.

Let's create an example:

(P1) Of the 133 people found guilty of homicide last year in Canada, 79% were jailed.
(P2) Socrates was found guilty of homicide last year in Canada.
(C) Therefore, Socrates was probably jailed.

In this case, we can be reasonably sure that Socrates is currently rotting in prison, based upon the statistics available. But there are definitely more certain and more uncertain cases.

(P1) In the 2016 American presidential election, 46.4% of voting Americans voted for Trump, while 48.5% voted for Clinton.
(P2) Jim is a voting American.
(C) Therefore, Jim probably voted for Clinton.

Clearly, this argument is not as strong as the first. It is only slightly more likely than not that Jim voted for Clinton. In this case we might want to revise our conclusion to say:

(C) Therefore, it is slightly more likely than not that Jim voted for Clinton.

In other cases, the likelihood that something is or is not the case approaches certainty. For example:

(P1) There is a 0.00000059% chance you will die on any single flight operated by one of the worst-rated airlines.
(P2) I'm flying to Paris next week.
(C) There's a less than one-in-a-million chance that I will die on my flight with one of the worst-rated airlines.

Note that in all of these examples, nothing is ever stated with absolute certainty. It is possible to improve the chances that our conclusions will be accurate by being more specific, or by finding out more information. We might like to know more about Jim's demographic profile (data such as where he lived and the voter preferences in that area) and his voting strategy as evidenced through his previous voting habits. We could also simply ask him who he voted for (in which case, we might also want to know when Jim is likely to lie).

5.18. Induction by Shared Properties

Induction by shared properties consists of noting the similarity between two things with respect to their properties and inferring from this that they may share other properties.

Companies that recommend products to you based on other customers' purchases will serve as a familiar example of this practice. Amazon.com tells me, for instance, that customers who bought the complete *Sex and the City* DVD series also bought *Lipstick Jungle* and *Twilight*.

Assuming that people usually buy things for themselves because they like them, we can rephrase this as:

(P1) There is a large number of people who, if they like *Sex and the City* and *Twilight*, will also like *Lipstick Jungle*.

I could also make the following observation:

(P2) I like *Sex and the City* and *Twilight*.

And then infer from there two premises that:

(C) I would also like *Lipstick Jungle*.

And I did. In general, induction by shared properties assumes that if something has properties W, X, Y, and Z, and if something else has properties W, X, and Y,

Induction by shared properties consists of noting the similarity between two things with respect to their properties and inferring from this that they may share other properties.

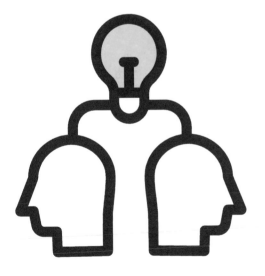

it's reasonable to assume that that something else also has property Z. Note that in the above example all of the properties were actually preferences with regard to entertainment. The kinds of properties involved in the comparison can and will make an argument better or worse. Let's consider a worse induction.

> (P1) Lisa is tall, has blonde hair, has blue eyes, and rocks out to Nirvana on weekends.
> (P2) Gina is tall, has blonde hair, and has blue eyes.
> (C) Therefore, Gina probably rocks out to Nirvana on weekends.

In this case the properties don't seem to be related in the same way as in the first example. While the first three are physical characteristics, the last property instead indicates to us that Lisa is stuck in a 1990s grunge phase. Gina, though she shares several properties with Lisa, might not share the same undying love for Kurt Cobain. Let's try a stronger argument.

> (P1) Bob and Dick both wear plaid shirts all the time, wear large plastic-rimmed glasses, and listen to bands you've never heard of.
> (P2) Bob drinks PBR.
> (C) Dick probably also drinks PBR.

Here we can identify the qualities that Bob and Dick have in common as symptoms of hipsterism. The fact that Bob drinks PBR is another symptom of this affectation. Given that Dick is exhibiting most of the same symptoms, it is quite reasonable to assume that Dick also probably drinks PBR.

PRACTICAL USES: A procedure very much like induction by shared properties is performed by nurses and doctors when they diagnose a patient's condition. Their thinking goes like this:

> (P1) Patients who have elephantiasis display an increased heart rate, elevated blood pressure, a rash on their skin, and a strong desire to visit the elephant pen at the zoo.
> (P2). The patient in front of me has an increased heart

rate, elevated blood pressure, and a strong desire to visit the elephant pen at the zoo.
(C) It is probable, therefore, that the patient here in front of me has elephantiasis.

The more a patient's symptoms match the 'textbook definition' of a given disease, the more likely it is that the patient has that disease. Caregivers then treat the patient for the disease that they think he probably has. If the disease doesn't respond to the treatment or the patient starts to present different symptoms, they will then consider other conditions with similar symptoms that the patient is likely to have.

5.19. Induction by Shared Relations

Induction by shared relations is much like induction by shared properties, except insofar that what is shared are not properties, but relations. A simple example is the causal relation, from which we might make an inductive argument like this:

(P1) Percocet, Oxycontin, and morphine reduce pain, cause drowsiness, and are habit-forming.
(P2) Heroin also reduces pain and causes drowsiness.
(C) Heroin may also be habit-forming.

In this case the effects of reducing pain, drowsiness, and addiction are all assumed to be *caused* by the drugs listed. We can use an induction by shared relation to make the probable conclusion that if heroin, like the other drugs, reduces pain and causes drowsiness, it is probably also habit-forming.

Another interesting example are the relations we have with other people. For instance, Facebook has compiled a great deal of information about you. But let's focus on the 'friends with' relation. They compare who your friends are with the friends of your friends in order to determine who else you might actually know. The induction goes a little like this:

(P1) Donna is friends with Brandon, Kelly, Steve, and Brenda.
(P2) David is friends with Brandon, Kelly, and Steve.

(C) David probably also knows Brenda.

We could strengthen that argument if we knew that Brandon, Kelly, Steve, and Brenda were all friends with each other as well. We could also make an alternate conclusion based on the same argument above:

(C) David probably also knows Donna.

They do, after all, know at least three of the same people. They've probably run into each other at some point. If they use a social network, it may also know whether these people attended the same school, or grew up in the same town, or frequented the same coffee shop, or something like that, and that information would also strengthen the induction.

5.20. Exercises for Inductions

Identify the form of the following deductive arguments: Modus ponens, modus tollens, hypothetical syllogism, categorical syllogism, disjunctive syllogism, adjunction, constructive dilemma, and destructive dilemma.

(a) If you don't have a pencil, you can't write the exam. You don't have a pencil. So, you can't write the exam.
(b) If you buy the farm, you can get kittens. If you buy a boat, you can go sailing. You're either going to buy the farm or buy a boat. Therefore, you can either have kittens or go sailing.
(c) If Lois has a bicycle, she also has a bicycle helmet. If Lois has a bicycle helmet, her hair will be flat. Therefore, if Lois has a bicycle, her hair will be flat.
(d) If you robbed that store, you would be found guilty. You were not found guilty. Therefore, you didn't rob that store.
(e) Either kittens are cute, or kittens are ugly. Kittens are not ugly. Therefore, kittens are cute.
(f) I have two buttons missing. I have a tail. Therefore, I have two buttons missing and I have a tail.
(g) All good muffins have chocolate chips. This is a good muffin. Therefore, this muffin has chocolate chips.

Supply the conclusion that results from the following premises:

(a) P1: All monkeys like bananas.
     P2: George is a monkey.

(b) P1: If this cupcake is less than a week old, George will eat it.
     P2: George will not eat that cupcake.

(c) P1: Either you're lying to me, or I'm stupid.
     P2: I'm not stupid.

(d) P1: If there's a monkey in the room, you can smell bananas.
     P2: If there's a cake in the room, you can smell cake.
     P3: There's either a monkey in the room, or some cake.

(e) P1: If you want to get ahead in life, you have to know your argument forms.
     P2: You want to get ahead in life.

(f) P1: If you have a boat, people call you 'Captain'.
     P2: If people call you 'Captain', you get a lot of street cred.

Identify a problem with the following inductive arguments.

(a) P1: 79% of men who take drugs prefer cocaine.
     P2: Princess Peach takes drugs.
     C: Therefore, Princess Peach prefers cocaine.

(b) P1: 60% of people who shop at Mountain Equip ment Co-Op like mountain climbing.
     C: Therefore, 60% of people like mountain climbing.

(c) P1: 100% of the people I asked said their name was Joe Brown.
     C: Therefore, 100% of people are named Joe Brown.

Identify these arguments as one of the following: *Inductive generalization*, *statistical syllogism*, *induction by shared properties*, and *induction by shared relations*.

(a) P1: Of the 10% of the population surveyed, most said they support the 'kittens for all' movement.
     C: Therefore, most people support the 'kittens for all' movement.

(b) P1: Kant's *Critique of Pure Reason* is a heavy book, is densely worded, and has a boring cover—and if you read it in a coffee shop, people think you're cool.
     P2: Heidegger's *Being and Time* is a heavy book, is densely worded, and has a boring cover.
     C: Reading Heidegger's *Being and Time* in a coffee shop will make people think you're cool.

(c) P1: 67% of people who attend university never have the opportunity to commit armed robbery.
     P2: Bob went to university.
     C: Therefore, Bob has probably never committed an armed robbery.

P1: 79% of men who take drugs prefer cocaine.
P2: Princess Peach takes drugs.
C: Therefore, Princess Peach prefers cocaine.

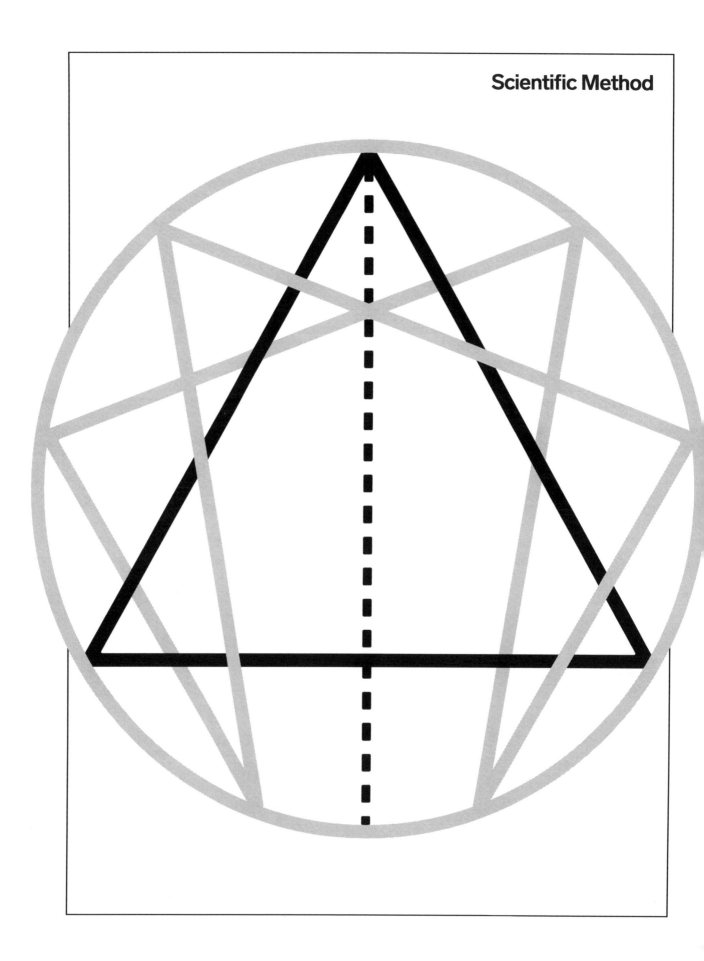

Chapter Six:
Science and Scientific Reasoning

The scientific method is the most powerful and successful method for discovering and creating knowledge ever devised. Every advance in engineering, medicine, and technology has been made possible by people applying science to their problems. It is adventurous, curious, rigorously logical, and inspirational—and it is even possible to be artistic and imaginative about scientific discoveries. And the best part about science is that anyone can do it. Science can look difficult because there's a lot of jargon involved, and a lot of math. But even the most complicated quantum physics and the farthest-reaching astronomy follows the same method, in principle, as primary school projects when you played with magnets or built a model volcano.

Evaluating scientific claims, however, can be tricky business. Often, we don't have the scientific background to be able to evaluate some scientific claim thoroughly. Sometimes, we have to trust the people who are making those claims, along with their peers, to let us know what the latest groundbreaking experiments show, or how the theory behind them works. Still, there are some basic standards any scientific theory should uphold, and it is possible to evaluate them based on these standards even if we're not scientists. This chapter introduces some features of scientific claims that allow us to evaluate them, irrespective of whether we are intimately familiar with the subject matter or not.

6.1. Scientific Method

The procedure that scientists use follows a standard pattern of logic, part of which is inductive, and part of which is deductive. So, like other inductions, its conclusions only offer you the likelihood or the probability that something is true rather than certainty that it is. But when it is done correctly, the conclusions it reaches are very well grounded in experimental evidence. Another part of it is deductive; and like other deductions, it gives you certain knowledge—but only about what's *false*, not what's true! These two parts have to be put together in a particular way. Here's a rough outline of how the procedure works.

Observation: Something in the world is observed and arouses a scientist's curiosity.

Hypothesis: An idea is proposed that could explain why the event he observed happened, or why it is what it is. This is the part of the procedure where scientists can be imaginative and creative.

Prediction: A test is planned that could prove or disprove the theory. As part of the plan, the scientist offers a proposition in this form: 'If my theory is true, then the experiment will have a certain, specified result.'

Experiment: The test is performed, and the results are recorded.

5(a) *Successful Result:* If the prediction he made at stage 3 came true, the idea devised at step 2 is *strengthened*. This part of scientific method is *inductive*, and not deductive. Next, it is time to go back to step 3 to make more predictions and do more tests to see if the theory can get stronger yet.

5(b) *Failed Result:* If the prediction did not come true, the theory has been *falsified*. This part of the scientific method is deductive: Scientists can't always be certain about what's true, but they can be absolutely certain about what's false. When predictions fail, they must go back to step 2 and devise a new theory to put to the test, and a new prediction to go with it.

Actually, a failed experimental result still represents a kind of success, because falsification rules out the impossible. This then frees up the scientist to pursue other, more promising theories.

Scientists often test more than one theory at the same time in order to eventually arrive at the 'last theory standing'. In this way, researchers can use a form of disjunctive syllogism to arrive at definitive conclusions about which theory provides the best explanation for the observation. Here's how that part of the procedure works.

> (P1) Either Theory 1 is true, or Theory 2 is true, or Theory 3 is true, or Theory 4 is true. (And so on, for however many theories are being tested.)
> (P2) By experimental observation, Theories 1 and 2 and 3 were falsified.
> (C) Therefore, Theory 4 is true.

Or, at least, Theory 4 has been *strengthened* to the point where it would be quite absurd to believe anything else. After all, there might be other theories that we haven't thought of and tested yet. But until we think of them and test them, we're going to go with the best theory we've got.

There's a bit more to scientific method than this. There are **paradigms** and **paradigm shifts, epistemic values**, experimental controls and variables, and the various ways that scientists negotiate with each other as they interpret experimental results. There are also a few differences between the experimental methods used by physical scientists (such as chemists), and social scientists (such as anthropologists). But this basic procedure of testing hypotheses by looking for

the evidence and ruling out what we know to be false is the same for all branches of science.

6.2. What Counts as a Scientific Claim?

While the word 'science' is relatively new, the concept is not. The word 'science' is derived from the Latin word *scientia*, which just means 'knowledge'. 'Scientist' is a word constructed to denote someone who engages in science, like an artist engages in art. ('Scientist' eventually won out over 'scientman' as our preferred term for someone who does science.)

Science, however, is not just any kind of knowledge. Throughout this book, you have been introduced to many kinds of claims. In general, critical thinking applies to claims that we can evaluate as true or false, plausible or implausible, etc. But not every true or false claim is a *scientific* claim. For instance, we can immediately exclude any kind of claim that cannot be evaluated as true or false. In addition, we can imagine all sorts of claims that—while they might be true or false—aren't true or false on the basis of scientific evidence. The reason that a scientific claim may be valued more than other claims (sometimes) is that we think that scientific claims are (1) provable; and (2) useful. At the same time, not every provable claim is scientific, nor is every useful claim, nor is every provable useful claim. We'll work out the details of this difficulty in the next few sections.

Before the word 'science' became popular, its subject matter was just called 'natural philosophy'. That's why everyone who gets a doctorate in a scientific discipline still gets a Ph.D.—a doctorate in philosophy. You may study for a Ph.D. in physics, chemistry, biology, or any other science, and what you'll get is a Philosophy Doctorate in Physics (for instance). The word 'physics' comes from the Greek word, φύσις, which means 'nature', and the earliest known Western philosophers were philosophers of nature. (As we saw in Chapter One, it is traditionally taught that Western philosophy began with Thales of Miletus, who sought to discover the first principle of nature—which he decided was water.)

We can already see the roots of modern-day science in the earliest philosophers, and especially in Aristotle, whose works are our primary source material on many of the views of other philosophers of his times. The first chapter of the first book of his *Metaphysics* (literally, the 'after-physics') is a discussion of what the best kind of knowledge is. Out of all of the things we claim to know, which claims can we count as 'scientific'? Aristotle didn't use the word 'science', but instead makes a distinction that is familiar to us all and will help us determine which claims among all of our claims are the scientific ones.

The key differentiation that Aristotle makes in this book is between the knowledge we receive through our senses and the knowledge we acquire through thought. Aristotle believed that perceptual knowledge would always be of particulars, but knowledge of universals is superior. That is to say, it is better to know something that pertains to each example of one type of thing than it is to know something only about some particular. He thus draws a distinction between those who have theoretical knowledge and those who only know about something through experience. In the end, he claims that the former kind of knowledge is better than the other, because it is able to examine causes and principles.[1] Now, consider the difference between these two claims:

(1) Fire is hot. Stay away from it.
(2) A combustion reaction is an exothermic reaction in which molecules combine with oxygen from the atmosphere to release energy in the form of heat. Introducing heat energy to other combustible materials encourages a combustion reaction, commonly known as 'burning'.

The person who knows that claim (1) is true is likely to live a long and healthy life that will not be cut short by jumping into a campfire. The person who knows that claim (2) is true will also not jump into campfires. The difference is that the person who understands claim (2) will be able to explain why they don't jump into campfires. Their knowledge will also be applicable to other sorts of situations. The person who knows what (2) means will be able to apply their knowledge in all sorts of situations, such as 'Don't store books in the oven', or 'Don't put your hand in the toaster'. (Your hand might not combust, but it will still really hurt.) The person who only knows claim (1), who knows to stay away from fire but doesn't know why, wouldn't be able to make the same kinds of inferences and would have to learn these things separately. The additional step, that of knowing the *why*, makes a claim more scientific—more provable and more useful.

It is a helpful rule of thumb to recognize that a more general claim is a more useful claim. That is, the more situations to which our claim might be applied, the more useful it proves to be. This rule of thumb will be later formalized; that is, in what sense it is 'useful', but it is easy enough to see that general claims are (in general) more useful than particular ones, simply because they can be applied more often. Consider the following claims. Which one is more 'scientific'?

(1) Bob has a bushy tail.
(2) Squirrels have bushy tails.

The first claim notices a feature of one individual. Let's say that Bob is some particular squirrel. We could make all sorts of observations about Bob, and our observations could be both accurate and useful, in a sense. If we want to be able to recognize Bob in the future, we may make a catalogue of Bob's features. Two of them are that he is a bushy-tailed rodent who steals seeds from the bird feeder. But claim (2) is more scientific because it gives us more general knowledge. We can apply (2) to any squirrel at all, and when we do, we can say something not just about Bob, but about *all squirrels*. General knowledge (knowledge of a *kind of thing* rather than knowledge of *a thing*) is more scientific. We might use (2) to define what makes a squirrel a squirrel, i.e., a member of its species, and then we are able to make all sorts of inferences that can be used to do what now call science.

---

1 Aristotle, Metaphysics, 982a1-2, tr. W.D. Ross in Complete Works of Aristotle, Jonathan Barnes ed. (Princeton: Princeton University Press, 1984).

Consider a biological claim:

> (1) A squirrel is a bushy-tailed rodent.

From this I could infer…

> (a) Anything that isn't a rodent isn't a squirrel;
> (b) All squirrels are rodents;
> (c) Anything that isn't bushy-tailed isn't a squirrel;
> (d) All squirrels have bushy tails;
> (e) Some rodents have bushy tails.

I could try to prove any of these claims, and I might even find that some of them don't hold. The first claim, that a squirrel is a rodent is true by definition. But what about the claim that all squirrels have bushy tails? I might have to revise that claim in light of further observations. What if I came across a squirrel that didn't have a bushy tail, because it had been burned in a campfire? I might then have to revise my claim that 'All squirrels have bushy tails' to say that 'All squirrels who haven't been burned in campfires have bushy tails', or better still, 'All squirrels who haven't suffered injuries or amputations of their tails have bushy tails'. All of these claims have a more scientific ring to them than any particular claim about Bob. Thus, generalizability is an important aspect of any scientific claim.

Something that might trip us up is the distinction between what is a scientific claim, and what it means to be 'scientifically proven'. Just because I can prove something using science doesn't make it a scientific claim. Consider every forensic science show ever:

> A team of socially awkward lab workers use scientific methods to determine whether or not Billy the Murderer was at the scene of the crime. They find some hair at the scene that has DNA matching Billy's. They also find some fibres that were dyed with the same chemical as the shirt Billy is wearing right now. They go to trial and claim that it is a scientific fact that Billy is a murderer.

It is still not the case, however, that in a science class you will learn, alongside other scientific truths like 'Water is H2O' and 'Gravity is a force that acts on

Scientific claims are both provable and useful. The philosopher of science, Karl Popper, takes these ideas and constructs a formal definition of what a scientific claim is—how it is proved and how it is useful.

objects with mass', 'Billy is a murderer'. The former claims are scientific, whereas the latter is not. We thus have two kinds of claims:

(1) Scientific claims (the topic of this chapter); and
(2) Claims supported by science.

Just because I *use* science to prove something does not make it a scientific claim.

6.3. A Formal Definition of 'Science'

The considerations above, about what makes a claim scientific or not, revolve around the ideas that scientific claims are both provable and useful. The philosopher of science Karl Popper takes these ideas and constructs a formal definition of what a scientific claim is—how it is proved and how it is useful. The discussion of what counts as a scientific claim around Popper's time necessitates the introduction of two new terms:

Verifiability: The possibility that a claim can be supported by additional observations.
Falsifiability: The possibility that a claim can be negated by additional observations.

These concepts do a lot of work to specify in what sense a scientific claim is 'provable'. Let's say I have some general claim: 'All kittens are evil', which I want to verify. I therefore decide to examine a number of kittens. If all the kittens I examine are, in fact, evil, then my claim is verified. To phrase it another way: every time I observe a kitten being evil, the observation supports my original claim, that all kittens are evil.

On what grounds would the same claim that 'All kittens are evil' be falsified? What observations would lead me to conclude that this hypothesis is false? I see a kitten not being evil, and I say it's just waiting for an opportunity and revise my original claim to 'All kittens are evil, but not all of the time'. I observe a bunch of kittens throughout their lifetimes, and I notice that some of them never did anything evil. Is my hypothesis therefore falsified? That depends.

According to philosopher Karl Popper, in order to

be 'scientific', a claim must be falsifiable as well as verifiable. In his book *The Logic of Scientific Discovery*, he constructs a more detailed argument for falsifiability as a criterion for qualifying a claim as scientific, but the general rule is this:

If there is no further observation that would falsify a claim, that claim is not scientific.

Returning my example above, if there is no further observation I would accept as proof of a kitten not being evil, the claim 'All kittens are evil' cannot be not scientific.

The concepts of verifiability and falsifiability serve as indicators of a claim's usefulness. We can now specify that the sense in which a scientific claim is thought to be useful is that one can attempt making predictions based on that claim. The extent to which those predictions turn out to be true are verifications of the claim's truth. The extent to which those predictions turn out to be false are evidence that the claim is no good. We can formalize this idea using the argument form *modus tollens* from earlier in this book (as Popper does in *The Logic of Scientific Discovery*).

Recall that the modus tollens form of argument goes like this:

If A, then B.
Not B.
Therefore, not A.

This is where we substitute in our scientific claim. If scientific claim A is *true*, then I would expect observation B. That is to say, my theory predicts a certain observation: If it is true that 'Objects with mass fall towards the earth', I can expect to observe any particular object with mass to fall down when dropped. My theory would be falsified only if I dropped something and it didn't fall down but remained suspended in mid-air. Contained in any scientific claim should be some way in which the claim could be proven false— we should be able to make some prediction that, were it not to come true, it would falsify the whole theory. I make a conditional statement:

> If it is true that all objects with mass fall towards the earth, this ball will fall when I drop it.

This statement contains a scientific claim and a prediction based on that claim. If I were then to observe a ball *not* falling toward the earth when I drop it, my modus tollens argument would be complete:

> If it is true that all objects with mass fall towards the earth, this ball will fall when I drop it.
> The ball does not fall when I drop it.
> Therefore, it is not true that all objects with mass fall towards the earth.

In light of this further observation, my theory would be *falsified*. I either have to give up on it or revise it in some relevant way. Say, for example, the ball didn't fall towards the earth because when I let go of it, it was already resting on a table top. In this instance, I would just revise my scientific claim to say: All objects with mass fall towards the earth unless impeded by some other object or force (like a table top, or the wind, etc).

What happens if my theory isn't falsified? Is it therefore proven? Why does Popper choose 'falsifiability' as opposed to 'verifiability' as proof that a claim is scientific? The reason is in the logic. Say my theory makes a prediction for what I will observe, and then I do observe it. Is it then true? Consider this bad argument:

> If it is true that all objects with mass fall towards the earth, this ball will fall when I drop it.
> The ball does fall when I drop it.
> Therefore, it is true that all objects with mass fall towards the earth.

This line of reasoning is tempting, but sadly, it is invalid. No matter how many times I see a ball fall towards the earth when I drop it, I can never say that my theory is verified, because the next one might not. The argument above has this form:

> If A, then B.
> B.
> Therefore, A.

And this, we know, is a formal fallacy called 'affirming the consequent'.

I can neither infer a general theory about balls, nor a general theory of things with mass from one ball dropping. Chapter 5 explained the rules of induction and how general claims may be made. For the most part, general claims can be proven false, but they cannot be proven true unless we've observed every one of the kind of thing we're trying to make a claim about. This is easier in some cases than others. If I say 'All five of the Von Trapp children have six toes', I might verify that claim by making five observations. If, on the other hand, my claim applies to 'all squirrels', then I would have to observe all squirrels in order to verify my claim. This is a tall order, and in general it's not necessary. We can make a reasonable inference based on some observations, but we can't then go on to claim that our theory is verified based those same observations. On the other hand, it only takes one observation to falsify a claim. Thus, falsifiability is the preferred quality according to which we say a claim is 'scientific'.

What happens when we determine that a claim isn't falsifiable? The topic of this chapter is scientific claims. What criticism can we make of claims that can't be falsified? It amounts to this: If a claim can't be falsified, it isn't scientific—but that doesn't necessarily mean it isn't true! Many non-scientific claims are true. Consider some other kinds of truth, like 'The play *Hamlet* takes place in Denmark'. I look it up in Shakespeare's work and it turns out to be true. Does that mean I've scientifically proved the setting of Shakespeare's play? Of course not.

6.4. Scientific Evidence and its Roots in Empiricism

When we say 'science', what we generally mean is 'empirical science'. The **empirical** part is what distinguishes our science from just any kind of knowledge. And when we say 'empirical', what we mean is knowledge based on observation. In this section, we'll examine the relationship between a theory and the evidence for that theory, and what kind of evidence counts as scientific evidence.

The **empiricist** philosophers arose in Britain as a reaction to the rationalists. The two schools debated the foundation of our knowledge, or what kind of knowledge is best founded. René Descartes (a rationalist) thought that our knowledge was founded in understanding itself. He used the example of melting wax in order to show that our knowledge could not come primarily from sense perception. In *Meditations on First Philosophy*, he writes:

Let us take, for example, this piece of wax: It has been taken quite freshly from the hive, and it has not yet lost the sweetness of the honey which it contains; it still retains somewhat of the odour of the flowers from which it has been culled; its colour, its figure, its size are apparent; it is hard, cold, easily handled, and if you strike it with the finger, it will emit a sound. Finally, all the things which are requisite to cause us distinctly to recognize a body, are met with in it. But notice that while I speak and approach the fire what remained of the taste is exhaled, the smell evaporates, the colour alters, the figure is destroyed, the size increases, it becomes liquid, it heats, scarcely can one handle it, and when one strikes it, no sound is emitted. Does the same wax remain after this change? We must confess that it remains; none would judge otherwise. What then did I know so distinctly in this piece of wax? It could certainly be nothing of all that the senses brought to my notice, since all these things which fall under taste, smell, sight, touch, and hearing, are found to be changed, and yet the same wax remains.[2]

The empiricist philosophers reject Descartes' assertions about the source of knowledge and maintain that we do, in fact, get all of our knowledge through sense perception. After all, if we didn't, where would it come from? Descartes makes it seem as though we have some **a priori** knowledge (*a priori* = prior to experience) about the notion of identity, whereas the empiricists would maintain that we get that notion and all other notions by inference from things we perceive—so we

know the wax is the same wax because we saw it melt.

The philosophy of the empiricists (John Locke, George Berkeley, and David Hume, to name a few) is where we get our notion of what counts as evidence within empirical science. Simply stated, we can't claim that our theory is 'scientific' unless it can be confirmed by observation. This is the origin of the scientific experiment. If a theory is to count as scientific, it must predict a particular observation, and we can confirm the theory by making that observation. If a theory can't be verified by experiment, it isn't scientific. And when we say 'experiment', we mean a procedure designed to measure a particular, predictable effect; one that should be evident if our theory is true. (It is also possible to design an experiment meant to falsify a theory; in that case, we would look for something that would not happen if our theory were true.)

Consider as an example Albert Einstein's general theory of relativity. According to his theory, gravity is the warping of space-time by massive objects. This contradicts Isaac Newton's earlier theory of gravity as an attractive force operating among objects with mass. But how does one demonstrate the warping of space-time? In 1919, Sir Arthur Eddington conducted an experiment designed by Sir Frank Watson Dyson that would provide evidence for the new theory. He considered the photon, a particle without mass. If Newton's theory were true, the photon should not be affected by the force of gravity. If Einstein's theory were true, the photon would be affected by gravity because the space in which it travels would itself be curved. Dyson's experiment measured the light coming from a faraway star system during a solar eclipse: He wanted to see whether the light's path would curve around the gravitational force of the sun. It did, so Einstein's theory was verified. (And Newton's was falsified.)

Was Einstein's theory scientific before it was verified? Yes, because it could be verified experimentally, even though it hadn't been yet. There was some effect which it predicted that would not occur if the theory were false. If there was evidence for Einstein's theory before the experiment, it did not actually prove Einstein's theory, because it wasn't scientific evidence. There's a particular kind of evidence that counts as

---

2 René Descartes, <u>Meditations on First Philosophy</u>, tr. Elizabeth Haldane (Cambridge: Cambridge University Press, 1911, p. 10.

proof of a scientific theory. While there may be many reasons to believe in something, not all of them count as scientific evidence. Here are some non-scientific reasons to believe in Einstein's theory:

- Einstein said it, and he's smart.
- Einstein says Newton is wrong, and I hate Newton.
- The holy book of my religion says the general theory of relativity is true.
- All of my friends believe in the theory of relativity.
- If I don't say that I believe in the theory of relativity, my physics teacher will hit me.

While all of these might be reasons to believe something, they don't count as scientific evidence. Scientific evidence is the observation of an effect predicted by a scientific theory.

There are also some features of scientific evidence that aren't true of other kinds of evidence. Observations predicted by a scientific theory should be **objective** and *replicable*. That is to say, anyone should be able to repeat Dyson's experiment and get the same results. And anyone who does so should observe the same outcome. Recall that in the opening section of this chapter, we said that scientific knowledge tends to be of a general nature. The reason that we don't take singular instances of something to be scientifically proved is that we can't reproduce them. 'Billy is a murderer' is not scientific knowledge, whereas, 'All cats are murderers' could be. (We could design an experiment to demonstrate that all cats, if given the appropriate opportunity, would choose murder over other available options.)

Why 'theory' and not 'fact'? The problem from our previous section remains: It is generally impossible to make all of the observations we would need to say that a theory is absolutely true. This is another truth of empiricism, one outlined in David Hume's *An Enquiry Concerning Human Understanding*. Hume makes the observation that even if we observe what we take to be a cause and effect relationship over and over again, we have no reason to think that the next time we try to make the observation, we'll see the same thing. This is because we're making an inference that we can't prove

experimentally. Embedded in how we conceive of scientific theories and their evidence (they predict things and can be confirmed by observing those predictions) is this one pesky inference that we can't prove: The idea that the future will resemble the past.[3]

Our theory becomes more certain the more times it successfully predicts an effect, but we must always account for the fact that the next time, it could be different. Thus, we should have a degree of certainty in a theory, but we can never say that it's 100% true. The higher the degree of certainty in the theory, the more certain I am that the next time I use it to predict an effect I will observe that effect. Consider some examples:

- I theorize that things fall to the ground when I drop them. I drop 1000 things, and they fall every time. I therefore infer that the next time I drop something, the probability that it will fall to the ground is 1000/1001.
- I theorize that Jenny always holds the door open for people. I've seen her do it 9/9 times I've observed. I infer that the next time I see someone approaching the door after Jenny, there's a 9/10 chance she'll hold the door for them.

A new problem arises when I try to infer the reasons why I'm observing what I observe. That is, according to empiricism, all my theory should do is predict an observation. When I try to come up with reasons to explain the observation, i.e., to create a theory that explores the causes and principles behind the observation, I might find that there are a number of ways any of my observations might be explained.

6.5. Underdetermination and Overdetermination

Ideally, I should be able to design an experiment that, if I observe what I set out to observe, proves my theory true and other theories false. What happens, though, if there are multiple theories that all predict the same observation as I do? In that case, my theory would be underdetermined.

The problem doesn't arise when I'm just trying to predict an observation. Rather, it occurs when I try

---

3 See David Hume, An Enquiry Concerning Human Understanding, Section VI: Of Probability.

to infer the *why* of what I'm observing. Why is it that Jenny always holds the door open for people? Is she polite? Was she raised in a door-holding household? Is she obsessed with door-holding? Does she think her door-holding will guarantee her access to an afterlife inaccessible to us non-door-holders? Is she always on her best behaviour when she thinks her science professors are watching? All of these possibilities would predict the same observation: That Jenny is always going to hold the door for people. How am I to determine which theory best fits the evidence, when the evidence for all of them is the same?

When we evaluate scientific claims, we want to keep an eye out for whether the theory is supported by the evidence to the exclusion of other theories. That is, when you look at a scientific claim, you want to consider whether or not the evidence for that claim could just as easily support a different claim.

Let's consider an example. I claim that I have a superpower that makes me invisible as long as no one is looking at me.[4] The fact that I'm not invisible when you look at me is evidence for my theory. The fact that I can be seen when people are looking at me similarly supports two incompatible theories: (1) I'm always visible; and (2) I'm visible only when I'm being looked at. Is there any observation that could be made to prove one theory over the other? In this scenario, we might try to look for evidence to disprove one theory rather than another. Is there any observation that could be made to disprove my claim?

It's not always possible to point to one observation that would prove one theory and disprove another. In these cases, the data is open to interpretation. We might be able to point to other reasons to prefer one theory to another, but we can't prove scientifically that we are correct. This is where principles like Ockham's razor apply. Consider these two competing theories for why people might scream when I hit them:

- When I hit someone, they experience pain, and pain causes people to scream.
- When I hit someone, they experience pain; the pain awakens the ghosts of their ancestors who invariably have unfinished business in the world of the living.

Why is it that Jenny always holds the door open for people? Is she polite? Was she raised in a door-holding household? Is she obsessed with door-holding? Does she think her door-holding will guarantee her access to an afterlife inaccessible to us non-door-holders? Is she always on her best behaviour when she thinks her science professors are watching?

4 You may recognize this superpower if you've seen the film <u>Mystery Men</u> (1999). There is a corresponding philosophical discussion according to which we try to distinguish between what is 'invisible' versus what is 'unseen'.

123

Once awoken, these ancestors attempt to communicate with the living through the organs of the living, but due to translation issues, they can't communicate using human words; their attempts to communicate their intent through the living comes through as an unintelligible scream, which to all observers, including the person screaming, appears to come from the person who's just been hit.

The second theory predicts the same observations as the first, but it introduces a lot of unnecessary considerations. If I have no reason to think that I need an additional explanatory factor to make sense of my observations, I shouldn't introduce any into my theory. Sometimes I do require additional explanatory factors, and my observations will justify introducing them into my theory.

We have to admit, in any case, that my preference for the simple theory over a complex one is not due to any scientific evidence; there's no set of observations that leads me to a scientific theory saying, 'Simple is always better than complex.' Ockham's razor is not itself a scientific principle.

Overdetermination is just the opposite of underdetermination. If my theory is overdetermined, that just means that I have more evidence for it than I need. I've excluded all of the other theories that would explain my observations, and then some. Especially in the physical sciences, you don't see too many people criticizing a theory for being overdetermined. (Sometimes in the social sciences you do—but that's a story for a future edition of this book.)

6.6. Confusing Necessary and Sufficient Conditions

In Chapter 4, we differentiated between necessary and sufficient conditions. In a conditional statement, a necessary condition is formalized as the consequent of a conditional statement, whereas a sufficient condition would be formalized as the antecedent of a conditional statement. For example, if ten dimes are sufficient to equal a dollar, I could make this formal statement:

If I have ten dimes, I have a dollar.

A necessary condition, on the other hand, is placed in the consequent position. If I need that dollar to buy a car air freshener at the gas station, my formalized conditional statement would look like this:

If I'm to buy that gas station car air freshener, I must have a dollar.

In this case, having the dollar isn't sufficient to buy the desired air freshener, because other conditions would also have to hold: The gas station must be open; there must be someone working; they have to have an acceptable scent in stock, etc., and if any of these additional conditions don't hold, I won't get my air freshener. This difference between necessary and sufficient conditions is the difference between whether an argument is valid or invalid, solid support for your theory, or just a fallacy. It is important, therefore, when I'm considering a scientific observation, whether what I'm observing constitutes a necessary or a sufficient condition for the effect that my theory is supposed to predict.

Let's take an obvious example. In Aristotle's *History of Animals*, he makes a claim about the breeding habits of eels that we now know to be false:

Eels are not the issue of pairing, neither are they oviparous; nor was an eel ever found supplied with either milt or eggs, nor are they when cut open found to have within them passages for milt or for eggs. In point of fact, this entire species of blooded animals proceeds neither from pairing nor from the egg. There can be no doubt that the case is so. For in some standing pools, after the water has been drained off and the mud has been dredged away, the eels appear again after a fall of rain. In time of drought they do not appear even in stagnant ponds, for the simple reason that their existence and sustenance is derived from rain-water.[5]

In this passage, Aristotle makes some observations from which he infers that eels must come from rain-

5 Aristotle, History of Animals, 570a4-12, tr. d'A.W. Thompson in Complete Works. (Oxford University Press, 1910).
6 A.S. Packard, 'The Reproduction of the Eel' in Nature 19, 174-174 (26 December 1878).

water. The observations are:

> Eels have not been observed to reproduce through intercourse.
>
> Eels have not been observed to have any sex cells inside their bodies.

Given that these methods of reproduction have been excluded from consideration, Aristotle then proceeds to report that eels appear after a rainfall and concludes that eels come from rain-water.

We can cut Aristotle some slack, because the breeding habits of eels are notoriously difficult to observe. (According to contemporary theory, eels venture out to sea to reproduce and change form several times throughout their life cycle.) A letter to the journal *Nature* in 1877 reports that eels had only been observed to have eggs in the previous year (1876)[6], and until that time Aristotle's theory prevailed.

Aristotle's mistake was to assume that a necessary condition (rain-water) was in fact a sufficient condition. That is, noticing that no eels were produced without rain-water, Aristotle assumed that the eels must in fact come from the rain-water, or that the rain-water was responsible for the eels' existence.

We see the same logic at work all the time in contemporary science. It is all too easy to make the logical leap from 'A is necessary for B' to 'A is responsible for B'. And when we use phrases like 'is responsible for', we tend to think of that as a sufficient rather than necessary condition. For example, were you to ask me 'Who's responsible for this mess?' and I blamed it on the cat, you would infer that the cat caused the mess. (And I would get off scot-free, even though what actually happened is I tripped over the cat and tried to grab onto the tablecloth to break my fall, dragging everything from the table onto the floor.) This kind of loose wording can be intentionally or unintentionally misleading, and it is prevalent in popular reporting on scientific discoveries. Modest wording doesn't sell magazines, so it's in a publication's best financial interest to overstate their findings as far as can be done without actually saying something false. Consider the following statement from brainworldmagazine.com:

> The hippocampus, as part of the brain's limbic system, is the structure responsible for the formation of memory. Without it, you wouldn't remember a great deal of your job training, or much else—as the hippocampus is also integral to spatial navigation...[7]

While it might be true that memories would not be formed without the hippocampus memories, this statement only tells us that the hippocampus is necessary to the formation of memory; not that it is sufficient. A more accurate report on the hippocampus' function would claim that it is involved in the formation of memory, or that it plays a role in memory. These phrasings make it clear that we're talking about a necessary rather than sufficient condition for memory formation.

Other ambiguous wordings suggest causal relations exist and have been scientifically proven when in fact they have not. Back in 2009, *Fox & Friends* reported on the causal link between beer pong and herpes. It is possible to imagine (as they did) how the causal relationship would work. If someone has a cold sore and their mouth touches a ball, which then goes on to someone else, the next person might contract the virus, they surmised. In fact, they picked up the story from a joke website. Still, the Centers for Disease Control had to issue a formal statement denying the causal link between beer pong and herpes.[8] In any case, your critical thinking skills should have kicked in when any such link was proposed—not only is beer pong not a sufficient condition to catch herpes, it isn't even a necessary one.

6.7. Science and Its Values

We tend to ascribe values to scientific claims. We say things like, 'Kale is good for you' or 'Copper is a great conductor'. When we say these things, we obscure what we really mean by the words 'good' or 'great'. When we say that 'Kale is good for you', we mean 'Kale contains nutrients that encourage the flourishing of the human body'. And if we say 'Copper is a great conductor', we mean 'Copper allows the flow of electrical current well in comparison to other substances'. It may seem

---

7 J. Sullivan. "Meet Your Brain's GPS: The Hippocampus" <u>Brain World</u>, 3rd May 2018. http://brainworldmagazine.com/working-memory-the-role-of-the-hippocampus/ 8 "Alleged CDC Beer Pong / Herpes Simplex study is a hoax" Press release from the Centres for Disease Control and Prevention, US Dept. of Heath and Human Services, 26 February 2009. https://www.cdc.gov/media/pressrel/2009/s090226.htm

When we say that 'Kale is good for you', we mean 'Kale contains nutrients that encourage the flourishing of the human body.' And if we say 'Copper is a great conductor', we mean 'Copper allows the flow of electrical current well in comparison to other substances'.

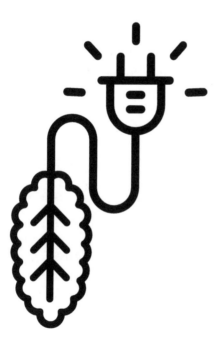

that these claims are also prescriptive: They might also mean 'You should eat kale!' or 'Use copper wiring in your home!' But this only makes the meaning even more obscure: Words like 'good', 'great', and even 'value' have more than one meaning, some of which may be moral, and some nonmoral. Exactly which meaning is employed when the word appears will depend on the sense of the word and the surrounding discussion. (And that's if we have avoided the fallacy of equivocation!) In this section we will focus on what it means to speak of *scientific* values, as distinct from other kinds of values.

The problem of obscured meaning is not just limited to claims about science; it covers all sorts of claims. For scientific claims, just as any other, we should always make sure that we're saying what we mean—the plain and bare truth. When I want to speak with that kind of scientific clarity, I don't say that my grocery store has 'the best' prices in town. I say that they have 'the lowest'—because 'best' could have various meanings. In a dog park I might say that my dog is a 'good dog', but that could mean his friendliness toward children, or his bravery as a protector, or that he has comb-able hair that I can spin into yarn, or that his meat is tasty, or any number of other qualities. But when I want to make a scientific claim about my dog I say something very specific, such as that he responds to verbal commands 78% of the time. When we use words like 'good, better, best', we assume a value system inherent in claims that we really want to be descriptive. If I want to be clear, I have to replace vague claims of 'good, better, best' with whatever measure I am using to say that such things are good, better, or best.

Examples:
'You have great eyesight' becomes...
'You can see things farther away than a lot of other people.'

Some go so far as to claim that there is a value system inherent in our scientific endeavours from the start. Medical science is the most open to these sorts of claims, and there are those who would claim that there wouldn't be any such thing as medical science if there weren't some inherent assumption of what the human body is supposed to be like and what it's supposed to do. If I don't make these assumptions, in what sense can I claim that someone is diseased or dysfunctional? The logic here points out the fact that I wouldn't be able to call someone disabled if there weren't some ability they were supposed to have but don't. But who says they were supposed to have that ability in the first place?

Consider the recent debate about whether deafness is a disability by nature, or rather a unique culture. On the one hand, some social systems in place claim that deafness is a disability and there are programs (and devices like cochlear implants) that propose to alleviate this perceived deficiency and help deaf people navigate the world more like hearing people. But what if we didn't perceive deafness as a deficiency? What if the ability to hear is just something that some people can do but others can't?[9] Is lactose intolerance a disability? What about my cat allergy? What about the fact that I can't drink more than 12 shots of tequila before passing out? The point is, sometimes cultural views sneak into our sciences, but when we identify those value claims we can correct for them. Sometimes this correction involves adopting different approaches, such as teaching sign language to deaf people instead of insisting on cochlear implants that some of them may not want. Sometimes it involves entirely abandoning some diagnoses of 'pathology' and related 'treatment' practices, such as the application of electrical shocks for homosexuality, for instance.

Value claims have always been apparent in scientific evaluations. In some cases, we can look and identify what, exactly, someone means when they make a value claim as part of a scientific endeavour. But bad scientific claims sometimes still sneak in. Consider these statements by Aristotle on eye colour in people and in animals:

> Of the eye the white is pretty much the same in all creatures; but what is called the iris differs. In some it is black, in some distinctly blue, in some greyish-blue, in some greenish; and this last colour is the sign of an excellent disposition, and is particularly well adapted for sharpness of vision.[10]

There are two value claims here, one of which is made explicit:

Greenish eyes are well adapted for sharpness of vision.

This claim lends itself to scientific verification. We could design an experiment to observe the sharpness of vision in green-eyed people in comparison to people with other eye colours and determine whether or not their vision was sharper. We could try to figure out what it is about the greenness of someone's eyes that allows for this sharper vision: Does this colour iris let in more light? Still, we should suspect Aristotle's motives for valuing green eyes and as well as sharpness of vision. Why hasn't he chosen some other quality of vision to highlight here? Are green eyes good for seeing in the dark? At a distance? Up close? Accurately? Did

"Greenish eyes are well adapted for sharpness of vision."

---

9 See, for instance: Harvey, Erica R. 'Deafness: A Disability or a Difference.' Health Law & Policy 2, no. 1 (2008): 42-57.

10 Aristotle, History of Animals, 491b35-492a3.

Aristotle choose to focus on sharpness just because he had already determined that green eyes were the best and now he has to explain why? If so, what was his real motivation?

The moral of the story is, even if a scientific claim is true, we should still examine how it is formed and why the scientist would choose to emphasize this truth rather than others. To claim that green eyes are best is to exclude a lot of people from having the 'best' sort of vision. That is, Aristotle's theory of the relative 'goodness' of eye colours could be interpreted as inherently discriminatory.

The other claim, that green eyes are a sign of an 'excellent disposition' is vague and unobservable. What do we mean to say that someone has an 'excellent disposition'? What disposition is 'best', and by what measure? This kind of claim lends itself especially well to a confirmation bias. If I assume from the outset that green-eyed people have the best dispositions, I can interpret anything I notice about green-eyed people afterwards as evidence for their being 'the best', which confirms my original assumption. For example, if I say 'Green eyed people have the best disposition', and then I notice "Green-eyed people are easily angered by small children', I may then go on to claim 'It is a sign of the best disposition to be easily angered by small children'. I then confirm my assumption: 'Green eyed people are easily angered by small children and therefore have the best disposition'.

The solution to the value problem of the sciences is to replace all value claims with literal statements of what it is we're observing, and the measure according to which we're making our observations. Epictetus recommended the same thing in his *Enchiridion*, the handbook for **Stoicism**, with the same purpose in mind: To acquire objective knowledge of the world.

> These reasonings have no logical connection: 'I am richer than you; therefore, I am your superior.' 'I am more eloquent than you; therefore, I am your superior.' The true logical connection is rather this: 'I am richer than you; therefore, my possessions must exceed yours.' 'I am more eloquent than you; therefore, my style must surpass yours.' But you, after all, consist neither in property nor in style.[11]

We should perform the same purge on our scientific knowledge. I should not say, 'My car is more fuel-efficient than yours; therefore, it is better.' I should say, 'My car is more fuel-efficient than yours; therefore, I will travel farther consuming an equivalent amount of fuel energy.' The additional claim, that fuel efficiency is better, may be true, but it is not scientific. I would need to make that claim explicit, particularly in what sense I claim that fuel efficiency is better. I make these addition claims apparent: 'A car that is fuel-efficient will produce fewer emissions'; 'Emissions from cars reduce air quality'; 'By "air quality", I mean the absence of particles in air that would make it unhealthy for me to breathe'; 'Therefore, fuel-efficient cars allow for the air to be less unhealthy for me to breathe'. And I like breathing air, and wish to preserve my health, so that's what I mean by 'better'.

It may be impossible to remove all claims of moral value from science. There are moral values so embedded in our thinking that we may not even recognize them as value claims. For example, the value claim above: 'I like breathing air' was made because I have a bias towards my own survival. But could I prove scientifically that my survival is of any objective value? Some would argue that science itself is a value claim. Why should I value observable, repeatable claims over any others? Are value claims about people, like 'Rob is a great guy' more or less important than value claims about objects, like 'Blueberries contain antioxidants'? How would I decide?

SUMMING UP: Thinking critically about the sciences is about determining the degree to which a claim is 'scientific' and whether it is conducive to the goals of science. That is to say, we want our scientific knowledge to contribute to an **objective** body of knowledge, verifiable by anyone (well, anyone who has the time, the equipment, and the training), that predicts the future behaviour of systems in nature. This does not, of course, mean we must purge value judgments from our thinking entirely. But it does

---

11 Epictetus, Enchiridion, XLIV. tr. Thomas Wentworth Higginson (Boston: Little, Brown and Company, 1891).

mean that when we are thinking *scientifically*, we should try reduce as much as possible the influence of our personal biases and embedded values. As noted in Chapter Two, it may be impossible to be entirely and perfectly objective, but it is possible to be objective enough to get on with the work of science.

I should not say, 'My car is more fuel-efficient than yours; therefore, it is better.'

I should say, 'My car is more fuel-efficient than yours; therefore, I will travel farther consuming an equivalent amount of fuel energy.' The additional claim, that fuel efficiency is better, may be true, but it is not scientific.

Popularity
Ignorance
Dilemma

Generalization
Authority
Division

Chapter Seven: Fallacies

WHAT IS A FALLACY? Simply put, a fallacy is an error in reasoning. A fallacy can arise for two reasons: (1) we mistakenly assume that we have proven our conclusion when we have not; or (2) we assume we have stronger evidence for the conclusion than there really is. Usually, this means that the kind of evidence needed to support the conclusion is lacking. A fallacy does not mean that the conclusion is necessary false, but that the premises provided are not strong enough to demonstrate that the conclusion is true. There are also fallacies that have faulty inferences at their base.

Why should we study fallacies? First and most importantly, so that you won't commit them! You want your reasoning to be sound and valid, and the surest way to meet these goals is to avoid fallacies. Second, learning about fallacies is a great way to correct biases in your own reasoning that may be too deep to spot without more focused analysis. You'd be amazed how much bad reasoning you may have learned from parents, family, friends, teachers, your culture, or the intellectual environment you've been raised in. This brings me to the third point: you want to learn about fallacies so you can spot the errors in reasoning others commit. Politicians, lawyers, newspaper reporters, bloggers, and Wikipedia are just a few of the guilty parties, but there are many more. Even worse, fallacies don't just happen by accident; they are often committed with some kind of intent in mind which is often to create a certain reaction. Identifying them enables you to make clear and educated choices about who and what to believe. This will help you avoid to falling prey to deceitful schemes or helping spread false informa-tion, and it will also enable you to communicate more effectively with others.

7.1. Appeal to Authority

(Latin: *Argumentum ad Verecundiam*) This is an attempt to prove a conclusion by an improper appeal to the opinion of an authority: The appeal is most easily identified as improper when the authority is irrelevant and/or unrecognized in the area.

Examples:
My mom says if I eat watermelon seeds, a plant will grow in my belly and I'll turn green. Because my mom said it, it must be true.

I think that the earth is flat because I'm a fan of the hip-hop artist B.o.B. and professional basketball player Kyrie Irving, and both of them say that the Earth is flat.

The President said that violent crime in the city of Chicago is absolutely out of control. He's the President; surely, he knows about these things.

I am a tiny potato, and I believe in you. You can do the thing.

It should be noted here that not all appeals to authority are faulty. When you are sick, you probably visit your doctor and take their advice, and when you get into legal trouble you proceed according to what a lawyer tells you. So, an appeal to authority can be relevant and proper when the authority you appeal to is recognized as having authoritative expertise in that area. We may also rely on it if we ourselves lack the necessary information or experience called for, and we cannot acquire the information we need for the argument ourselves. To appeal to statements made by Buzz Aldrin about the moon's surface is a proper application of authority. Likewise, to appeal to statements made in a local newspaper about when a newly-built bridge will open to the public is also a proper application of authority. When we look at reasonable doubt, we'll discuss some ways to decide whether a given authority can be trusted, and when they probably shouldn't.

7.2. Appeal to Force

(Latin: *Argumentum ad Baculum*) This covers any attempt to make someone accept a proposition or argument by using some type of force or threat, possibly including the threat of violence. After all, threats do not establish any truth whatsoever.

> Examples:
> Company policy concerning customer feedback is 'Either it's perfect (100%) or we failed (99% or less)'. Anyone who doesn't support this will be fired.

> I believe that the Baccus Players should perform 'Antigone' this year, and if they perform anything else, I'll burn down the theatre.

It is important to be able to tell the difference between the appeal to force argument, and a straightforward description of bad consequences that might befall someone who takes a certain course of action. Thus, an argument like this one:

> If you drive while drunk and are caught by the police, you will probably go to jail.

…is not actually a case of appeal to force. This example does not say anything about the rightness or wrongness of drunk driving. It simply describes the

legal standing of the act, and its likely outcome. Of course, the sense in which an argument like this is expressed may also matter here. For instance, if someone were to say:

> If you go outside without your jacket and sweater, you'll catch a chill. You might even get pneumonia and die!

…much would depend on whether the speaker is a caring and anxious parent looking out for the welfare of her child, or a grumpy old curmudgeon who would like nothing more than to see you catch a chill and die. Much may also depend on whether the utterance of that appeal produces psychosomatic effects in the hearer. But I digress.

7.3. Appeal to Emotion

Any attempt to make someone accept a proposition or argument by arousing and exploiting their emotions is likely to partake of this fallacy. The most usual form this fallacy takes is an appeal to pity (Latin: *Argumentum ad Misericordiam*) but the general form is any argument in which a strong emotional appeal is meant to subvert someone's rational thinking. Remember: Your feelings, by themselves, do not establish truth. Your feelings might help prompt you towards a *prima facie* interpretation of things. But that's not the same as knowing for certain that a proposition is true or that an argument is sound.

> Examples:
> The defendant should not be found guilty of this crime. Her life has been filled with endless abuse, a lack of love and respect, and so many hardships.

> You and I met in a past life. I know this because when I first met you, a powerful feeling of recognition swept over me.

> The Montreal Canadiens are going to win the Stanley Cup this year. I just know it!

> "Search your feelings, you know it to be true!"—Darth Vader.

7.4. Appeal to Tradition

(Latin: *Argumentum ad Antiquitatem*) This fallacy happens when someone cites the historical preferences and practices of a culture or even a particular person, as evidence for a proposition or argument being correct. Traditions are often passed down from generation to generation, with the explanation for continuity being 'this is the way it has been done before', which is of course not a valid reason. The age of something does not entail its truth or falsity.

Examples:
We have turkey for Thanksgiving dinner and duck for Christmas dinner every year, because that is what my parents and grandparents always had.

Whenever I buy a new broom for the house, I always cut off the top ten inches of the handle. My mom did that when she bought a new broom, and so did my grandmother before her.

It is, however, important to consider these arguments carefully. It is not always reasonable to dismiss an argument just because it recounts the way things have always been if there is no other justification for continuing to do things that way. Some customs in religion, jurisprudence, the arts, etc., gain their force and their appeal because they partake of honoured tradition. For example:
When Muslims face Mecca to pray, they are participating in an ancient cultural and spiritual tradition which reminds them of their religious commitments and unites them into a global and historical community.
The key indicator here is whether we adopt or dismiss an idea because it's old, *and for no other reason*. There must also be a reason why it matters that an idea is old.

7.5. Appeal to Novelty

(Latin: *Argumentum ad Novitatem*) This fallacy is the opposite of appeal to tradition, in that it is the claim of the newness or modernity of something is presented as evidence of its truth and superiority. But, of course, the mere novelty of the idea or proposition does not imply its truth or falsity.

Examples:
String theory is a new and rising research area in particle physics, and therefore it must be true.

The latest *Star Wars* movies are better than original series films from the 70s and 80s because the newer ones have younger actors and more up-to-date techniques and equipment for the special effects.

The care we took with the 'Appeal to Tradition' fallacy applies here too. It can also be wrong to adopt or dismiss an idea or a way of doing things for no other reason than just because it has never been tried before.

7.6. Appeal to Ignorance

(Latin: *Argumentum ad Ignorantiam*) This is an attempt to argue for or against a proposition or position because there is a lack of evidence against or for it: I argue X because there is no evidence showing not-X.

Examples:
There is intelligent life on Neptune, for sure. Science has not found any evidence that there isn't life there.

This man is a terrorist. Look: He's never shown us that he's not a terrorist, has he?

7.7. Shifting the Burden of Proof

As we saw in the discussion of the fallacy of ignorance, an absence of evidence doesn't prove anything one way or another. A special variation of the fallacy of ignorance can happen when a speaker tries to someone else responsible for providing the relevant evidence. The 'burden of proof' is the responsibility to bring forth the evidence that some statement is true, and this responsibility always falls on the person who asserts the argument under consideration. Speakers who try to make someone else take up this burden commit the fallacy of *shifting* the burden of proof away from themselves onto someone else.

Examples:
I believe that the stars out in space are actually not what scientists say. What's really out there is a giant wall made of stones and bricks, and there's a fire on the other side of the wall, and what people call stars are actually little holes in the wall where the light of the fire shines through. Don't believe me? Well, go ahead and prove me wrong!

I think the City of Gatineau should erect a 30-foot statue of Marilyn Monroe. After all, how could anyone possibly dislike Marilyn Monroe?

Aliens must exist. Until scientists study every planet in the universe and show me there aren't any aliens any-where, I will continue to believe that they exist.

7.8. Appeal to Popularity

(Latin: *Argumentum ad Numeram*) Here, a speaker attempts to use the popularity of a position or premise as evidence for its truthfulness. This is a fallacy because the popularity of something is irrelevant to whether it is true or false. It is one that sometimes is difficult to spot or prevent committing because common sense often suggests that if something is popular it must be true and/or valid.

Example:
All the mothers in my child's daycare are giving quinoa to their kids, so it must be the best thing for them.

The iPod is a great product. Ten million people bought one.

Most people believe that driving a sport utility vehicle is safer than driving an ordinary car. Ten million SUV owners cannot be wrong.
The singer George Whats-His-Name holds concerts in

football stadiums and always attracts a crowd of 50,000 people or more. His music must be really good.

Sometimes the number of people who believe something can be relevant, but those are usually cases where the proposition at stake is the popularity or distribution of something. For example:

I've seen lots of people wearing green bowler hats this year. They must be becoming very fashionable. And since I want to be fashionable, I'm going to get one for myself.

The argument here is not directly about the popularity of green bowler hats, but instead about the speaker's wish to be fashionable; i.e., to wear the same thing as many other people.

7.9. Fallacy of Accident

(Latin: *a dicto simpliciter ad dictum secundum quid*)
The fallacy of accident is also known as the fallacy of sweeping generalization. It is an attempt to apply a general rule to a situation with disregard for relevant exceptions to that rule. In other words, it is taking a general rule and attempting to apply it like a universal one (something that has no exceptions). Often what is being applied is what we would call 'rules of thumb', which are considered to be scientifically vague bits of reasoning that have a cultural and temporal context.

General rule: All birds can fly.
Exceptions: Flightless birds like kiwi, penguin, emu, ostrich, and rhea.

If you were raised in a large city like Montreal, you may only see flight-capable birds in a park or in someone's yard and your rule of thumb would most likely be like the one above: 'All birds can fly'. Thus, what we are familiar with often determines the rule of thumb and what is 'normal'. We can discuss possible exceptions to the rule, where birds that are flight-capable cannot fly, such as when the bird is a hatchling, or has broken a wing. One committing this fallacy

Person A: All Scotsmen love eating haggis and listening to bagpipe music.

Person B: My brother-in-law is a Scotsman and he doesn't like haggis at all.

Person A: Then he must not be a true Scotsman.

would take instances like these and categorize them as 'abnormal' and still continue to argue that all 'normal' or 'quintessential' birds can fly.

Sometimes the exception might be denied, as when someone insists that the general rule being discussed must be very narrow. This is sometimes called the 'no true Scotsman' defence, taking after examples like this:

> Person A: All Scotsmen love eating haggis and listening to bagpipe music.
> Person B: My brother-in-law is a Scotsman and he doesn't like haggis at all.
> Person A: Then he must not be a true Scotsman.

7.10. Amphiboly

Amphiboly is a fallacy of ambiguity, where the ambiguity in question arises directly from the poor grammatical structure in a sentence. The fallacy occurs when a bad argument relies on the grammatical ambiguity to sound strong and logical.

> Example:
> *I'm going to return this car to the dealer I bought it from. Their ad said 'Used 1995 Ford Taurus with air conditioning, cruise, leather, new exhaust and chrome rims.' But the chrome rims aren't new at all.*

There are other kinds of amphiboly fallacies, like those of ambiguous pronoun reference:

> *I took some pictures of the dogs at the park playing, but they were not good.*

In the above, the amphiboly occurs because it's unclear whether the dogs or the pictures are 'not good'. Sometimes the amphiboly arises from something as simple as the position of a comma:

> Let's eat grandma!
> Let's eat, grandma!

And there is amphiboly when modifiers are

misplaced, such as in a famous Groucho Marx joke:

> 'One morning I shot an elephant in my pajamas. How he got into my pajamas, I'll never know.'

7.11. Fallacy of Composition

(Also known as exception fallacy) This is the fallacy of assuming that when a property applies to all members of a class, it must also apply to the class as a whole.

> Examples:
> Every player in the NHL is wealthy; therefore, the NHL must be a wealthy organization.
>
> The atoms that make up my body are all invisible. Therefore, my body is invisible!
>
> Each of the monthly payments for this new car is really small. Only around $200/month. It must be a really inexpensive, affordable car!
>
> All the players on that team are great players. This team must therefore be a truly great team.

7.12. Fallacy of Division

(Also known as false division, or faulty division) This fallacy assumes that when a property applies to the class as a whole, it must also apply to every member of that class as well.

> This machine is very heavy. Therefore, all the parts of the machine will be very heavy too.
>
> Students at Heritage College study all kinds of subjects: Nursing, electronics, early childhood care, fine arts, and so on. Therefore, when John goes to Heritage College, he will study nursing, electronics, early childhood care, fine arts, everything!
>
> It's safe to eat ordinary table salt—so it must also be safe to eat pure sodium and chloride, because that's what salt is made of.

7.13. Straw Man Fallacy

Like the red herring, a straw man tends to happen when one person is criticizing or attacking another's position or argument. It occurs when she misrepresents or purposely distorts the position or argument of her opponent in order to weaken it, thus defeating it more easily. The name vividly depicts the action. Imagine two fighters in a ring: One of them builds a man made of straw (like a scarecrow), beats it up horribly, and then declares victory. While doing this, his or her real opponent stands in the ring, completely untouched. The straw man is considered to be one of the commonest fallacies; in particular we see it in used in political, religious, and ethical debates.

> Examples:
> The Leader of the Opposition is against the purchase of new submarines and helicopters. Clearly, he is okay with our country being defenceless and open to invasion by our enemies.
>
> The members of Black Lives Matter say that they are fighting racism. But they are actually hypocrites, because they are implying that white lives don't matter.

Notice how the second example there is also a formal fallacy. Categorical propositions do not automatically imply their own double-negatives: If all black lives are things that matter ('All S are P'), it does not follow that all nonblack lives are things that don't matter ('all not-S is not-P'); there could be other things that are also P. Straw man fallacies are often constructed around non-sequiturs like that.

7.14. Red Herring

(Latin: *Ignoratio elenchi*) This fallacy is committed when someone raises an irrelevant issue in the middle of an argument, derails the original discussion, and causes the argument to contain two totally different and unrelated issues. You recognize the insertion of a red herring in a discussion when you begin your argument about one thing and end up arguing about something else entirely. If not caught and removed, this fallacy makes any premises that were used logically out the outset unrelated to the conclusion. It is a distraction tactic, and often used to avoid addressing criticisms or attacks by an opponent. This device is very commonly seen in political debates. It is also often seen in debates when someone makes an excuse for not doing something he was asked to do.

Examples:

The 'Occupy Wall Street' protesters complain that corporations and their money control Washington. But their camps are messy and disorganized and are known to have homeless people and drug addicts living in them, and they are making life hell for the shop owners in their area.

I don't believe that climate changed is caused by human activity, because Al Gore made that movie *An Inconvenient Truth* even though he isn't a scientist. Filmmakers who are not scientists shouldn't make films about science.

Question: "Did you clean your room?" Answer: "Well I started, but it got too hot up there. You know, we really need to get the air conditioning fixed. And why haven't you taken me shopping for summer clothes yet?"

The fallacies of Red Herring and Straw Man look similar, and it's easy to mistake one for the other. As a general rule: Straw man involves deception, and red herring involves distraction.

7.15. Abusing the Man

(Latin: *Argumentum ad Hominem*) This is any attempt to disprove a proposition or argument by launching a personal attack on the author of it. A person's character, or any of her actions that are unrelated to the discussion, does not necessarily predict the truth or falsity of a proposition or argument. Ad hominem arguments, and genetic fallacy arguments in general, fail because they say nothing about the propositions being discussed. They are types of criticisms that

attack something by raising facts that are perhaps tangentially related to the argument, but are logically irrelevant.

Examples:

We shouldn't listen to those Antifa protesters. They are all just a rabble of troublemakers, and they only care about themselves.

Jane says that it is statistically very likely that other planets in the galaxy have intelligent life. But she dabbles in the occult and reads Tarot cards, so she can't be taken seriously.

A variation of this fallacy is called poisoning the well. It is a way of attacking someone's honesty, so that all future arguments presented by that person will be preemptively rejected, or if not rejected then immediately subject to unnecessarily severe scrutiny. The name arose from an exchange between British novelist and Protestant clergyman Charles Kingsley and the Catholic theologian John Henry Cardinal Newman. Kinglsey argued that Newman's claims could not be trusted because, as a Catholic, his first loyalty is to the Pope and not to the truth. Newman replied that in such a situation, no Catholic could discuss anything with anyone: Kingsley, he said, had 'poisoned the well of discourse'.

There can be some circumstances in which facts about an argument's origins, or its speaker, may be relevant:

- When the speaker is raising an argument about a topic in which he probably does not have relevant skills, or adequate knowledge.
- When the speaker being criticised is biased; that is, when the speaker holds on to some value or belief even after that value or belief has been shown to be wrong.
- When the speaker being criticised is probably in a conflict of interest; for instance, when the speaker is likely going to directly and personally benefit from having his argument accepted.

Those circumstances are sometimes good prima facie grounds for reasonable doubt, but they are not grounds for automatically rejecting an argument. For instance, when a businessman who produces and sells electric cars makes an argument for why the economy should let go of fossil fuels and transition to renewable energy sources, the fact that he stands to profit from the sale of electric cars does not discount his argument about the need for renewable energy. In general, even when a fact about the argument's source is relevant to the analysis of the argument, it is still better to study the argument's own merits and flaws when deciding to accept or reject it. After all, having good grounds for reasonable doubt *is not the same* as finding the logic of an argument unsound. With that in mind, consider whether the following are plain cases of *ad hominem*, or whether there is any merit to them:

> Jones says we should decriminalize marijuana, because that would free the police to concentrate on more serious matters. But you'd expect him to say that: He's a pot smoker himself.

> The safety report about genetically modified food can't be trusted. It was written by scientists who work for the same company that makes the genetically modified seeds.

7.16. False Cause

(Latin: *Post hoc ergo propter hoc*) This fallacy comes about when one argues that because X happened immediately after Y, that Y was the cause of X. Or, when concerning event types: Event type X happened immediately after event type Y; therefore, event type Y caused event type X. In a sense, it is jumping to a conclusion based upon coincidence, rather than on sufficient testing, repeated occurrence, or evidence.

> Examples:
> The sun always rises a few minutes after the rooster crows. So, the rooster crowing causes the sun to rise.

> Once the government passed the new gun laws, gun

"The sun always rises a few minutes after the rooster crows. So, the rooster crowing causes the sun to rise."

violence dropped by 10%; therefore, the new gun laws are working and caused the occurrence of gun violence to drop.

7.17. *Non-Sequitur* Fallacy

(Latin: 'does not follow') A logical fallacy that is most often absurd, where the premises have no logical connection with or relevance to the conclusion.

> Example:
> The police have not been able to crack this cold homicide case, so they've all decided to donate blood to the Red Cross.

> As your lawyer, I need you to answer this question: What do you think of my haircut?

7.18. Fallacy of the Undistributed Middle

(Also known as undistributed middle term) This is a formal fallacy that occurs in a categorical syllogism when the middle term is not distributed into at least one premise. According to the rules of categorical syllogism, the middle term must be distributed at least once for it to be valid.

> Example of the form: All Xs are Ys; All Zs are Ys; therefore, All Xs are Zs.
> Example in words: All ghosts are spooky; all zombies are spooky; therefore, all ghosts are zombies.

7.19. Naturalistic Fallacy

(Latin: *Argumentum ad Naturam*) The naturalistic fallacy occurs when a person bases their argument or position on the notion that what is natural is better or what 'ought to be'. In other words, the foundation for the argument or position is a value judgment; the fallacy is committed when the argument shifts from a statement of fact to one of value. The word 'natural' is loaded with positive connotations—just like the word 'normal'—so there is praise implied when it is used. One commonly sees this fallacy in moral arguments.

> Example: It is only natural to feel angry sometimes; therefore, there is nothing wrong with feeling angry.

7.20. Complex Question Fallacy

(Also known as a loaded question, trick question, or fallacy of presupposition) This fallacy asks a question that has a presupposition built in, which implies something (which is often questionable) but protects the person asking the question from accusations of false claims or even slander.

> Examples:
> Was it from The Pirate Bay or some other site that you illegally downloaded your MP3s?

> I heard a lot of noise in my back yard last night. So, did you climb the fence to get in, or pick the lock on the gate?

> Which church do you and your wife attend?

To pick apart the last example: If addressed to a man, it assumes that he must be married, that his partner is a woman, and that both of them attend church—even though that might not be the case.

7.21. Equivocation

(Also known as doublespeak) This is a fallacy where one uses an ambiguous term or phrase in more than one sense, thus rendering the argument misleading. The ambiguity in this fallacy is lexical and not grammatical, meaning the term or phrase that is ambiguous has two distinct meanings. One can often see equivocation in jokes.

> Examples:
> If you don't pay your exorcist, you can get repossessed.

> A feather is light, and whatever is light cannot be dark; therefore, a feather cannot be dark.

> Hamburgers are better than nothing. And there's noth-

ing better than a good steak. Therefore, hamburgers are better than steak.

All men are mortal. No woman is a man. Therefore, no woman is mortal.

My uncle has a law practice. But that means he's not a good lawyer: After all, he's only practicing.

7.22. Begging the Question

(Latin: *Petitio Principii*) This is also sometimes called circular fallacy: It is the fallacy of attempting to prove something by assuming the very thing you are trying to prove. In its form, the conclusion occurs as one of the premises, or concerning a chain of arguments the final conclusion is a premise in an earlier argument.

> Examples:
> All of the statements in Smith's book *Crab People Walk Among Us* are true. Why, he even says in the preface that his book only contains true statements and first-hand stories.

> It's always immoral to lie to someone because the act of prevarication is contrary to moral principles.

> He's in jail. Innocent people don't go to jail, only guilty people do. So, clearly, he's guilty!

7.23. False Dilemma

(Also known as false dichotomy, black-and-white fallacy) This fallacy arises when only two choices are offered in an argument or proposition, when in fact a greater number of possible choices could exist between the two extremes. False dilemmas typically contain 'either…or' in their structure.

> Either you help us kill the zombies, or you love them.

> Our internet security law is designed to catch sexual predators who use the internet to lure their victims. So, either you support our law, or you are sheltering the paedophiles.

> You are with us, or you are with the terrorists.

> Either you were hallucinating, or those lights you saw in the sky were alien spacecraft!

7.24. Hasty Generalization

(Also known as argument from small numbers, unrepresentative sample) This fallacy occurs in the realm of statistics. It happens when a conclusion or generalization is drawn about a population and it is based on a sample that is too small to properly represent it. The problem with a sample that is too small is that the variability in a population is not captured, so the conclusion is inaccurate.

> Examples:
> My grandfather drank a bottle of whiskey and smoked three cigars a day, and he lived to be 95 years old. Therefore, daily smoking and drinking cannot be that bad for you.

> I don't believe that global warming is happening. After all, the last five years have been cooler than usual.

7.25. Faulty Analogy

This one occurs when someone uses an analogy to prove or disprove an argument or position, but this analogy is too dissimilar to be effective. There are two important things to remember about analogies: No analogy is perfect, and even the most dissimilar objects can share some commonality or similarity. Analogies are neither true nor false, but come in degrees from identical or similar to extremely dissimilar or different.

In some ways the fallacy of faulty analogy is a lot like the argument by shared properties. However, the fallacious version of the argument pretends to be a deduction, whereas the argument by shared properties is an induction, and it can be measured for how strong or weak it is.

> Not believing in the monster under the bed because you have not yet seen it with your own eyes is like not believing the Titanic sank because no one saw it hit the bottom.

Dogs are warm-blooded, nurse their young, and give birth to puppies. Humans are warm blooded and nurse their young. Therefore, humans give birth to puppies.

During your years at college, you had almost no free time. Now you say you want to do a night course with a local artists' club. You'll end up with no free time again.

The anti-poverty activists blockaded one of the bridges over the city when I was driving to work this morning. They were loud and aggressive, and they wasted a lot of people's time: They're just as bad as the Nazis.

7.26. *Tu Quoque*

(Latin: 'you also') This is the fallacy of asking 'But what about you?' It is the rhetorical device that is often used by people who are accused of something; for instance, of harming someone or making mistakes. They might want to deflect attention away from themselves by accusing another person, perhaps the accuser, of committing the same mistakes or harms. But this is only a deflection technique: It is not proof (nor disproof) of anything. In this respect, *tu quoque* is a variation of some other fallacy, such as red herring, or *ad hominem*.

> Speaker 1: This man running for office campaigned against same-sex marriage, but he was caught by the police in an airport bathroom with a male prostitute. I can't vote for him.
> Speaker 2: But what about your candidate's emails? She used a private email server for government business. She's just as bad!

7.27. Slippery Slope

This fallacy involves arguing that taking some particular action will inevitably or necessarily lead to other (usually bad) consequences, without providing enough reasons why the further consequences are inevitable.

> Examples:
> If we legalize gay marriage, pretty soon people will want to marry their sisters and brothers, their children, and even their animals!

If we allow more English schools in Quebec, eventually we will have to allow more English-speaking businesses. Then whole towns will become more and more English, and the French language will practically disappear!

As a general rule (although there are exceptions), people use the slippery slope argument in order to make others afraid of something that in reality they have no good reason to fear.

7.28. The Fallacy Fallacy

Here, the presence of a fallacy in an argument is furnished as proof that the argument is unsound. But this is not, strange as it may be to say it, proof that the *conclusion* of the argument is false. When someone assumes that the conclusion must be false because the argument leading to it is a fallacy, philosophers often call this the fallacy fallacy. An argument that is a fallacy is an unsound argument; but the conclusion of a fallacy might be true for some other reason.

> Examples:
> Eating Tide Pods is bad for you because my mom, my teacher, and my older brother said so. (Appeal to Authority—but eating Tide Pods really is bad for you!)

> 999 people out of 1,000 surveyed say that they'd prefer to travel from New York to Boston by car rather than by ox cart. (Appeal to Popularity—but in fairness, cars are much faster and more comfortable than ox carts.)

If you want to point out that someone has committed a fallacy but you would like to not be an asshat about it, you can say something like this: 'Your conclusion might be true, but your premises don't support it. Perhaps you would like to try a different argument?'

Remember, the point of philosophical discussion is not to win, nor is it to show off how smart we are. The point is to advance everyone's knowledge. Thus, the reason for studying the fallacies is not to humiliate and silence those who commit them. It is to identify everything that doesn't serve the case, and gently blow it away so that we can try again.

142

Chapter Eight: Reasonable Doubt

Reasonable doubt is the most practical and least theoretical branch of logic. It handles the basic question of why, if at all, you should believe something. To answer that question, the principles of reasonable doubt help you to understand and examine how information moves through a society's intellectual environment, how it changes as it moves, how it reaches your mind, and, once it reaches you, how your own biases and presuppositions might affect it, including when you communicate it on to others.

Most people are familiar with the term 'reasonable doubt' from watching courtroom dramas on television or in film. It is an important legal concept used by judges and juries to help them decide whether an accused person is innocent or guilty. But reasonable doubt is something that can also be applied to many more situations. You might be asked to spend money on something. You might be invited to join a club, organization, or association of some kind. You might be asked to endorse a certain religious, political, or moral belief; for instance, by signing a petition, attending a rally, voting, or by sharing images and articles on the internet. You might be asked to do something that you have never done before. In such situations, and others like them, it can be very useful to think of such requests as propositions, and then decide whether they are believable. There are some fairly straightforward ways to do this, and if you find that the argument is weak, or incomplete, or objectionable, or for any reason fishy, it is probably wise to invoke your reasonable doubt.

8.1. What is Reasonable Doubt?

As we saw in the discussion of good thinking habits, reasonable doubt is related to healthy **skepticism**. We defined healthy skepticism as 'a general unwillingness to accept that things are (always) as they appear to be'. Reasonable doubt is like a refinement or a specialization of the habit of healthy skepticism. Let's define it here as the suspension of one's acceptance of some statement or proposition, due to an absence of sufficient support for that statement. Here are some questions you can ask yourself to help you decide whether some reasonable doubt is warranted in a given situation.

- Is there decent and readily available evidence which proves that the proposition is true?
- Can you see that evidence for yourself?
- Can the proposition be put to some kind of test, especially a scientific test which could definitively prove that it is false?
- Does the argument in support of the proposition pass the test of **Ockham's razor**? In other words, is it simple?
- Is the person who asserted the idea someone you have good reason to trust?
- Is it consistent with other propositions that you are already reasonably sure are true?
- Is it consistent with your **worldview**?

The more of these questions you answer with 'no', the more grounds you have for reasonable doubt. You can also ask critical questions about a few alternative propositions. For instance:

- Is there decent evidence that supports some other proposition, and/or which contradicts the one you are considering?
- Are there other, perhaps simpler ways to interpret the evidence that supports the proposition? (**Ockham's razor** again!)
- What additional implications or conclusions can be drawn from the proposition? Are they morally unacceptable, or inconsistent with the speaker's original intentions or worldview, or inconsistent with some other part of the argument, or questionable for some other reason?

Again, if you can answer these questions with a 'yes', you probably have a good basis for reasonable doubt.

A proposition is not automatically disproven just because someone could reasonably doubt it. You might have all the reasons listed above for why you should reject the proposition, and then later discover that it was true after all—but in such a situation, you have not made a logical mistake. The point of having reasonable doubt is that you should not be too quick to believe anything and everything offered to you. Rather, you should accept only those propositions which are supported by the best information and the strongest argument available to you at the time. If that information changes in the future, the good critical thinker also changes his or her beliefs accordingly. In general, reasonable doubt means withholding one's acceptance of the unsupported statement until some acceptable source of support can be found. So, having reasonable doubt is like taking a 'wait and see' attitude because it is open to the idea that the support for the statement may exist. But until that support appears, it assumes that the statement is likely to be false. Depending on your level of curiosity, and perhaps also how much free time you have, you may choose to go looking for that support. But if there are decisions to be made or problems to be solved, and good grounds for reasonable doubt in your mind, you will almost always be better off basing your decision, or the solution

to your problem, on the best quality information that you already possess.

Here are a few examples of such situations where you should engage your reasonable doubt:

- A salesman offers you an amazing deal, but the offer seems too good to be true.
- Your employer asks you to do something that falls outside your usual (or even contractual) range of responsibilities.
- An advertiser makes an improbable or bold claim about the capabilities of a product he's selling.
- A politician makes a bold claim about an opponent's character, history, or true intentions.
- Someone invents an unlikely new technology: Superfast computers, 'miracle' medicines or weight-loss pills, cold-fusion nuclear power, clean fossil fuels, perpetual motion machines, hi-tech invisibility cloak, transparent aluminium, etc.
- A charity or a humanitarian aid organization asks you to donate to a worthy cause, but critics say the organization might be a front for a private, for-profit corporation, or a missionary recruitment effort for a religious group. Or, the critics might allege that most of the money collected by the organization goes to pay the leadership, or to advertise to raise more funds, and that very little goes to its projects.
- A film, video game, music album, or book suddenly becomes popular, and you want to decide whether it really is as good as it seems everyone around you says it is (and therefore, whether you should buy it too).
- A new friend tells you an unusual story about his family background; for instance, that he is the heir to a prestigious noble title, or is secretly very rich, or was personally involved in an important historical event.
- You think you might have had a paranormal experience such as seeing a ghost, UFO, angel, or the like—or someone you know might be describing such an experience.
- A health problem you might be experiencing feels like it might be worse than what your doctor tells you it is.
- Someone shares with you a news article that made him or her angry; someone else says that the same article is 'fake news'.

By the way: Scientists have identified what they believe to be the area of the brain responsible for belief and doubt: It's the ventromedial prefrontal cortex. This area of the brain deteriorates in old age a little faster than other areas, which explains why elderly people tend to fall for scams somewhat more readily than younger people. (If you are not an elderly person yourself, you may want to keep this in mind and help safeguard the interests of your grandparents.) Here are the summary remarks from the researchers who discovered this, as published in the scientific journal *Frontiers in Neuroscience*:

'Belief is first, easy, inexorable with comprehension of any cognition, and substantiated by representations in the post-rolandic cortex. Disbelief is retroactive, difficult, vulnerable to disruption, and mediated by the vmPFC. This asymmetry in the process of belief and doubt suggests that false doctrines in the 'marketplace of ideas' may not be as benign as is often assumed. Indeed, normal individuals are prone to misleading information, propaganda, fraud, and deception, especially in situations where their cognitive resources are depleted. In our theory, the more effortful process of disbelief (to items initially believed) is mediated by the vmPFC; which, in old age, tends to disproportionally lose structural integrity and associated functionality. Thus, we suggest that vulnerability to misleading information, outright deception, and fraud in older persons is the specific result of a deficit in the doubt process which is mediated by the vmPFC.'[1]

And with that observation in mind, let's get underway.

8.2. Doubting Your Own Eyes and Ears

Most of the time, it's perfectly rational to believe that something is true when you've seen or heard it for yourself. Yet there are several factors that can alter your perceptions of things, and if those factors are in play, it can be reasonable to doubt your own senses.

Our expectations, stereotypes, and bad thinking habits affect what we see, and how we remember what we see. In 1947, psychologists Gordon Allport and Joseph Postman conducted an experiment in which they showed people a drawing of two men, one black and one white, confronting each other on a subway car. The white man held a knife in his hand. Later, the people were asked to describe the picture. Around half of them said the knife was in the black man's hand. Psychologists Boon & Davies replicated the experiment in 1987, and the picture they used depicted two white men, but the man with the knife wore a business suit and the other wore workman's clothes. Again, many people recalled later that the knife was in the workman's hands.[2] In these examples, the viewer's stereotypes and prejudices caused them to construct certain memories differently in their minds. Those who recalled the pictures wrongly genuinely believed that the picture was as they described it later. They were not deliberately telling lies. But because of unconscious expectations based in stereotypes operating unconsciously in their minds, they got the picture wrong. This affects all kinds of situations where eyewitness testimony is important: Criminal investigations, for instance. Because people's perceptions can be distorted in this way, police detectives prefer hard physical evidence over eyewitness testimony when investigating crime scenes and bringing evidence to prosecutors. Eyewitnesses are often too unreliable.

Expectation, as a form of **observer bias**, tends to happen when we have a strong enough desire for something to be true. We will interpret our personal experiences in the way that best fits our desires. One of the most common ways in which we do this is when we see human faces in objects where no such shapes exist. Psychologists call this effect **pareidolia**, which we can define as a psychological phenomenon in which vague and ambiguous sensory information is perceived as meaningful. And this happens because the mind is almost always working to organize the sensory information it receives, the better to understand it. The 'face on Mars', the hill in the Cydonia region of the planet Mars that resembled a human face in a 1976 photograph, is a well-known example of this. Other examples of pareidolia include astronomer Percival Lowell's diagrams of 'canals' on the surface

1 Asp, Manzel, Koestner, Cole, Denburg, and Tranel. 'A Neuropsychological Test of Belief and Doubt: Damage to Ventromedial Prefrontal Cortex Increases Credulity for Misleading Advertising' Frontiers in Neuroscience, 2012; 6:100. 9 July 2012. **2** Boon, J. C., & Davis, G. M. (1987). Rumours greatly exaggerated: Allport and Postman's apocryphal study. Canadian Journal of Behavioural Science / Revue canadienne des sciences du comportement, 19(4), 430-440.

of the planet Mars, first published 1895. The case of a piece of toast that had a burn mark resembling the face of Christ is another famous example.[3] The people involved in these examples strongly wanted to believe that what they were seeing is what they thought it was, and their strong desires affected their perceptions.

Sometimes, the mere verbal suggestion that things might be a certain way is enough to make people expect to see them that way. In 2007, close to Halloween, I tried this out myself. On a visit to a cornfield maze with some children I mentioned that the cornfield had been the site of a War of 1812 battle, and that the ghosts of some of the soldiers had been seen there once or twice over the years. Sure enough, half an hour later, one of the children ran out of the maze panting with fright and claiming to have seen one. He hadn't, of course. But the darkness, the creepy music fed through hidden speakers that the farmer had placed in the maze, and my suggestion of what he might have seen, was enough to produce in his consciousness the expectation of a certain experience, which he then imposed on his perceptions. (He may also have been merely intending to please me by confirming my story.) Some reality TV shows exploit the psychological power of suggestion to create the expectation of ghosts, aliens, or whatever other thing the show might be about in the minds of the show's participants.

Environments where the sensory information is vague or ambiguous can also influence our expectations, and they can affect what we think we see and hear. The situation might be too dark, too bright, too hazy, too foggy, or too noisy. Clouds, smoke, garbled voices, multiple sources of loud noise, blurry photos, strange smells, etc. might obstruct your senses. Because of pareidolia, the mind will often impose an organized pattern on the ambiguous sights and sounds. Similarly, you may want to consider doubting your own eyes and ears when your senses are physically impaired. You might be sick, injured, stressed, tired, dizzy, excited, on drugs, hypnotized, distracted, disoriented, or drunk. Certain illnesses, such as diabetic myopia, can also affect one's eyesight. Each of these situations constitutes a kind of impairment and can lead you to perceive things in the world inaccurately. It is often under such

circumstances that people have paranormal or supernatural experiences of seeing ghosts, UFOs, angels, etc. Putting aside the possibility for the moment that such things could be real: If you are seeing a thing like this when visual conditions are bad, or while impaired, it may be warranted to discount your first thoughts about what it is you are seeing.

Another curious source of error in the interpretation of our personal experiences is called the **nocebo effect**. This was discovered during clinical trials for experimental drugs, when patients given the placebo reported experiencing the real drug's side-effects. In one recent experiment, two groups of patients were given a skin cream and one group was told that the side-effects included increased pain sensitivity. The nocebo effect was triggered by the information that the patients received, including the packaging on the box, and the price. The cream with the more colourful box and the higher price triggered the nocebo effect more often. But both creams were placebos that contained no medically active ingredients at all.[4] A 'nocebo', then, is the opposite of a placebo. It is a physical condition similar to an illness, an allergic reaction, or other medical symptom, and the patient is often experiencing real physical pain. But there is in fact no physical or chemical trigger present. The symptom is physical and real, but its true cause is entirely psychosomatic. Although it may sound counterintuitive, the best way to cure someone of a nocebo symptom is not to tell the person their pain isn't real. Rather, it's to tell the person that the condition is not serious and won't last, and that other people who have had the same symptom after exposure to the (non-existent) cause ended up recovering quickly.

8.3. Doubting Your Common Sense

How trustworthy is 'common sense'? Most of the time, it is about as trustworthy as anything you may have learned from your intellectual environment and your worldview. But it is equally as open to criticism as anything else you might believe. For example: Many people believe, on the basis of common sense, that shark attacks are common, that flying in an airplane

3 'Woman 'Blessed by the Holy Toast', BBC News, 17 November 2004.
4 'Why Side-Effects May Seem Worse for High-Priced Drugs' CBC News, 18 October 2017.

is the most dangerous way to travel, that exposure to cold air will make you sick, and that having a shower will help you sober up more quickly after a night of heavy drinking. But all of these common-sense beliefs are actually false. Only around ten people per year are attacked by sharks, out of the many millions of people who, at this moment, are swimming or boating in the world's oceans. People got sick more often during colder months not because of cold air, but because they huddled together in their (warm) houses more often, and thus swapped germs more often. Statistically, in terms of the number of deaths per year, and the number of deaths per vehicle-mile, it is much more dangerous to drive a car than to fly in a commercial aircraft. And when you shower after drinking, your liver processes the same amount of alcohol in your bloodstream as it would have done if you sat in your living room and watched television instead.

One of the reasons that common sense is not always reliable is because it changes all the time, and it can be very different from one community to another. For example, about a century or so in the past, common sense used to lead people to believe that animals don't feel pain, that kings rule their countries by divine right, and that no one would ever walk on the moon. But today, common sense tells us that all three of those beliefs are false. So, the next time that someone tells you that something is common sense, then ask yourself whether that thing is common, or whether it is really sensible. There's a good chance that it's neither.

Another reason you may need to occasionally doubt your common sense is that people often appeal to common sense to disguise the habits of self-interest and face saving. In this way, common sense is not a body of knowledge, but a kind of device for self-deception.

As a general rule: Whether a proposition is true or false has nothing to do with whether it is part of your common sense. It might be true, or it might be false, but that will depend on whether it is supported by good reasons, arguments, and evidence, and not on whether it happens to be common, or seem sensical.

Of course, this is not the only way people use the phrase 'common sense'. Sometimes, people will refer

Many people believe, on the basis of common sense, that shark attacks are common, that flying in an airplane is the most dangerous way to travel, that exposure to cold air will make you sick, and that having a shower will help you sober up more quickly after a night of heavy drinking.

to common sense when they are criticizing another's choices or holding them responsible for their actions. In this way, common sense means having a proper understanding of the likely consequences of choices and actions. And 'having no common sense' means lacking enough foresight to predict the consequences of one's actions. This is a somewhat different use of the term. In that case, when someone tells you to 'use your common sense', try to think of everything that applies to the situation that she is talking about, and what should be done about it. Making careful observations and asking the right questions (skills discussed back in Chapter 2) are helpful here.

8.4. Doubting Your Emotions, Instincts, and Intuitions

Your emotions, gut feelings, and instincts should also be doubted once in a while. That is not the same as suppressing or denying them, of course. One's emotions can sometimes play a very useful role in the process of reasoning. Contemporary culture places a lot of emphasis and importance upon emotional knowledge: The lyrics of pop songs, and the dialogue in well-loved films and television shows, encourage us to 'do what your heart tells you', 'do what feels right', and 'if it makes you happy, it can't be bad'. Pop psychologists, self-help books, and motivational speakers might also encourage you to 'follow your bliss', 'visualize success', and 'believe in yourself'. They might claim that we should always maintain a positive, optimistic attitude, and avoid excessive self-criticism or self-doubt, because they say such 'negative energies' will attract bad fortune, sabotage our endeavours, and turn us into failures. But just like everything else, it is important to examine and evaluate what your heart tells you, just as you examine your common sense, your worldview, and anything that anyone else tells you.

Most emotions are triggered responses to an event, situation, or perception that is either happening 'out there' in the world or in your own mind and body. Sometimes the emotions are responding to things we may be only barely consciously aware of: Subtle details, mnemonic associations, subliminal symbols, and

the like. In this way, your instincts and emotions can be very helpful. They can warn of danger, guide you toward beneficial ends, or (at the very least) inform you that there is more going on in the situation than is obvious at first glance. Many emotions are also triggered by our psychological desires and attachments, for instance, the attachment to one's home, workplace, friends and loved ones, or future goals. We might experience irrational fear, anger, or even depression when one of those attachments is threatened, which can be an indicator of how deeply attached to such things you are. In this way, your instincts and emotions can provide you with useful knowledge, especially self-knowledge.

At other times, however, your emotions can get in the way of clear thinking. Stereotypes, prejudices, obsessive or criminal behaviour, and even self-destructive behaviour are often supported by strong emotions. Someone who is excessively optimistic about his or her success in a business venture, for instance, might not fully understand the risks involved, or the true influence of factors beyond her control. Therefore, she is more likely to make bad decisions. Someone who lives in fear of dangers that don't exist or which are very remote (someone afraid of being involved in a plane crash, or being abducted by aliens, perhaps?), or dangers that are very remote (being bitten by a shark?) is not being benefitted by his emotions.

Furthermore, an emotional state is almost never a good enough reason, *by itself*, to explain or justify someone's actions. You might accept the explanation of a man who said that he ran from the burning house because he was afraid of dying there. But you would probably reject the explanation of a man who said he set fire to someone's house because doing so gave him pleasure. You might believe that man was telling the truth about his reasons, but that is not the same as accepting or supporting those reasons. It can also happen that you are emotionally attached to something that you shouldn't be. Someone who, for instance, is absolutely convinced that he will get the job, or win the bicycle race, or get a very high mark on his essay because he 'just knows' that's what will happen, and he is convinced of this for no other reason than because he 'feels it in his heart' is almost certainly setting himself up for an embarrassing failure. And finally, it is possible to be mistaken about one's own feelings and mistaken about the right way to act upon them. A man who visits the home of a woman he loves two or three times a day, and who peers into her windows, and leaves notes under her door, and follows everything she does on her computer social networks is not really loving her: Rather, it would be more accurate to say he is stalking her.

In cases where your emotions and instincts seem to be pulling you one way or another, or making you feel something and you are not at first sure why, observe and question them just as you would any other aspect of your situation.

- Do you know exactly what you are feeling? Can you put a name on it?
- Can you identify what event, situation, attachment, or perception is stimulating the feeling?
- Is the feeling interfering with your ability to do something?
- Is the feeling interfering with your objectivity? (Don't be too quick to say 'no'.)
- Is a physical state in your own body contributing to the feeling? For instance, are you sleep deprived, or hungry, or ill, or have you had too much coffee lately?
- What are other people in the situation feeling?
- Are you feeling nothing at all? (This can be as much an indicator of your feelings as an overwhelming emotion.)
- Has the feeling been invoked by something that someone has said? And if so, can the statement be examined on its own merits, like any other argument?

Diagnostic questions like these can be hard to ask. Caught up in the moment, it might not occur to you to slow down, calm yourself, and observe and question your own feelings. But if you can cultivate the habit of casting reasonable doubt upon your own instincts and intuitions when it seems there is a risk that they may lead you astray, you are more likely to make better, more intelligent decisions.

8.5. Confirmation Bias

Suppose that there is decent evidence available that supports whatever it is you are asked to believe. Even then, there are several ways in which people 'skew' or 'twist' their handling or their interpretation of that evidence, to allow them to continue believing whatever they may want to believe, whether it is rational to believe it or not. The name for this kind of faulty reasoning is **confirmation bias**. The term was coined in Peter Watson, an English psychologist, in 1960. It refers to the way people tend to favour evidence that supports beliefs they already have, as well as to ignore evidence that does not support those beliefs. But when we downplay or ignore evidence that goes against our beliefs, we can end up making bad decisions. For instance, we might judge the riskiness of some action poorly. We might not fully understand new information which becomes available. People put money into bad investments, vote for corrupt politicians, reinforce stereotypes, ignore health problems in their own bodies, and sometimes even reinforce feelings of depression and fear, because of the way they suppress evidence that goes against what they believe about themselves, other people, or their situation.

Three of the most common ways that people commit confirmation bias is by resisting contrary evidence, looking for confirming evidence, and preferring available evidence.

Resisting contrary evidence means avoiding, ignoring, re-interpreting, or downplaying evidence that goes against what you believe. Political activists, scientists, investors, religious believers, and people from all kinds of professions will do this when they feel their most cherished ideas are threatened. But if you want to test some statement to find out if it's true, you need to look at more than just the evidence that confirms it. You also need to look for the evidence which refutes it as well, and in both cases, you should assess how relevant or strong the evidence is.

Another part of confirmation bias is the habit of preferring confirming evidence. This means favouring evidence that supports or agrees with whatever you already believe. When we are particularly committed

"The CN Tower in Toronto has a secret deck, just above the topmost viewing platform, which has special quantum-radio broadcast machines that control people's minds." *

or attached to a certain idea, we often trick ourselves into seeking out and using only the confirming evidence. This can lead us to miss out on other kinds of evidence that are equally relevant. As a result, we can end up accepting a proposition that isn't true, or failing to properly understand a given problem. And we can harm our own interests in all the same ways that resisting contrary evidence can do. To cite a real-world example: In the years leading up to the banking collapse of September 2008, there were many people in the banking and investment industries who knew that a crisis was coming. Profits from debt refinancing, sales of derivatives, sub-prime mortgages, and the like could not rise forever, they said. But those people were told to keep their objections quiet because the system, at the time, was still profitable. Some of these critics were threatened with being fired if they persisted with their warnings. But their warnings came true, with catastrophic results for the world economy.

Here's the example that philosophy professors almost always use: The proposition 'all swans are white'. If you wanted to find out whether this proposition is true, you could look for white swans. However, even if you saw nothing but white swans, you would not be able to deductively claim that the proposition is true. At the most, you could claim 'all the swans I've seen so far are white'. Therefore, you should also look for black swans. The more white swans you see, the stronger your claim becomes. But one sighting of one black swan is all that it you need to deductively prove that the proposition is false. (That example, by the way, also illustrates the difference between **deductive** and **inductive** reasoning (see Chapter 5). Also of note: I suppose someone could say, 'Well a black swan is not a true swan!' But that would be a case of the 'No True Scotsman' fallacy.)

Although it is not, strictly speaking, a part of confirmation bias, there is a third way that people inadvertently bias their handling of evidence: Preferring available evidence. This means preferring the evidence that is easy to find. The evidence might be memorable, or very impressive, or simply psychologically persuasive. It might be the evidence that happens to come up on your social media stream, as your friends share the website links or the memes that amuse or interest them. It might be the evidence that happens to appear in the first three or four items on a search engine result list. But the easy evidence is not necessarily *all* the evidence!

One more topic to consider in relation to observer bias is the **Dunning-Kruger effect**. Named two psychologists from Cornell University, David Dunning and Justin Kruger, this is the kind of observer bias in which people believe that they are more highly skilled than they really are. As a result, people may end up taking on tasks that they are not prepared for, or they might incorrectly judge the competence of others.

8.6. Lack of Evidence

Probably the most important occasion when you should exercise reasonable doubt is when you are told something is true, but there's no evidence you can see that supports it. Or, there might be evidence which favours the statement, but that evidence is very slim and unreliable. Or perhaps the evidence can be interpreted differently, to support much simpler conclusions. Here are some examples:

> Whenever American presidents visit Canada, their hidden purpose is to invite Canada to join the USA as its 51st state.

> The CN Tower in Toronto has a secret deck, just above the topmost viewing platform, which has special quantum-radio broadcast machines that control people's minds.

It is also reasonable to doubt a proposition when it's impossible for you to find out the evidence for yourself. The claim might be one which no one could verify. Or, the best means to test the claim might require expensive equipment or scientific training that you don't possess. Or, there might be someone stopping you from verifying the claim for yourself. For example:

> I have invented a machine that uses cold fusion to produce cheap and abundant electrical power. It will fit under your kitchen counter—soon every household in the world will have one! But for proprietary reasons I will not allow outside investigators to open the box and see how it works.

In cases like these, a lot depends on how much you are willing to trust the speaker. In this example the speaker might not want to open the box because he is afraid that someone might steal his patent. A professional third-party investigator, such as an engineer or scientist, could be bound by a legal contract to not infringe his copyright. If you happen to know that the person is a competent entrepreneur with a graduate degree in nuclear physics, you might be willing to trust him, at least for a little while. But if you happen to know that he has a degree in theatre, not physics, then you should probably keep walking.

The overall point is that you should not always automatically believe what people tell you. Rather, you should proportion your willingness to believe according to a few guidelines, such as:

THE TRUSTWORTHINESS OF THE SPEAKER. Is she an expert in the relevant field? Is she someone you personally know? Is she someone who has proven to be trustworthy before? Is she acting from genuine care for you, some kind of self-interest, or some mix of both? Etc.
THE TRUSTWORTHINESS OF THE CLAIM. How consistent is the claim with what you already know to be possible or likely? Or, how contrary?
THE AMOUNT OF WORK YOU'RE BEING ASKED TO DO. Are you being asked to spend a little bit of money? A lot of money? Vote a certain way? Eat or drink something that will affect your health? Give some personal information away (your phone number, street address, etc.)? Make some public declaration of belief? Do something that will take five minutes? An hour? A year?
THE AMOUNT OF TRANSPARENCY YOU'RE GIVEN. If someone asks you to believe something without showing you what's behind the curtain, you are almost always better off doubting it.

As a final note about evidence: Claims that assert something amazing, unlikely, or wild, or even just especially unusual, are often called **extraordinary claims**. We can create a maxim of reason to help us remember not to fall for manipulations and trickery: 'Extraordinary claims require extraordinary evidence'[5]. And if that extraordinary evidence is lacking, it's best to assume the claim is false.

8.7. Contradictory Claims

Probably the most obvious occasion when you should invoke your reasonable doubt is when you are given two or more propositions and they cannot both be true at the same time.

Suppose, for example, you log into your favourite social network, and you get a 'friend' invitation from someone famous. Suppose it's Jodie Whittaker, the actor who currently stars in the BBC sci-fi television series *Doctor Who*. The proposition you are asked to believe, in this situation, is that the person asking to be added to your list really is the actor she says she is. But you probably have another proposition in your mind which states that famous actors do not send requests like that to people they do not know. These two propositions cannot both be true at the same time: They contradict each other. So, what you have to do is decide which of these you have greater reason to believe, and which you have greater reason to doubt. In this example, you have much greater reason to believe the second proposition, which is much more consistent with other things that are well known about celebrities. And you also have some excellent alternative ways to explain who might really be trying to 'add' you: A friend of yours who wants to play a practical joke on you, for instance. Or it might be a salesman, or a con artist, a stalker whose real profile you have blocked, or someone else who is trying to gain access to information about you.

When evaluating two or more contradictory claims, it could be the case that one of them is true; however, on the other hand, it may also be the case that they are all false. But when the claims contradict one another, it cannot be the case that they are all true

at the same time. Here are a few more examples:

> The stars in the night sky are actually pinpoints of light shining through little chinks in a cinder-block wall which surrounds our solar system.

You probably should not accept this claim because it conflicts with just about everything scientists around the world have discovered about the stars.

> There are sharks and piranhas living in the Ottawa river.

This claim conflicts with a few basic facts about sharks and piranhas, and about geography, all of which are easy to find out.

Sometimes you might be given two statements that don't contradict any practical knowledge you have about the world, and that don't contradict your world-view, but they do contradict each other. For example, consider these two statements:

> Next summer, Heritage College will receive a multi-million-dollar extension. When the work is done, our building will be twice as big!

> Next summer, the Heritage College building will be demolished and replaced with another, brand new, much bigger building.

Either one of these statements might be true, and they are both fairly consistent with other things that you might know about the building, such as that it is slightly overcrowded, etc. But they clearly cannot both be true at the same time. So, in this situation, you should doubt *both* of them, and then ask a few teachers or administrators what they might know about the situation.

Contradictory claims are also one of the ways you can spot a scam or a confidence trick. We'll see more about such things later on.

8.8. Conspiracy Theories

A common kind of extraordinary claim is the

---

5 Popularised by the American scientist and television presenter Carl Sagan, in his 1980 television series <u>Cosmos</u>. The earliest version of this maxim is likely this one from French scientist-philosopher Pierre Simon Laplace (1749-1827): "The weight of evidence for an extraordinary claim must be proportioned to its strangeness."

conspiracy theory. For example, many people believe that the manned moon landings made between 1969 and 1972 were filmed in a studio; the governments of the United States and other powerful countries are controlled by a secret society called the Illuminati; and the terrorist attacks of 9/11 were an 'inside job'. They also may believe that some of the vaccines given to babies, such as the MMR vaccine, cause recipients to develop learning disabilities, and can even stunt their brain growth. Some people believe that the vapor trails in the sky left behind by jet aircraft contain mind-altering chemicals that governments use to pacify the populations in cities and keep them obedient to the laws. **Extraordinary claims** like these are often called **conspiracy theories.**

This is how the American writer Mark Twain defined a conspiracy: 'A secret agreement of a number of men for the pursuance of policies which they dare not admit in public.' For our purposes, let's define a conspiracy theory as one that attempts to explain some event or situation in the world by saying it is the work of a secret group of people, or a group of people who work in secret, and who have nefarious aims. Part of why conspiracy theories seem compelling is because they often provide (usually false) answers to some of those philosophical questions which form part of our worldviews. They offer a reassurance that the world is intelligible, even if it's not especially just or fair; they suppose that events which appear to be random are under someone's control, even if that someone is a villain. And by researching or promoting a conspiracy theory, believers can gain a sense of purpose and agency in the world.

Sometimes there is at least *some* evidence available that seems to support the theory. For instance, those who believe the moon landings didn't happen often point to the photos from the lunar surface, in which there are no stars in the sky. Those who believe in secret government-type conspiracies point to the 'occult' symbol of a pyramid with an eye on the top on the back of the American $1 bill. And those who believe in various 9/11 conspiracies note that the World Trade Center towers fell in a way that strongly resembles a controlled demolition.

But in most conspiracy theories, there are usually other, and far simpler, ways to explain the evidence. To continue the examples given above: There are no stars in the moon landing videos because their feeble light is drowned out by the glare of the moon's surface, dispersing the light of the sun. This is the same reason we do not see the stars on earth during the day: The glare of the sun, dispersed in the atmosphere, drowns them out. The 'Illuminati Pyramid' on the back of the American $1 bill was placed there as a symbol that the American union is both glorious, and unfinished. It also has to do with the deistic and humanist ideas espoused by the authors of the U.S. Constitution. And the World Trade Center towers fell in an apparently controlled way because they were designed to do so in the event of a fire, just like all modern skyscrapers. Remember your Ockham's razor! If other explanations are simpler, and require fewer presuppositions, you should prefer those other explanations, until or unless extraordinary evidence appears.

Scholars who study conspiracy theories have found that they tend to have these four assumptions in common:

- They concern groups, large or small, rather than individuals;
- The group has illegal or sinister aims.
- The group's activities are highly organized, not accidental.
- The planning for their activities is carried out in secret, not in public.[6]

These four assumptions don't appear equally in all conspiracy theories. A given conspiracy theory will emphasise one or two of those assumptions above the others, but most of them will have all the elements present to some degree. They can also come with some variations. For instance, some conspiracy theories do concern individuals. But those individuals are often members of, or even the leaders of, some kind of group: The CEOs of large corporations, the heads of powerful governments or churches, etc.

To the list given above, I would like to add the following features, not all of which are universal, and

---

6 Young & Nathanson, Sanctifying Misandry (McGill / Queens University Press, 2010).

not all of which are assumptions of the theory. But the more complex the theory, the more likely these features will appear:

- They attempt to create fear in order to generate support for some value program, or for some commercial venture (they're selling books, health supplement pills, weapons, etc).
- They divert attention away from real social problems and real injustices.
- The community of the theory's believers often have derogatory names for non-believers, which strip the non-believers of their rationality or even their humanity: 'Sheep', 'dupes', 'the herd', 'the ignorant masses', or (my personal favourite groaner) 'sheeple'.

If the explanation for some event involves these assumptions, and especially if these assumptions are closed to critical questioning (like a value program), you've probably found a conspiracy theory. Here, you should definitely invoke your reasonable doubt!

Some of you might have heard the phrase 'Just because you're paranoid doesn't mean they are not out to get you!' In the same way, just because some extraordinary claim bears these signs of a conspiracy theory doesn't mean the claim is false. But it *does* mean you are almost certainly better off assuming the claim is false. In the spirit of open-mindedness, it's fine to remain open to the idea that someday you may indeed see some extraordinary evidence in support of the extraordinary claim—but until that day arrives, it's best to let the claim go.

8.9. Doubting Experts and Professionals

Given that we don't always have the time or the opportunity to figure out things for ourselves, we have to rely on experts at least some of the time. This is natural and normal, and not a problem. But we must still decide when it is rational to trust an expert, and when it is rational not to. And in some specialized fields, if you are not a professional in that field, you are probably not in a very good position to judge whether

the expert has done a good job. It is also sometimes the case that professionals and experts are in a position to harm as well as help their clients. So, how do you know who is an expert, and who is not? And how do we decide whether a given expert can be trusted?

One of the most frequently quoted definitions of a 'profession' was written in 1914 by United States Supreme Court judge Louis Brandeis. He said a profession is:

> …an occupation for which the necessary preliminary training is intellectual in character, involving knowledge and to some extent learning, as distinguished from mere skill; which is pursued largely for others, and not merely for one's own self; and in which the financial return is not the accepted measure of success.[7]

We might criticize this definition by saying that its emphasis on service to others renders it too narrow. There are certainly experts who practice their profession in order to benefit themselves. Yet the point that Brandeis was trying to reach was that such service to the public is an essential part of what makes a professional person trustworthy.

Let's define an expert here as someone who is much more knowledgeable in a particular subject area or field than most other people are, due to some combination of experience and specialized training. Experts tend to have:

- Extensive formal education and training from college or university, or some other reputable institution relevant to their field.
- A lot of experience: Several years at least; and the more, the better.
- A decent reputation among other experts in the same field, and among clients.
- A history of professional accomplishments.

Yet even when it is appropriate to call someone an expert, there are still circumstances in which it may be prudent to doubt what that person says. Here are some examples:

---

7 Louis Brandeis, Business—A Profession (Boston, USA: Hale, Cushman, & Flint, 1933), p. 2.

<u>Profession</u>: an occupation for which the necessary preliminary training is intellectual in character, involving knowledge and to some extent learning, as distinguished from mere skill; which is pursued largely for others, and not merely for one's own self; and in which the financial return is not the accepted measure of success.

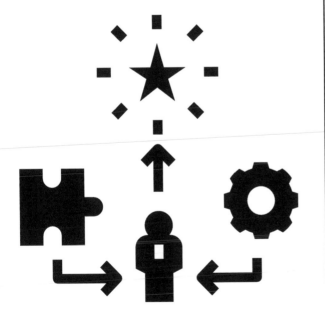

- The person is speaking about a topic outside of his or her actual training and experience, and yet claims to be an expert in that field.
- The person admits he's not an expert in some field, but he relies on his reputation or fame in a second (perhaps unrelated) field to establish trustworthiness in the first field.
- There are sufficient reasons to believe that the expert is inappropriately influenced or biased (for instance, by the corporation that funds his or her research), or that he is involved in a conflict of interest.
- When various experts disagree with one another about the matter under consideration.

Regarding the third point: Many academic science journals now encourage their contributors to put a 'conflict of interest statement' in their published articles, to help allay concerns about whether corporate or government power influenced their research. Such statements usually look like this: 'The authors declare that the research was conducted in the absence of any commercial or financial relationships that could be construed as a potential conflict of interest.'

The fourth point deserves a closer look, too. Experts disagree among themselves all the time, and this one way that they keep their skills sharp and their judgments sound. But most of the time, most experts in a given field will have a general consensus about the most important principles of their field. It would be weird, for instance, if there was a lot of disagreement among aeronautical engineers concerning whether propeller-driven aircraft need to have wings, or if archaeologists disagreed over whether aliens had built the Pyramids of Egypt. (The truth is out there.) But when the experts have a lot of disagreement among themselves, non-experts should stand back and exercise some reasonable doubt. When the experts who agree with some claim are the great majority, and those who disagree with that claim are a very small minority, then we have less reason to doubt it. For example, the overwhelming majority of qualified scientists in relevant fields believe that climate change and global warming are real, and they are caused by human activities. In late 2012, Dr James Powell, executive director of the National Physical Science Consortium, surveyed 13,950 articles published in peer-reviewed, professional scientific journals. He found that only 24 of them claimed that the theory of global warming was false.[8] Clearly, then, there is no controversy among climate scientists about the causes of global warming. When Jim Bridenstine, a climate change denier, was appointed head of NASA, for example, he was able to see the data for himself, and he changed his mind after only one month.[9]

Here are a few further points to consider. It is possible to doubt what an expert says without at the same time doubting that they are an expert. It's also not rational to believe something just because an expert said it's true, and for no other reason (which would be to commit the fallacy of appeal to authority). Finally, there are some questions which, while we can seek advice opinions from experts on them, we are still going to have to resolve for ourselves. Moral, social, religious, and political questions are among the kinds of questions each person should decide, by means of reason, on his or her own.

8.10. Scams, Frauds, and Confidence Tricks

One of my associates once saw a job listing on Craigslist, a popular internet forum, in which a purported employer was looking for a mystery shopper (a person who poses as a normal customer at some business, and then reports about his or her experience back to the employer). She was sent a cheque for $3,000 and then asked to wire-transfer the money to an address in a foreign country, and then report about her experience with the money transfer service. But when she brought the cheque to the bank, she was told that the cheque had the wrong signature and could not be cashed. Had she deposited the cheque using an ATM or a cheque-cashing service, she would have transferred the money to the destination, and then the bank would have eventually discovered that the cheque was bogus and cancelled it. The result would have been that my friend would have been cheated out of $3,000 of her own money.

All scams and confidence tricks depend on two main factors for success: The victim's self-interest (especially his or her desire for money, sex, social prestige, a job, or even love and attention), and the victim's gullibility. They are successful when victims want something desperately enough, and don't ask too many questions. Scammers and con artists tend to be creative, persuasive, and original; they also constantly change or improve their strategies, so that their scams become harder to detect and thus more successful. Some con artists will research their victim's history and find out things like what the person wants, what their weaknesses are, what events in their past have caused them shame or anger, and so on. These facts are then used to manipulate the victim when they eventually interact. However, all cons depend on a fairly small number of basic strategies. I will describe a few of them so you are forewarned, and will not become a victim:

DECEPTION: Effective con artists use lies and half-truths to make themselves, or their situation, appear to be something other than what it really is. Almost all confidence tricks rely on some amount of deception. For instance, the scammer might dress in a costume or disguise in order to appear very rich or very poor. They might pretend to be a professional in a field they actually know nothing about, or they might set up a web site to pretend they have a legitimate business.

DISTRACTION: Some con artists keep your attention focused on something unrelated, while they or an accomplice steal from you when you're not looking. Think of the person who steals your purse or your wallet while pretending to accidentally trip and knock you down and then help you to your feet again.

FLATTERY: Con men often open their game by being friendly and amiable, and quickly become admiring and deeply respecting. Some con men might pretend to fall in love with their intended victim. Since most people enjoy being praised and admired, this strategy helps make the victim more receptive and agreeable to the con man's claims and requests that come later.

8 Powell, James. 'The State of Climate Science: A Thorough Review of the Scientific Literature on Global Warming'. Science Progress, 15 November 2012. 9 Eric Niiler, 'Nasa's Jim Bridenstine agrees humans are responsible for climate change' Wired, 17th May 2018.

TIME PRESSURE: People who have been led to believe that an important decision must be made in a very short amount of time tend to make bad decisions.

VULNERABILITY: The con artist might present herself as someone in pain or in a position of weakness; for instance, as someone suffering a serious disease, or someone persecuted unjustly by the law. This technique manipulates the sense of empathy that most people have for the suffering of others.

OBEDIENCE: Most people still defer, at least somewhat, to lawyers, judges, police officers, professors, priests, rich people, and just about anyone who looks like they possess some kind of social authority or power. This is true even in societies that claim to be democratic and equal. Therefore, con men sometimes present themselves as persons with authority, in order exploit people's willingness to defer and to obey.

CONFORMITY: Taking advantage of the fact that most people will do what they see many other people doing, the con artist and accomplices will do something in order to make it easier for their victim to do it too. Think of people who start crossing a road before the lights have changed because two or three others have already started crossing ahead of them.

Although all cons involve these basic psychological strategies, some specific applications of those strategies have been so successful and so widely used that they have been given names. Here are a few of them:

'BIG STORE' is named after the Marx Brothers movie, and it involves renting out a large building, such as a storefront or a warehouse, and filling it with furniture and people to make it appear like a well-established business. Potential customers, not knowing that they're buying stolen goods in a black market, think that they're buying legitimate goods in a law-abiding business.

'PHISHING' is when the con artist sends an email that looks like it comes from a legitimate business, bank, or government agency. The message asks the victim to 'verify' or 'confirm' personal details that may have been lost or subjected to a computer virus attack. The sensitive information they are attempting to collect may include email and other passwords and bank account numbers.

The 'SHELL GAME' and 'THREE CARD MONTY' are two similar sleight-of-hand tricks in which a pebble or other small object is placed under one of three cups or shells or similar objects. The position of the cups is then mixed up by sliding them back and forth across the table quickly, and then the victim is asked to bet some money on which cup has the pebble. What the victim does not normally see is that the pebble has been moved separately, and is hiding elsewhere, such as in the con artist's palm.

'BAIT AND SWITCH' is a con in which a victim is offered a chance to buy something, or must do something, to get something else in return. They might be shown the product or the reward that they have been offered—but once the money changes hands or the service is performed, the product or reward turns out to be something very different than what was promised. It's called 'bait and switch' because the product you wanted to buy (the bait) is switched with something else when you aren't looking, or when it passes through a place where you can't see it.

'HONEY TRAP' is an aggressive kind of scam in which a sexually attractive person lures the victim to a private location with an expressed or implied promise of sexual intimacy. Once the victim has been lured to the private place, he or she might be robbed, blackmailed, held captive, photographed in a compromising position, kidnapped, harmed in other ways, or even killed.

'RUSSIAN BRIDE' is a less aggressive version of Honey Trap. In this type of scam, the con artist creates fake personal ads with dating websites or matchmaking services, poses as a single person in a distant country, and starts a long-distance relationship with the victim. Eventually, the con artist will ask for money to emigrate to the victim's country, and possibly to move household furniture and children too. But once the money is sent, the con artist disappears.

'PONZI SCHEMES' are a species of financial investment fraud. A con artist posing as a businessperson will offer prospective victims a chance to invest in some low- or medium-risk enterprise, with the promise of an excellent return on their investment. But in reality, there is no enterprise. The con artist uses money from his second investor to pay his first investor. Then he uses money from his third investor to pay the second one, and so on. (In a variation of this scam called the 'PYRAMID SCHEME', the con artist freely admits that there is no enterprise to invest in and promises to pay earlier investors with new money from subsequent investors.) This procedure can be very difficult for victims to spot, since at least some investors think they are getting their money's worth. A successful pyramid scheme operator can eventually become exceedingly rich if he's canny. But the system depends on a constant flow of money from new victims to keep working. If the flow of new investment should slow down or stop, the scheme collapses.

'PSYCHIC SCAMS' involve a con artist who claims to possess magical powers. For instance, he might say he can communicate with the dead, or with angels or other supernatural beings, or with aliens, or even with God. For a price he will convey to the victim messages from a recently deceased person (or animal!) He might also claim to be able to detect and remove curses, or he might offer to cast magical spells that will bring the victim money, good heath, love, a better job, or some other kind of worldly benefit. Leaving aside the question of whether ghosts or magic or gods actually exist, the fraudulent medium exploits the victim's belief in the paranormal to part him from his money.

'ADVANCE FEE FRAUD' is a type of scam where the victim is asked to do something and is promised a large sum of money as the reward, but they must pay the con artist a small sum in advance as part of the deal. A common version of this is called the

'NIGERIAN MONEY SCAM' or '419 SCAM', named for the section of Nigerian criminal law that covers fraud. In this type of scam, the con artist sends an email message to multitudes of people in which he poses as someone from a foreign country and asks for help opening a bank account in your country. He'll say this is needed to transfer a very large sum of money as part of an inheritance, a tax-avoidance plan, or some similar deal. You are also offered a share of that large sum of money. But once you open the account, you will be asked to make deposits there to keep the account 'active' or 'viable' or something like that—and your share of the big sum never arrives. Another variation, which dates back to the 19th century, is called the 'SPANISH PRISONER'. In this one, a person asks for help transferring money to an individual who will help break a rich friend out of a jail (in Spain). The con artist asks for some money in advance in order to bribe the guards, and then promises a share of the money that the rich prisoner will surely pay as a reward when he is free. A more recent variation is the 'CASTING AGENT' scam, in which the scam artist poses as a talent scout for a film studio or modelling agency. The con artist asks for large up-front fees for professional photo shoots and promises the victim that well-paying jobs will soon follow. The photos for the victim's portfolio might arrive, or they might not—but the jobs never do.

'AFFINITY SCAMS' are scams in which the con artist poses as a member of a tightly integrated small community of some kind, such as a church, or an ethnic enclave in a large city (Chinatown, Little Italy, etc.). The con artist pretends to be a member of the group, and ingratiates himself to the leaders and prominent members of the group in order to improve his credibility among other members. That much is perhaps better described as a fraud, than a scam. And in general, an affinity scam is a step in a larger strategy. Once the con artist's credibility is established, he can target people for other types of scams more easily.

8.11. Information and Media Literacy

Most of the topics we've covered so far here in Reasonable Doubt relate to information that reaches you from local or nearly local sources: Your friends, your own experience of the world, people you might meet in your community. The concept of '**information literacy**' presented here is the technique of reasonable doubt applied to information that comes from mass-communication technologies and industries.

Mass media overwhelmingly dominates the intellectual environments of most modern countries: Television, radio, film, computer games, newspapers, magazines, the internet. Perhaps only the very poorest parts of the world, or the few communities not yet organized by states or the global capitalist market, are free from its influence. The information presented in these media passes through numerous 'filters' on its way from the place where it was created to the place where it reaches your mind. Some of these filters are part of the machinery of transmission, such as cameras, microphones, radio transmitters and receivers, computer networks, printing presses. Other filters are in the people who process the information: Journalists, informants, editors, technicians, lawyers, advertisers, writers, publishers, and owners. Each individual along this path has a chance to influence the context of information according to their worldview.

Through the effects of all those filters, media does more than simply transmit information; indeed, there is no such thing as a 'plain fact' in the media. Through those filters, media also transmits criteria for what counts as a 'fact' in the first place—along with values, worldviews, social and psychological pressures, framing languages, precedents for behaviour, models of an overall way of living, and so on. So, in addition to transmitting facts, media also transmits prescriptions for how to think about those facts, and how to feel about them.

Earlier in this text, I said that **framing languages** probably cannot be avoided; here, I can add that the framing techniques of media are also probably unavoidable. That is not necessarily always a drawback. Nevertheless, the media's influence over your intellectual environment is also an influence over your worldview, and thus an influence over your consciousness and identity. Media literacy is therefore a requirement for all persons who would prefer to decide for themselves who they will allow to influence them, and to what degree. Media literacy involves being selective about which media you will follow and believe, yet also being wide-ranging enough to see what media is influencing others. We will cover more tips like this later in the chapter. But first:

8.12. The Business Model of Media

The first thing that needs to be acknowledged when analysing information in the mass media is that mass media are businesses and are operated for the purpose of making money for owners and investors. In a capitalist economy, almost no one seriously doubts this; even the best journalists and entertainers, however much they may also care about knowledge and truth and art, still have to gain and keep their paying customers. The business model of media needs a separate discussion here, for two reasons. One is that it's not the same as the propaganda model of political communication (however much there may be some appearance of overlap). The second is that the business model of media makes no judgment about the *content* the media. So, you could read a serious newspaper whose journalists care about justice and truth, and then read a tabloid magazine whose purpose is to entertain and distract you, or to infuriate you. In both cases the business model is the same.

Since this is the case, we need to ask: What are media organizations in the business of selling in order to earn their profits? Most people believe media companies are in the business of selling information, but this is only partially true. In general, very little of a media organization's budget, typically less than 20%, comes from reader or viewer subscriptions. Public broadcasting is a notable exception: Viewer subscriptions form a much larger part of a public broadcasting organization's income than in privately-owned commercial broadcasting. But the majority of public broadcasting revenue comes from government, and another large portion comes from sponsorships (which is really advertising by another name).

A second answer to the question 'What does media sell?' is that media sells advertising space. But that's also not quite correct. Space and time in which to display advertising are indeed the units of measure for the media product, but they are not the product itself. Advertisers are the buyers of the media product, and the actual media product that they are buying is the audience. A media organization, be it a newspaper, a website, or a television station, is in the business of selling audiences to other businesses.

The content of media, whether it is a news report, a comedy show, or even a pornographic film, is that which attracts someone to join an audience. Content is thus comparable to the 'bait' on a fishing hook. Regardless of the social importance or the artistic merit of that content (or the lack thereof), its purpose in the business model of media is to lure an audience toward the advertising message (the 'hook'), and then to keep them attending to that message.

Media organizations are therefore very careful to ensure that the content they provide remains interesting to their audiences. The content will therefore tell you that you're beautiful, that your values are good and right and just, that the problems of the world are someone else's fault, and that you don't need to change yourself or any part of your life (or, not very much, and with very little effort). Even the kind of news which mostly provokes 'outrage'—the kind that makes the audience angry, or which tends to make people fearful or hateful of some social group (think of conservative media provoking anger against Muslims, or liberal media provoking anger against conservatives, etc.) —still confirms the audience's values and thus keeps them attending. Note that the advertising in the media might communicate a different message than the content of media. Advertising in women's publications, for example, regularly create anxiety in the audience for being insufficiently beautiful, sexual, popular, or the like. We will see more later about how advertising deliberately seeds anxiety in people's minds in order to move them to buy a product that promises relief from that anxiety. Here let it be noted that media

Former Google employee Tristan Harris said that such features exploit a design flaw in the human mind: 'All of us are jacked into this system... Our minds can be hijacked. Our choices are not as free as we think they are.'

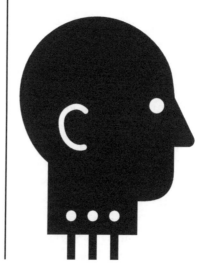

10 Ward, Duke, et.al., 'Bran Drain: The Mere Presence of One's Own Smartphone Reduces Cognitive Capacity' Journal of the Association for Consumer Research (University of Chicago Press Journals), Vol.2, No.2, April 2017. 11 Quoted in Olivia Solon, 'Ex-Facebook President Sean Parker: Site Made to Exploit Human 'Vulnerability'' The Guardian, 9 November 2017.

has to strike a careful balance between affirming the audience's beliefs and values with the content, and disturbing the audience's sense of life-satisfaction with the advertising. Too much affirmation, and the audience won't buy the advertised products; too much disturbance, and the audience will leave.

Internet social media makes for an interesting pure-type example of this. If you are like most people, the thing you most want to see in the media is your own life. So, that is exactly what companies like Facebook and Twitter put on public display for you: Your photos, your feelings and opinions, your friends and relations, your hobbies and pastimes, on display for dozens, hundreds, or thousands of people. When the content provided by a media company is generated by the audience members themselves, the cost of providing that content is very low. By the way, this also partially explains the rise of game shows and reality television: These types of programs don't require as many writers and designers, so they can be produced cheaply. Internet social media is like another kind of reality show, in which you are both the audience and the star.

Social media also has psychotropic addictive functions that help keep your attention fixed to the screen. These functions, originally created to 'send little bits of positivity' to users (that's how Justin Rosenstein, the Facebook engineer who invented the 'Like' button, described it) serve to keep one's attention by providing a steady stream of small rewards and incentives. The result of this stream of small rewards is to keep people constantly distracted. One study found that the mere presence of a smartphone, whether it is being used or not, is enough to distract you and thus reduce your cognitive capacity.[10] Former Google employee Tristan Harris said that such features exploit a design flaw in the human mind: 'All of us are jacked into this system…Our minds can be hijacked. Our choices are not as free as we think they are.'[11] Loren Brichter, the designer who invented the pull-to-refresh feature used in many social media apps, said that he did not originally intend the function to be addictive, but he acknowledges that it became so: 'Pull-to-refresh is addictive. Twitter is addictive. These are not good

things.'[12] Nir Eyal, a technology industry consultant, wrote that most social media apps are now deliberately designed to be addictive:

> The technologies we use have turned into compulsions, if not full-fledged addictions. It's the impulse to check a message notification. It's the pull to visit YouTube, Facebook, or Twitter for just a few minutes, only to find yourself still tapping and scrolling an hour later… The products and services we use habitually alter our everyday behaviour, just as their designers intended. Our actions have been engineered.[13]

These services engineer behaviour by providing small respites for the tiny and barely-perceived stressors of everyday life:

> Feelings of boredom, loneliness, frustration, confusion and indecisiveness often instigate a slight pain or irritation and prompt an almost instantaneous and often mindless action to quell the negative sensation…As product designers it is our goal to solve these problems and eliminate pain—to scratch the user's itch.[14]

The purpose of keeping people attending—even to the point of addiction—to their social media, is to gather data about users' preferences from their 'likes' and other feedback mechanisms. The company can analyse this data to find out what kind of products you might want to buy, so that it can sell *you* (your time, your attention span, your curiosity) as a member of an audience to an advertiser. Free 'cloud computing' email services do this too, by scanning keywords in your emails. Search engines do the same with your search keywords and your selection of displayed search results. Much of this information about you can be found and used by other companies, such as when:

- A website lodges a 'cookie' on your hard drive to track what other websites you look at.
- A website you use sells information about how you use its site, to another company.
- Quiz games that are shared on social media ('Which *Game of Thrones* Character Are You?' and the like) might

12 Quoted in Paul Lewis, 'Our minds can be hijacked': The tech insiders who fear a smartphone dystopia'. The Guardian, 6 October 2017.
13 Nir Eyal, Ryan Hoover: Hooked: How to Build Habit-Forming Products (Portfolio, 2014) p. 1.
14 ibid, p. 48.

send the answers you provide to a political research company. These answers reveal your political views, your level of activism for those views, and the like, and they allow the company to target political ads at you more accurately. (To find out how this technique was used to influence national elections in several countries, you may wish to research the Cambridge Analytica scandal.)

- Cookies on websites, and also apps on your phone, use the IP address of your router, or the GPS locator on your phone, to figure out where you are. This information can be used to fix prices for things you buy online. People who log on from an affluent neighbourhood may see a higher price than those who connect from a less affluent neighbourhood. (In the industry, this is called 'dynamic pricing'.) In late 2018, researchers found that Google tracks the location of your phone even when you deliberately disable its location-tracking services. [15]

- You don't lock up the privacy settings on your social media account (or your phone, or other devices), leaving everything you post on your social media account open to the world.

- A social media company re-writes its privacy policies and Terms of Use policies in order to make more information about you available to its buyers, or grants them permission to use that information in new ways.

Your social media data might also be used by other companies for other purposes besides targeting ads at you. During a hiring process, for instance, a company's recruiters might go through a candidate's publicly visible photos and comments. Or, they might ask candidates at the job interview to give their passwords so they can see what's not available for public view. After being hired, employers may require employees to do some marketing for the company using their social media accounts; for instance, by posting about the company's sales and events.

It is primarily for reasons like these that we do not need to suppose there's a conspiracy among media owners, businesses, and governments that is designed to keep audiences in the dark about what's really going on in the world. It's enough to see how the owners of a media outlet must work hard to avoid alienating or

annoying the audience. For example, if a news broadcast were to show a story about child slave labourers mining rare earth minerals for use in the manufacture of cell phones, most viewers would change channels and watch a sitcom instead. Media providers know that audiences generally don't want to hear that kind of news—the kind which implies we might be complicit in something unjust, or that implies we may have to change an important part of our lives. Or, even if none of that is the case, many audiences simply do not care about the plights of impoverished brown-skinned people in distant countries. Broadcasting this story would cause the loss of *at least two* audiences: The people who were enjoying the show, and those who might be in the market to buy a new phone. And without an audience, the business has nothing to sell.

Similarly, media organizations will also take care not to annoy or alienate their shareholders and their advertisers. If a media outlet were to anger too many of its advertisers, it would soon find itself with a product that no one wants to buy. If it angered its shareholders, they would withdraw their investment capital. And if reporters and journalists annoy their editors and managers, they may find themselves sacked. On that point, here are the words of Canadian news media owner Conrad Black:

> If newspaper editors disagree with us, they should disagree with us when they're no longer in our employ. The buck stops with the ownership, [and] I am responsible for meeting the payroll. Therefore, I will ultimately determine what the papers say, and how they're going to be run. [16]

Taken together, it may appear as if the media is indeed involved in a conspiracy to placate and pacify the public. But remembering Ockham's razor, there's no need to take the explanation quite that far. It's sufficient to see that the business model requires editors and journalists and owners to regulate (or self-censor) themselves; that is, to make decisions that preserve the size and quality of the product they sell (the audience) and which keep the buyers of that product (the advertisers) happy.

---

15 Ryan Nakashima, "Google tracks and records your movements even if you turn off Location History" Los Angeles Times / The Assocated Press, 13th Aug. 2018.
16 Conrad Black, quoted in James Winter, 'Black's Plans'. The Globe and Mail, 12 March 1994, p. D7.

Given these forces affecting the news, how can you keep yourself intelligently informed about events and topics that interest or affect you? The main thing to do is to read about events in multiple news sources, not just one. Among mainstream corporate news services, some will be politically right leaning, a few will be left leaning, and some centrist. Pick a service for each of these three positions and read all three of them. If you have access to the internet, you can read about world events in newspapers and broadcast media of different countries. Also, look for independent news outlets that rely on volunteer or 'citizen journalists' for their content, and make most of their money from volunteer donations or reader subscriptions. With less of their revenue stream coming from advertisers, independent media tends not to have the same problem with advertiser-friendly bias that corporate media often has. But in exchange for this advantage, independent media tends to be more politically partisan (for one side or another of the political spectrum). It also tends to have fewer resources for in-depth investigative journalism, and fewer resources to protect themselves from lawsuits.

Journalists are professionals, and all of them entered the profession because they think it is important for people to know what's going on in the world. (Well, that's what one would hope!) Most of the time, professional journalists do their best to be as objective and as impartial as possible. If any bias appears in the work of a journalist or a media company, it is not a reason to distrust the industry as a whole. Nonetheless, as noted earlier, there is no such thing as a 'plain fact' in mass media. Information is always subject to various forces that affect how, when, and in what frame, and after what judgment calls, it gets presented. We always have to do our own thinking in order to be fully informed when we need to make decisions like how to spend our money, how to vote, or when to take a stand on a pressing public cause.

You may also want to consider exercising more caution about how much information, and what kinds of information, you allow the publishers of digital media to collect about you. If the right to privacy is important to you, you may want to consider following

guidelines such as these:

- Assume that anything you post on your Facebook, Twitter, Instagram, or other social media pages, can and *will* be seen by anyone in the world, regardless of your privacy settings. Don't post anything there that you wouldn't post on a telephone pole at a busy street corner.
- Don't assume that someone who is your Facebook friend today will always be so. Therefore, even when you post things 'friends-only', don't post anything that someone could use against you.
- Use different passwords for your bank account, your social media, your email, and so on.
- Use an email address provided by your university (if they provide one) or by your ISP; avoid email accounts provided by free online services.
- Be suspicious of any business or media organization that asks for your street address, phone number, or eerily specific security questions such as the street you live on or your mother's maiden name. Be especially suspicious if you are asked such questions by a quiz or an entertainment app ('What's your stripper name?' or other such silliness.)
- Use cash for your purchases as often as you can, in order to avoid leaving a digital record of your purchases. Retailers often record what you bought, when you bought it, the total cost of your purchases that day, etc., and they use that information to predict what you may want to buy next, and sometimes to predict what's going on in your life: a job change, a pregnancy, etc.
- Do not give your credit card number to any organization from which you don't intend to buy anything.
- Get a protective wallet for your bank cards and your passports. This will prevent criminals from covertly scanning the chips in your cards and devices and gathering information about you which could be used for identity theft.
- Limit your use of social media, perhaps to less than 20 minutes a day. Pick one or two days a week in which you do not use your social media at all.
- Do not send nude or compromising photos of yourself to anyone using social media, including your closest friends.

- When you host parties, ask guests to observe a 'no pictures' rule. If someone wants to take pictures anyway, ask them to get permission from everyone who will be in the picture.

8.13. Analysing the Form and Content

Critically analysing the content of media is different than analysing its delivery mechanisms; it's also very different than analysing arguments. The rhetoric of media is often about emotional rather than logical persuasion, and this can make it difficult to determine the strength of the argument being presented. Our familiarity with different media and our viewing habits can affect how critical we can be. If you are used to watching films passively as entertainment, it is important to be aware of the things you ordinarily accept as part of the cinematic experience, such as the emotional quality of the score, or the use of close-up shots in certain scenes. These can have implicit premises that serve in both the arguments made by media and in their rhetoric.

To begin analysing the content of media, you want to carefully describe what you are seeing. What is the medium? Is it mostly words, pictures, sound or a combination of these? What is the subject of the piece, and how is it portrayed? Are the colours dark, is the focus sharp or blurry, is the lighting bright or dim?

Once you have a basic description, ask yourself what information the piece conveys and what you would need to know in order to understand it more fully. If it looks like an old film, you might want to know if it is really old, or it was just shot to look that way. Think about how this would change the message. Does it matter who made the piece? Would the message seem different if it was created by a man rather than a woman, or by someone of a different cultural background?

Using this information, you can begin to interpret the medium. What do you think it means? What message is the author trying to communicate? What other messages are also being communicated? Think about the emotional tone of the piece, and the attitude it takes to its subject. What values does it express or omit? If the piece presents itself as objective/scientific/journalistic, what elements contribute to or detract from this? If had a more personal and reflective nature instead would it still be as compelling?

Media are meant to be communicative, so think about who the intended audience is and the purpose of the piece with regards to this audience. It can be very interesting to compare commercials (for instance) for which you are and are not in the intended demographic group. What makes a commercial appeal to you, or not? What makes a film or game entertaining to you? How would a different audience respond? Evaluate the success of the piece in achieving its purpose. How did it intend to make you feel about the subject? How did it really make you feel?

Reflect on the cultural impact of the medium and how it might influence others. Draw on all of your other observations to think about this. Does it portray the subject in a culturally acceptable way? (This is harder to do than it sounds. For example, if you are a straight, white, middle-class man, you might not know how to judge the portrayal of gay, black, unemployed women.) Does it present it in a new light, or in a way that conflicts with other values? This can be very subtle. We often think that films made for entertainment, because they don't pretend to be objective or scientific, shouldn't be taken seriously. The film *Jaws* is about a man-eating shark, and it aims to scare viewers with tense music and sharp scene cuts. *Jaws* was a fictional film, but presenting sharks as predators to humans changed people's attitudes towards sharks and had a negative impact on shark conservation. By contrast, the BBC's *Blue Planet* documentaries show the underwater world of fish and marine mammals as a pristine environment without any human presence. While these films are beautiful, the way they present the marine environment hides the significant impact of humans on the oceans.

Finally, given the discussion of the business model of media affects their content, you may want to consider how the content has been framed in order to avoid alienating audiences, advertisers, and shareholders. Here are some of the ways in which this happens, especially in news media:

Selection of events to report or not report: Obviously, if a news outlet chooses to say little or nothing about a certain event, it has shown some bias in its reporting of the facts, even if what little it does say is factually correct, and even if decisions have to be made (for reasons of limited space, time, etc) about what will and what will not be shown.

Selection of point of view: As a general rule, any newsworthy public event can be examined from multiple points of view. Consider, as an example, a story about a bomb attack in a foreign country. The reporters could take the view of the victims and empathize with their suffering, or they could take the view of the attackers and emphasize their grievances. Or the reporters could draw attention to third parties harmed by, or benefitted by, ongoing violence in the region.

Selection of framing language: Nouns, metaphors, and adjectives used by the journalists will often give away their point of view. War reporting is where this is most obvious: One side of a conflict might be referred to as 'troops' or 'hordes' or 'terrorists', while the other side might be referred to as 'soldiers', or 'brave women and men', or 'our boys', or 'freedom fighters'.

Preference for drama: One of the most effective ways to draw an audience is to report stories involving conflict, tension, or controversy. As it is often said in the newspaper industry: 'If it bleeds, it leads.' Another way to attract attention is to use words or images that elicit sympathy: Pictures of dead or injured children, for instance. Sometimes journalists will report two or more sides of a story even when one of those sides is relatively insignificant. This can make a controversy appear larger than it really is. For instance, very few people believe that the works of William Shakespeare were written by someone other than Shakespeare. But in the interest of 'balance' and 'fairness', a journalist might give equal time to someone who believes Shakespeare's plays were ghost-written by Francis Bacon. This creates the impression of a dramatic and vigorous debate, and that kind of drama attracts audiences.

Marginalization: This is a term that dates back to the days when newspapers were laid out by hand, without computers. A story that the editors wanted to downplay might be given only a small amount of space on the page, near the margins (hence, 'marginalization'), or on the back pages. Similarly, an event that the editors want to draw special attention to could be given a more 'front and centre' position, with tall block-capital letters.

Passive reporting: This is what happens when journalists don't do their jobs. An agency that calls a press conference typically gives journalists a press kit along with access to people for interviews, and photo-ops for their cameras. Passive reporting happens when the journalists simply copy the information from their press kits into their reports without doing any of their own writing, researching, or follow-up. Reporters do this for many reasons: Sometimes they are so busy that it's easier to just copy and paste the text from the press kit. But organizations who want their information presented in the best possible light sometimes manipulate the environment of the press conference to make the journalists more comfortable: Offering free food and drink, bringing in sexy people from local modelling agencies to work as servers, and so on.

Disinformation: Some media companies willingly publish disinformation on behalf of political parties, businesses, churches, or other organizations that they support, or whose worldviews they share. Some will also publish disinformation strictly in order to make money. We'll see more of this when we discuss fake news.

8.14. Propaganda and Disinformation

In our everyday language the word '**propaganda**' tends to have a bad connotation. It refers to a message from a government or political party that tries to garner support for a political cause by emotionally manipulating people—but the word does not necessarily have to refer to such shady tactics. Propaganda is a type of communication from a political organization that is disseminated for the purpose of raising support for that organization's causes and policies, whatever those might be, and whether the means of persuasion is rational or emotional or something else. Governments publish propaganda all the time, as do all political parties, although some might do so more often than others. Corporations, labour unions, military forces, churches, charities, and all kinds of other public institutions publish propaganda to raise support for their own purposes, too. A political scientist of my acquaintance defines propaganda as any government communication, or any partisan communication of any kind, including innocuous messages such as when a government office might close for the holidays—but I think that definition is probably too broad to be useful.

You should examine propaganda claims with the same critical and skeptical eye that you use to examine advertising, news, or just about anything else spread by mass media. Such claims might be true or false, but it's the evidence and the argument that determine this, not any patriotic symbols that may decorate it. One should be especially vigilant of **disinformation**.

Disinformation is a specific type of propaganda: It also attempts to raise support for a political cause, but here the goal is to influence people (to vote or spend money or speak out in support of a cause) by deliberately spreading falsehoods. It might describe an event that never took place, or one that did take place, but which happened very differently than the way they retell it. Disinformation might accuse a person or group of doing something they did not do. It could warn of a threat from an enemy or a source of danger which does not exist, or which in reality is fairly trivial. It may discredit or divert attention away from well-evidenced facts or well-documented historical realities.

Almost all political parties and governments spread disinformation once in a while; some more than others, and some have done so in the past more than they do now, or vice versa. Corporations sometimes spread disinformation about the quality or safety of their products, or of their competitors' products. They may also spread disinformation about the state of the economy or about some situation in the world in order to keep their investors confident, or to maintain market share. Military forces also sometimes do this to trick their enemies into false beliefs about the strength of the force that faces them.

Disinformation also differs from propaganda in a second way: Its function is not only to spread lies, but also to construct a fictitious reality, supported by a set of tightly inter-connected lies, half-truths, talking points, pseudo-facts, '**alternative facts**'[17], and a carefully constructed worldview. In this fictitious reality, the main criterion is political usefulness. That is to say, its function is to make the producers of disinformation appear to be right, true, just, and wise, no matter what they say. It must serve this function whether or not the content of the message corresponds to an observable reality, and whether or not the message has logical consistency. As counterintuitive as it may seem, the producer of disinformation does not always need to have any particular policy or position to promote. This is because the main goals of a disinformation campaign are to glorify its producer, to dominate intellectual environments, win arguments, silence critics and opponents, and position its own **framing language** (and hence its **worldview**) as the normal and natural framing language for any and all public discussions. This is where disinformation can be distinguished from ordinary propaganda: It aims to do more than influence you to vote or spend your money a certain way. Ultimately, it has the ambition of dominating your mind.

Disinformation may refer to actual events, but it must describe them in whatever light glamorizes the producers of disinformation. Its message will normally appear to come from very trustworthy and reliable sources, which helps make it seem credible and persuasive. However, this also makes it very hard to identify whether or not a given piece of propaganda is actually disinformation. It is effective because most people tend to trust and believe what they see and hear and read in sources that look authoritative, and most people tend to trust speakers who seem confident, self-assured, and convinced. Here are some examples from the 20th century:

- U.S. senator Joseph McCarthy's 'communist conspiracy', 1950–54.
- The Nazi campaign against the Jews, which falsely accused them of doing things that are just too horrible

9 The term 'alternative facts' was coined by Kellyanne Conway, who was a senior aide in the White House during the first few months of Donald Trump's presidency (at the time of writing she is still 'counselor to the President'). She was explaining why the President's press secretary, Sean Spicer, claimed that Trump's inauguration ceremony drew the largest crowd of any inauguration, contrary to the evidence of photographs and city transit ticket sales. C.f. John Swaine, 'Donald Trump's Team Defends 'Alternative Facts' after Widespread Protests'. The Guardian, 23 January 2017.

The term 'alternative facts' was coined by Kellyanne Conway, who was a senior aide in the White House during the first few months of Donald Trump's presidency.

(at the time of writing she is still 'counselor to the President')

to reprint here, 1933–1945.

- The corporate-funded denial of climate change and global warming.
- The non-existent Iraqi 'weapons of mass destruction', which was the stated *casus belli* for the invasion of Iraq in 2003.

Disinformation is often extremely difficult to identify, at least at first. It frequently requires a lot of research, many courageous questions, and much time to pass, before the true state of affairs is revealed. As when recognizing conspiracy theories, one should remember that extraordinary claims require extraordinary evidence. But this, too, can be difficult to apply, because the disinformation source may actually present the extraordinary evidence to the public. (The trouble is that such 'evidence' is often fabricated from nothing, or taken out of context, or mixed with half-truths and lies, or just as extraordinary as the claim it supposedly supports.) However, there are a few general features of a disinformation campaign which, if you spot them, may give you reason to doubt it.

EXCESSIVE SIMPLICITY: The worldview and the framing language of a disinformation campaign tend to presuppose a highly simplistic understanding of things. Elsewhere in this textbook I have described simplicity as a good thinking habit, and as a quality of the preferable explanation for things, so this statement may seem incongruous. But a disinformation communique tends to simplify things that are by nature complicated, such as diplomatic, economic, or scientific matters. It also tends to ignore or suppress tricky or subtle details, which nonetheless remain relevant.

DISCREDITING CRITICAL KNOWLEDGE SOURCES: The producers of disinformation want people to think that they (and often only they) provide the truth about whatever situation is the object of the propaganda. So it is necessary for them to undermine trust in any source of knowledge that could expose their lies. In much the same way that a criminal on trial might undermine a jury's trust in the witnesses to his crime, so to make the jury think he is innocent, a corrupt politician or corrupt political party might try to undermine the public's trust in the news media, or in scientists, or the police, or anyone who could provide evidence of the corruption. This effort often involves the promotion of **conspiracy theories**, or the regular repetition of a slogan about the media's (or other group's) supposed biases against the politician or the party. The effort may also involve discrediting the very notion of truth itself, as when for example, a politician or a political spokesperson asks us to look at **alternative facts**,[18] or declares that 'truth is not truth'.[19] (Not every instance of discrediting truth itself is an instance of propaganda. Some people may do this in order to save face, to avoid the embarrassment of having been caught making a mistake.)

Seizing the First Impression: Most people believe the first thing they are told about some event or situation. People often continue to believe it (or something like it) even when told something different about it, especially if the first impression is also coupled with some of the other features of propaganda noted here (fake authorities, etc.) Seizing the First Impression is also, by the way, an effective form of counter-propaganda, or inoculation against propaganda.

Absolutist moral assumptions: As part of its excessively simple presentation of complicated things, the disinformation campaign often only portrays 'good guys' and 'bad guys', with almost no shades in between. Within the fiction-based worldview created by the campaign there is normally no room for any discussion of alternatives. In this way, the worldview presupposed by a disinformation campaign resembles a value program.

Fear: In the worldview of disinformation, there are clearly-identified 'bad guys' who are always portrayed as a source of danger. They might be said to threaten the economy, or the state, or people's safety or morals. Racist or xenophobic beliefs are frequently included here: The campaign might claim that the 'bad guys' should be considered suspect because they have lower standards of hygiene, or they are prone to criminality, less intelligent on average, or involved in criminal conspiracies, or that they do not share the target audience's cultural and religious values.

Unstated assumptions: The disinformation campaign presents a set of fictitious 'facts', and then suggests implications or hints at possibilities, using framing words, rhetorical or leading questions, provocative images, and the like. The target audience is thus prompted to reach certain conclusions on their own. This technique is often used when the explicit statement of the assumption would damage the campaign, for instance if the conclusion to be reached is racist or sexist, or if it is clearly a logical fallacy. A related concept is the 'dog whistle' (discussed below).

Time pressure: If the disinformation includes a call to action, it is often claimed that the action must be taken quickly. War propaganda often includes an element of time pressure.

Mixing truths and falsehoods: Disinformation campaigns might include a few clear truths and demonstrable facts among their propositions. Mixing truths together with half-truths and lies and expressing such truths with the right kind of framing language, can help make the overall picture presented by the campaign appear more believable. Viewers are made to feel that if one or two of their messages turn out to be true, the rest of their messages is probably also trustworthy.

Fake, inaccessible, or misquoted authorities: Among the falsehoods which make up part of the disinformation, there may also be testimony from scientists, policy analysts, or other relevant experts and witnesses. Later, it may be revealed that these people cannot be reached by the public, or that their actual reports have been suppressed or partially censored, or they don't even exist at all. One should always be suspicious of statements like 'The experts agree that…' when such statements are not coupled with information about who those experts are, what their qualifications are, who they work for, or how their opinions were surveyed. (See section 8.9, above.) Out-of-context quotations from actual experts, or from political rivals, may also be used to make it seem as if that person said something very different from what was actually intended.

Shifted accusations: Upon being accused of something, such as lying, or harming some group, or

---

18 Mark Moore, "Conway: Trump spokesman gave 'alternative facts'" New York Post, 22nd January 2017.
19 Melissa Gomez, "Giuliani Says 'Truth Isn't Truth' in Defense of Trump's Legal Strategy" The New York Times, 19 August 2018; "Trump lawyer Rudy Giuliani: Truth isn't truth" BBC News, 19th August 2018. Mr. Giuliani made that declaration in a "Meet The Press" interview that broadcast on NBC Television on 19th

even conducting a disinformation campaign, the disinformation producer replies by accusing rival persons or parties of doing something similar. A shifted accusation is a means of controlling the framing language of a discussion, and a means of ensuring that the disinformation creator remains always on the attack, and never on the defence, in any given argument. They will often present clear fallacies like the red herring and *tu quoque*. However, coupled with other qualities like time pressure, or fear, people tend to ignore the fallacy and accept the shift.

BLACK PROPAGANDA, AND FALSE FLAGS: A disinformation message might disguise its true source, for instance by appearing to have come from one party, when in fact it came from another. Or, it might describe a real event, with credible witnesses and documentary evidence, that was secretly carried out by persons disguised as members of a different party than their own. The term 'false flag' comes from military and espionage contexts, and it refers to ships flying the flag of a different country than the one they're actually registered with, or soldiers wearing the uniforms of a different army than their own. This can become complicated, or rendered absurd, when members of one group publicly accuses another group of perpetrating a false flag; such an accusation can serve as an act of propaganda in its own right, for instance, as an attempt to 'poison the well'.

GASLIGHTING: This technique, named for the film *Gaslight* (1940), involves a set of lies, and a framing language to support them, constant repetition and reinforcement over weeks or months or more, and a campaign of belittling and patronising someone or the members of some group. The aim is to make people doubt their own interpretation of events, to doubt their memories and their perception of reality, to break down their trust in their own judgments of things, and ultimately to break down their ability to think for themselves. Between individuals and in small groups, gaslighting is a kind of bullying; a form of psychological abuse. From a propagandist, gaslighting is perhaps the very essence of disinformation. Like black flags, however, members of one group might accuse another group of gaslighting them or others; this, too, muddies

the water concerning who is doing the gaslighting, and dilutes the real meaning of the term.

CODE WORDS AND 'DOG WHISTLES': These are key words or phrases which mean different things to different sections of the audience. To one audience, a certain word or phrase may appear insignificant, reasonable, even banal. To another group, the same word or phrase signals that the speaker is a member of that group, and that he's prepared to pursue that group's political goals. They're sometimes called 'dog whistles' in the sense that they call upon the members of that group to gather together, much as a dog owner might whistle to call his dog to his side using a whistle that only the dogs can hear. Code words are a way of publicizing one's true political beliefs and intentions to one group but not to another, and a way of publicizing one's intentions whilst preserving 'deniability' about them; that is, whilst remaining coy about those intentions to those who might find them abhorrent. Knowing a few such code words, then, is one way to tell whether someone is using disinformation as part of their political plan.

'FIREHOSE OF FALSEHOODS'. This technique involves flooding the media with false statements, some of which are so obviously and outlandishly false as to be ridiculous. As described by Christopher Paul and Miriam Matthews, the researchers who coined the term, the firehose of falsehoods has several distinct features: "high numbers of channels and messages," a "shameless willingness to disseminate partial truths or outright fictions," "rapid, continuous, and repetitive," and "it lacks commitment to consistency," and it "lacks commitment to objective reality".[20] The technique works because most people treat information as trustworthy if it comes to them from multiple sources and in high volume. Firehoseing is also a means of dominating a discussion: it forces other voices in the media to waste time correcting the falsehoods (to little effect), making them less able to put forward their own ideas and arguments.

MARKETING TECHNIQUES: Disinformation often uses some of the same techniques advertisers employ to persuade us to spend our money. Some of these include celebrity endorsements, **weasel words**, constant repetition, provocative images, and so on. If it comes from a government, it might use patriotic symbols such as national flags, portraits of respected leaders, references to historical events, and so on. If it comes from a religious group, it might use religious symbols, or quotations from holy books, etc.

The scope of possible types of disinformation goes beyond this brief outline, but these are perhaps the most important points. A given disinformation campaign might only have some—and not all—of these features, but that does not disqualify it. The more of these features you think are present in a given piece of propaganda, then the more you may want to engage your faculties of reasonable doubt.

Another thing you can do is go to a fact-checking agency, to see if any professional research has been done on the topic. Most such agencies can be reached on the internet, and some publish their findings in newspapers and magazines as well as in their own web sites. Here is a short list of them:

- FactCheck.org (USA)
- PolitiFact.com (USA)
- FullFact.org (United Kingdom)
- Snopes.com (primarily for memes and urban legends)

As counter-intuitive as it may seem, responding to propaganda with facts, evidence, and refutations tends not to persuade people to abandon false beliefs. Such efforts often reinforce people's false beliefs.[21] Most people prefer to continue believing whatever they already believe, however they came by it. And it can be very hard to change anyone's mind when peer pressure, or a sense of selfhood and identity and group membership, or a 'firehose' of media messaging, also reinforces their (false) beliefs. The most successful ways to resist propaganda are:

- warn people in advance to expect propaganda,
- explain to them how propaganda works,
- regularly repeat any available retractions and refutations of the propaganda,
- and provide alternative **narratives** (not just facts) to

fill in the empty space left behind by the refuted false-hoods.[22]

8.15. Fake News

Sometime around the year 2015, a new kind of content appeared in the mass media: **Fake news**. The ubiquity of fake news has led some scholars who study media, culture, and society, to surmise that we now live in 'the era of **post-truth**' and of 'post-factual politics', by which they mean: 'Circumstances in which objective facts are less influential in shaping public opinion than appeals to emotion and personal belief'.[23]

Fake news of one kind or another has probably existed for as long as there have been any forms of mass media. However, the kind of fake news that's new(ish) is peculiar to internet-based social media. It depends on web sites that social media users can share with their contacts, who in turn share it with theirs, and it can propagate among these hosts much like a virus. The common phrase 'to go viral' refers to the kind of information that media consumers share among themselves so frequently that the content appears to have a life of its own. Researchers at MIT, for instance, found that false stories on Twitter travelled about six times faster than true stories. They also found that "false news reached more people than the truth; the top 1% of false news cascades diffused to between 1000 and 100,000 people, whereas the truth rarely diffused to more than 1000 people."[24]

Fake news will have some, often many, of the same features as disinformation in general: Excessive simplicity, fictitious or misquoted sources, fear mongering, etc. Yet not all fake news publishers are propagandists, in the strict sense of being sponsored by a government, political, or other public type of organization. Some fake news publishers are in it strictly for the money. Fake news also tends to have some features of its own that distinguish it from typical propaganda:

- 'Click-bait' headlines, often carefully worded to raise one's curiosity and promise the satisfaction of that curiosity if the web link is clicked upon. 'He came home one night, and you won't believe what he saw his

21 Zakary L. Tormala and Richard E. Petty, "Source Credibility and Attitude Certainty: A Metacognitive Analysis of Resistance to Persuasion," Journal of Consumer Psychology, Vol. 14, No. 4, 2004. 22 Stephan Lewandowsky, Ullrich K. H. Ecker, Colleen M. Seifert, Norbert Schwarz, and John Cook, "Misinformation and Its Correction: Continued Influence and Successful Debiasing," Psychological Science in the Public Interest, Vol. 13, No. 3, December 2012;

daughter doing!' 'When you read these 15 facts about green tea, you'll never drink it again.' Or, the headline provokes outrage and/or a heightened sense of drama: 'He admitted to faking the evidence that put twenty men behind bars.' 'Revealed: The secret plot to take away your freedoms!'

- Professional, easy-to-read graphic design and URL, superficially similar to well-known and better trusted news sources.
- Headlines that have little or nothing to do with the content of the article.
- More spelling and/or grammar errors than you would expect from a professional media source. (This happens when the creators of fake news rush their work.)
- And especially: Extraordinary claims *without* the required extraordinary evidence.

Fake news can also be spotted by what it *lacks*: Features you would expect to see in a real media source.

- Fake news articles often have no author by-line. Many legitimate news articles don't have by-lines either (they might instead say 'Staff writers', or they'll name a news wire agency like Reuters or Associated Press). But fake news articles are much less likely to display by-lines.
- Fake news websites tend to have no 'About' page for the site as a whole. Or, if it has an 'About' page, that page will usually lack contact info for the site's owners and its chief editorial staff. Or the 'About' page will say that the site is satire, entertainment, or 'fantasy news', but that admission might be deliberately hidden away in a place that is difficult to find.
- Inline hyperlinks on fake news pages tend not to lead to other articles. Most have no inline links at all. Or if it does have links, they usually lead to website home pages, and not to articles.
- Fake news tends to have no confirmation of the general details of the story in any other news outlet.
- Fake news sites normally don't have a statement of the site's editorial policies.
- Fake news sites tend to have no ombudsman or other instrument whereby the public can report (or complain about) misleading or offensive content.

Fake news, its related concepts in **rhetoric** (such as **truthiness**, **alternative facts**, etc.), and the intellectual environments dominated by **post-truth**, benefit from a psychological phenomenon called **mere repetition bias**. This is a kind of bias in which people believe something because they have seen it or heard it many times, and perhaps seen or heard it from multiple sources (different social media, friends and neighbours, etc.) Fake news and other forms of propaganda works by regular, frequent, and consistent repetition, leading you to feel mentally 'exhausted' and therefore more willing to accept their claims and less willing to form your own judgments.

Fake news may seem like harmless fun, and sometimes the promoters of disinformation will even frame it as a joke. But it can, and regularly does, influence what we think and believe, and thus it can influence how we talk, vote, spend money, interpret real news, and relate to other people (especially those who have differing political or religious commitments). It's now well known that fake news influenced the results of national democratic decisions, such as the United Kingdom's 'Brexit' referendum, the 2017 independence referendum in Catalonia, and the 2016 presidential election in the United States. There are fake scientific journals which operate as pay-to-publish scams for contributors ('predatory publishers', they're often called), and which can influence scientists or policy makers in business and in government to make bad decisions or to waste money.[25] Fake scientific authorities are responsible for, among other things, supporting the anti-vaccine campaign, resulting in numerous deaths from preventable diseases.[26]

Fake news can also inspire people to undertake harmful and/or criminal courses of action, including hate crimes and terrorist attacks. One famous example of this occurred during the 2016 United States presidential election campaign: A popular item of fake news claimed that the Democratic Party was operating a paedophilia ring, with a Washington DC pizzeria as its headquarters. There was no truth to this; nevertheless, emails from the Democratic Party's chief fundraiser that had been leaked to the media suggested a loose connection between the restaurant's owner

23 Oxford English Dictionary, entry on 'Post Truth'; see also "'Post-truth' declared word of the year by Oxford Dictionaries' BBC News, 16 December, 2016. **24** Vosoughi, Roy, Aral, "The spread of true and false news online" Science, Vol. 359, Iss. 6380, pp. 1146-1151. 9 March 2018. **25** Alan Burdick, "'Paging Doctor Fraud": The Fake Publishers That Are Ruining Science.' The New Yorker, 22 March 2017. Carl Straumsheim, "'Predatory' Publishing Up" Inside Higher Education, 1st October 2015.

and party fundraisers. At first the fake news story was only carried by satire sites, but soon it was picked up by conspiracy theorists. Finally, a man visited the restaurant and opened fire inside it with an AR-15 rifle. No one was physically injured that day, but the shooter was sentenced to prison.[27]

Some of the fact-checking organizations noted above are helpful in sorting out what's fake and what's real. And in general, if you come to believe that a certain media publisher is a source of fake news, it's a good idea to avoid that publisher entirely. Consider alerting friends of yours about the fake news, to help clear up the intellectual environment you share with them, though this may cost you your friendship with those who continue believing the fake news.

8.16. Advertising and Marketing

All advertising serves just one purpose: To sell something. In general, all advertising tries to do this in one, or both, of these two ways:

- Making a favourable claim about the qualities of the product; or
- Creating a favourable feeling in the mind of the viewer that is to be somehow associated with the product, for instance by being informative, or inspirational, or entertaining.

But all advertising, at its heart, delivers only one message: 'Your life sucks, and my life is awesome, so buy my product or service and your life can be awesome too!' Some ads may present this message in an informative or entertaining way. Some advertisements even have what deserves to be called artistic merit. But the job of advertising is not to help people make informed and rational choices about how to spend their money: It is to influence people to spend their money in very specific ways, on very specific products and services. Thus, we are always justified in approaching claims made in advertising campaigns with reasonable doubt.

Fake news and other forms of propaganda works by regular, frequent, and consistent repetition, leading you to feel mentally 'exhausted' and therefore more willing to accept their claims and less willing to form your own judgments.

26 "Russia trolls 'spreading vaccination misinformation' to create discord." BBC News, 24th August 2018; Jessica Glenza, "Russian trolls 'spreading discord' over vaccine safety online" The Guardian, 23 August 2018; Lena H. Sun, "Anti-vaccine activists spark a state's worst measles outbreak in decades" The Washington Post, 5th May 2017.

Here are some of the most common ways that advertisers do this:

IDENTIFICATION/ASSOCIATION: Using key words, images, sounds, or even provocative shapes, the product is presented in close association with something desirable. The most common object of association here is sex. By filling the space with images of beautiful and sexually available people, most of them women posed and dressed to get the attention of a male audience, advertisers play upon some of the deepest and most human psychological instincts. But advertisers might also associate their products with good health, exotic locations, celebrities and their accomplishments, or a lifestyle of some kind, be it a life that is adventurous, fun-filled, wealthy, wholesome, or enviable for some other reason.

SLOGANS AND JINGLES: Catchy tunes, rhymes, clever puns and word play, and the like can hold our attention for years. To this day, whenever I see certain brands of breakfast cereal in the grocery store I hear the song that accompanied TV ads for that cereal back in the 1980s replaying in my mind.

MISLEADING/VAGUE COMPARISONS: Sometimes advertisers want to compare their products to other similar products that you might buy instead. But since they also want you to buy their products, they have to present the comparison in a slanted way. For instance, the text of an ad for a headache pain medicine might say 'Now 30% more effective!' Well, more effective than what? It doesn't say. Or, a car commercial might show two cars together with their prices and boast that you will 'Save $15,000 when you buy a MonsterCar!' But the price of the competition's car includes all the optional features like power windows and GPS navigation, whereas the price of the MonsterCar doesn't include those features.

WEASEL WORDS: These are words which appear to make a definite claim about the product, but actually don't. For example, the marketing text for a lottery might say 'You might have just won ten million dollars!' Well, you *might* have, but the realistic likelihood of *actually* winning that prize is very small. A campaign for a department store holiday sale might say 'Up to 60% off everything in the store!' But, in fact, only one product in the store is marked down that much, while everything else is marked down between 20 and 30 percent. Words like 'possibly', 'up to', 'as much as', and 'many' serve as weasel words when they are just vague enough to mislead and manipulate the viewer, without telling an outright lie.

PUFFERY/EXAGGERATED CLAIMS: Puffery is an exaggerated claim that is obviously untrue but gets your attention anyway. I once saw a billboard advertisement for women's cosmetics that made the claim: 'We make women so beautiful, other women will want to kill you.' Taken at face value, this statement is clearly, painfully false. But the statement still creates the impression in the viewer's mind that women who use that product will become enviable. Similarly, television commercials for trucks or fast cars might tilt the camera, to make the vehicle look like it can easily drive up a nearly vertical slope. The image tells no lies, but most people don't notice the camera tilt, especially if the shot lasts only half a second, and the impression left on the viewer is a misleading one.

PUSH POLLING: This is a type of advertising technique normally used by political campaigns. Large numbers of individuals are contacted directly, usually by telephone, and invited to participate in a survey. But the caller is not actually collecting data. Instead, the caller is trying to influence the contacted person's thinking about an issue (and her vote!) use a series of leading questions, rhetorical questions, and carefully chosen framing words. It might drop vague hints about the bad behaviour of a political opponent, or an innuendo about the unreliability or untrustworthiness of a party.

As when you are exposed to something you suspect might be disinformation or fake news, you should treat advertising claims with a large dose of reasonable doubt.

Everyone who uses media needs to do so intelligently, and to do their own thinking and sometimes research as well, in order to preserve their free minds and to make truly autonomous decisions about what to believe and what to do.

27 'The Saga of 'Pizzagate': The Fake Story that Shows How Conspiracy Theories Spread' BBC News, 2 December 2016; 'Pizzagate: Gunman Fires in Restaurant at Centre of Conspiracy' BBC News, 5 December 2016.

ghtWro
ustEvilMu
goodUnjus
rtuousS
kedr

Chapter Nine:
Moral Reasoning

In the discussion of reasonable doubt in the last chapter, we learned how to decide what to *believe*. And now in this discussion of moral reasoning, we will learn how to decide what to *do*. In this sense, moral reasoning is the most practical part of the process. When we reason about morality we build arguments, just like when we reason about anything else. But arguments involving moral propositions have to be constructed in a special way. This is partly to help us avoid the **naturalistic fallacy**. But it is also to help ensure that our arguments about morality are consistent.

9.1. Features of Moral Arguments

The main thing that makes an argument about morality distinct from other kinds of arguments is that moral arguments are made of **moral statements**, at least in part. A moral statement, as you might guess, is a statement about morality: It is a statement that says something about what's right or wrong, good or evil, just or unjust, virtuous and wicked. Moral statements are not like other propositions: They do not talk about what is or is not the case. Rather, moral statements talk about what should be the case, or what should not be the case. Look for moral indicator words like 'should', 'ought', 'must', 'is right', 'is wrong', and the like, as well as for the language of character-qualities, like 'temperance', 'prudence', 'friendship', 'coldness', 'generosity', 'miserliness', and so on. Sometimes, sentences written in the imperative voice (i.e. sentences which are commands) are moral statements in which some of

the moral indicator words have been left out. Thus, a sentence like 'Share your toys!' could mean, '*You should* share your toys!' But to be fully logical, it's necessary to phrase imperative sentences that way in order to fit them into moral arguments, and to then determine whether they are sound. It's also easy to fall into the fallacy of **equivocation**. Words like 'good' can have a moral and a non-moral meaning: We don't use the word 'goodness' the same way when we speak of good snow boots and good people.

With that in mind, which of the following are moral statements, and which are not?

- Peter should keep his promise to you.
- Peter did keep his promise to you.
- Human stem cell research is wrong.
- Some people think that human stem cell research is wrong.
- My mother is a good person.
- My mother tries to be a good person.
- This pasta dinner is really good.
- Finish your dinner!
- It's wrong to cheat on tests.
- Information gathered from terror suspects by means of torture can't be trusted.
- Torturing people suspected of terrorism is barbaric and criminal.
- You've always been a good friend to me.
- Proper etiquette demands that we treat guests with respect.

As stated above, moral arguments are made of

moral statements. This means that the conclusion is a moral statement, and at least one of the premises is also a moral statement. As we saw in the discussion of deductions, nothing can appear in the conclusion that was not present somehow in at least one of the premises. So, if you have a moral statement for a conclusion, you need a moral statement somewhere in the argument as well. Without it, the argument is an instance of the **naturalistic fallacy**, and it's unsound. Consider these examples:

(P1) It's wrong to steal candy from babies.
(P2) Little Sonny-Poo-Poo is a baby.
(C) Therefore, it's wrong to steal candy from Little Sonny-Poo-Poo.

In this example, P1 is a general claim about moral principles, and P2 is a factual statement. Together, they lead us to the conclusion, which passes a moral judgment about the particular case described in P2.

(P1) Jolts of electricity are very painful.
(P2) Some of the prisoners have been interrogated using electric jolts.
(C) It is wrong to torture people using electric jolts.

In this example, both P1 and P2 are both factual claims. But the conclusion is a moral statement. Since there's no moral statement among the premises, this argument is unsound. Now there might be an implied, unstated general moral principle which says that it's wrong to inflict pain on people. And some readers might unconsciously fill in that premise and declare the argument sound. But remember, when examining an argument, the only things you can examine are those that are actually in front of you.

9.2. A Taxonomy of Moral Theories

How do we know that it's wrong to steal candy from babies, and wrong to inflict pain on people? We know this because somewhere in our intellectual environments and our worldviews, we learned a few general moral principles. And there are lots and lots of moral

theories that might form part of your worldview. Here's a kind of 'family tree' of the most successful theories of ethics philosophers have developed over the centuries.

1: **Deontology**, or Duty-Ethics: These are theories which claim that there are actions and choices that are inherently, intrinsically wrong, no matter what the consequences.
    1a. Divine Command
        1a.1 From scriptures [theology]
        1a.2 From personal experience [mysticism]
    1b. Natural Law theory
    1c. Kantian Deontology
    1d. Rights
        1d.1. Natural Rights
        1d.2. Human Rights
        1d.3. Civil Rights

2: Consequentialism: These theories claim that there is no such thing as an intrinsically, inherently wrong choice or action. The rightness or the wrongness of an act or the choice depends on the consequences.
    2a. **Utilitarianism**
        2a.1. Act Utilitarianism / Hedonistic [Bentham]
        2a.2. Rule Utilitarianism / Lexical [Mill]
        2a.3. Objective List

3: **Areteology** / Virtue Theory: These theories state that the weight of moral concern is on the character and identity of the person who acts and chooses, as well as the habits he or she develops in the course of making certain choices frequently and consistently.
    3a. Ancient Mythological [Celtic, Norse, Greek, Germanic, etc.]
    3b. Teleological [Aristotle]
    3c. Religious [Aquinas, El-Farabi]
    3d. Non-Teleological [Hume]
    3e. Will to Power [Nietzsche]
    3f. Modern Virtue [MacIntyre, Hursthouse, Foot, Crisp, Slote]

4: **Justice**: This field of ethics may look like deontology, since it is concerned with duties and is neither concerned with consequences nor with moral identity. However, unlike other forms of deontology, justice is concerned with groups rather than with individuals. Justice looks at the morality of power-relations, and the distribution of wealth and resources in a community.

    3a. Aristocracy

        3a.1. Classical *Res Publica* [Plato, Aristotle]

        3a.2. Theocracy [Augustine, Aquinas]

        3a.3. Feudalism

        3a.4. Oligarchy and Mercantilism

    3b. Social Contract Theory [Hobbes, Rousseau.]

    3c. Liberalism

        3c.1. Classical Liberalism [Locke, Mill.]

        3c.2. Capitalism [Smith]

        3c.3. American Libertarianism [Nozik, Rand]

    3d. Communitarianism [Taylor]

    3e. Distributive Justice [John Rawls, etc.]

    3f. Socialism

        3f.1. Marxism [Marx, Engels]

        3f.2. Communism [Žižek]

        3f.3. Social Democracy

By the way, I have drawn this family tree with three roots in the base, in accordance with the observation by philosopher Jonathan Glover that ethics is founded in three main psychological traits that he termed the 'moral resources'.

Different ethical theories base morality either on self-interest or else on one of the moral resources. They tend to urge the claims of one of these factors to be *the* basis of morality…Sympathy for others is at the heart of utilitarianism. Respect for other people, as a form of recognition of their moral standing, is the centre of Kantian ethics and of moralities based on rights. Concern with one's own moral identity is one source of ethics centred on virtue.[1]

In the next sections, we'll look at some of these theories of ethics in detail.

1 Glover, J. Humanity: A Moral History of the 20th Century, p. 28.

9.3. Utilitarianism

Jeremy Bentham (1748–1832)

John Stewart Mill (1806–1873)

Henry Sidgwick (1838–1900)

Peter Singer (b. 1946)

Derek Parfit (1942–2017)

Statement of the theory: The morally right action is that which results in the best consequences. An action holds no intrinsic value; its value depends solely on its consequences.

By far the most widespread and popular ethical theory today, **utilitarianism** is very practical, and in most situations, it offers a quick and straightforward solution to most ordinary moral problems. It has turned out to be very historically influential in the last 200 years or so, especially in major public concerns such as women's suffrage, the reform of prison conditions, the abolition of slavery, and the welfare of animals and of children. Because of its emphasis on calculating benefits, harms, and preferences, this school of thought has also profoundly influenced modern economics and econometrics.

The core of the utilitarian theory combines three main points. First, actions and choices should be judged only by their consequences: Nothing else matters. Right actions are, simply, the ones with the best consequences. Second, the only consequence that needs to be examined is the amount of utility that the action produces for everyone affected by the action. Utility is usually interpreted as 'happiness' but can also mean 'pleasure', 'benefit', or 'well-being'. Its converse, disutility, usually means something like 'unhappiness', 'pain', or 'suffering'. The right actions are those that produce the greatest net result of utility over disutility. And third, when calculating the utility that is gained or lost as a result of one's choices, no one's utility is more important than anyone else's; no one deserves, *a priori*, to be happier than anyone else. As Jeremy Bentham said, 'Each to count for one and none to count for more than one.'

Modern utilitarianism was originally developed for use by legislators in the British Parliament. Bentham's idea was that lawmakers should ask themselves what consequences the policy or decision under consideration was likely to produce. He listed a number of ethical criteria by which to measure utility, including duration, intensity, number of people affected, and so on. Adding up all of these criteria in an almost mathematical way, he believed, would make it possible for legislators to come to morally correct decisions fairly quickly. When considering any moral dilemma, the right choice is the one that produces 'the greatest benefit for the greatest number of people', or the greatest net benefit over pain for all those who are affected.

There are several different types of the theory. *Act Utilitarianism*, which was espoused by Bentham, measures the utility in the actual outcomes of one's choices. *Rule Utilitarianism*, generally attributed to John Stuart Mill, holds that one should follow moral rules which have been shown by experience to produce the greatest benefit for the greatest number of people. This may look like a form of deontology, since it comes down to obeying moral rules—but note that the rules gain their authority only from the consequences that tend to flow from following them. Thus, we have rules like 'don't kill', 'don't tell lies', etc., because we know that people who follow such rules tend to produce utility for themselves and others. Those who break such rules tend to produce disutility. If there is some situation in which following a rule will clearly produce disutility, then the rule should not be followed.

And the core concept of the theory, utility, also comes in different types:

THE PLEASURE PRINCIPLE: As noted, utility is normally defined in terms of pleasure and pain, or happiness and suffering. This can mean physical pleasure and pain, but the definition can also easily include emotional and intellectual pleasures and pains, such as love or depression. It can additionally include social conditions that harm people in other ways, such as political repression. In this type of utility, all pleasures are equal: Thus, the pleasure of playing a game of conkers can be about as good as the pleasures of reading Chaucer. Some pleasures might last longer, or be more intense, or affect more people, and so fare better in the calculus. But if all other factors are equal, so is the value of the utility or disutility that could be gained.

SATISFACTION OF DESIRES: Utility is defined in terms of the fulfilment of people's interests, and of people getting of what they want and avoiding what they do not want. Sharing some common features with economic theories about consumer behaviour, this understanding of utility probably has the greatest prestige and appeal.

LEXICALITY: This is an innovation of Mill's that was intended to meet objections to Bentham's hedonistic theory: it asserts that some things are more worth desiring than others. The pleasures of Chaucer really can trump the pleasures of a game of conkers, since the latter (well, according to Mill) is a higher-order pleasure.

OBJECTIVE LIST: Utility is defined in terms of an objective list of 'goods' that, as experience has shown, tend to improve people's quality of life. There can be multiple lists for different cultures, societies, and times in history, which allows the theory some flexibility.

CRITICISMS OF THE THEORY: Probably the most obvious criticism of utilitarianism is that its central principle, 'utility', can sometimes be ambiguous. Measuring happiness and pleasure, as some forms of utilitarianism requires, is a bit like measuring a cloud with a ruler. Are sado-masochists experiencing happiness by inflicting pain on each other? The re-defining of utility as 'satisfaction of preferences' helps address this criticism, but it has problems of its own. Some people do not know what their desires are; some find that once their wants have been satisfied they are still unhappy; some might have wild or impossible desires; and some might have a desire to hurt others.

Another criticism is that sometimes the actual

consequences of one's actions are hard to identify precisely. Your choices might affect some people directly, others indirectly, and some only remotely. So, which of them do you include in your utilitarian calculus, and which do you exclude? What about unintended or unforeseeable consequences? And depending on how you measure utility, an action can be conceived as having very different moral worth. Do you add up the average happiness of all people involved? In that case, the net utility can be increased by getting rid of those who bring down the average for everyone else. (Think of 'ethnic cleansings' here). Or do you maximise the total happiness? In that case, utility could be maximised by some enormously large population of people all of whom experience very little utility individually.

A third criticism has to do with the way utilitarianism might force certain consequences that could be considered unjust. There can be situations in which the choice that produces greatest balance of happiness over unhappiness also results in a lot of harm or suffering for people who don't deserve it. Think of a magistrate forced to imprison or execute an innocent man in order to prevent a riot or a war, etc. In classical utilitarianism, it can be acceptable to do that which burdens or harms some, in order to benefit many others. As the character Spock from Star Trek once said, 'The needs of the many outweigh the needs of the few, or the one.' Committed utilitarians regard this as a strength of the theory (and rightly so). But this can sometimes mean that an unjust act could be compensated for by other consequences that produce enough benefit to outweigh the harm in their calculations. Those who believe in any of the more rule-oriented moral views, such as the Ten Commandments or similar religious moral teachings, cannot logically accept that claim. With the rule-oriented view, no amount of utility could compensate and outweigh the harm caused by punishing an innocent person, for instance.

9.4. Deontology

Immanuel Kant (1724–1778)
W.D. Ross (1877–1971)

In classical utilitarianism, it can be acceptable to do that which burdens or harms some, in order to benefit many others. As the character Spock from Star Trek once said, 'The needs of the many outweigh the needs of the few, or the one.'

Statement of the theory: The right thing to do is that which is in accord with one's moral duty as determined by reason. The rightness of wrongness of the action is intrinsic to the action itself.

Duty-based or rule-based statements of ethics has been around for centuries, but the philosopher who did the most to lay out the logical structure of such statements was Immanuel Kant. As he saw it, the right thing to do has nothing to do with consequences and outcomes: It is the choice you make, the action in itself, which matters. And to be moral, the action has to be in accord with moral laws. So, to figure out whether a choice you are about to make is in accord with moral law, he proposed a procedure called the **categorical imperative**: 'Act on that maxim which you can at the same time will that it shall be a universal law'. Basically, the idea is to ask: 'What if this course of action was a moral law for everyone? Would it still be possible to do it? If some course of action became self-defeating if everyone did it, then you shouldn't do it either. For example, if you were considering telling a lie to someone, even an innocent and harmless one, you should consider what would happen if everyone told lies, all the time. The result would be that no one would ever trust anything anybody says, so when you tell your lie your listener would know perfectly well that it's a lie, which defeats the purpose of telling the lie in the first place. As another example, you might think it convenient to throw fast-food wrappings out your car window. But if everyone did that all the time, there would be huge piles of litter on roadsides everywhere, as well as traffic hazards from flying garbage, and a terrible smell. Civic authorities would have to bring in workers and equipment to constantly clean it up, thus making the disposal of food waste less convenient for everyone. So, it is wrong to do it. Kant's idea is that reason cannot consent to an action which, if it were a law for everyone, would make it impossible to do the action.

Kant also formulated a second, more pragmatic version of his moral principle, called the **practical imperative**: 'Act in such a way that you always treat humanity, whether in yourself or in another, as an end in itself, never as a means to an end'. In this second formulation of the theory, Kant named an object of special concern, 'humanity', as a thing which deserves the utmost respect at all times. 'Humanity', here, means that which Kant thought made human beings special: Our capacity for reason and free will. Kant thought that reason and freedom were intertwined with each other, and he thought they were so important that anything which exploits, reduces, interferes with, or subverts them is always wrong. He was not simply saying that one should complain or retaliate when someone tries to take your freedom away. Rather, it is a matter of respecting reason and freedom wherever you find it, 'whether in yourself or in another'. A choice is always morally wrong if it exploits someone's else's freedom, or if it uses another person as a means to an end, presumably a selfish end. For example, you might think that buying a pack of chips in a shop uses the shopkeeper as a means to an end, but the shopkeeper is (presumably) freely exchanging his merchandise for your money, so there's no moral problem here. But exploiting the shopkeeper's generosity to get a pack of chips for nothing is using his freedom as a means to an end, and thus intrinsically wrong.

The 19TH-century Scottish philosopher William David Ross produced a theory of '**prima facie** duties' (i.e. 'first glance' duties), which further clarify deontological thinking and help make it practical. Ross identified seven such basic principles:

- Fidelity: To keep one's promises, speak the truth, be loyal to friends, etc.
- Reparation: To compensate others for any harms or burdens one might have caused them.
- Gratitude: To show genuine thankfulness for benefits received from others.
- Non-maleficence: To refrain from causing harm to others.
- Justice: To treat people equally; to treat others in accord with what they deserve, etc.
- Beneficence: To do good to others, to show respect and kindness to others, etc.
- Self-improvement: To seek education, to develop one's natural talents, etc.

Ross believed that in any given situation, one or more of these duties may apply. Some duties may carry more weight than others, and each person must evaluate this on their own, following something like Kant's imperatives. In cases where two or more of these duties conflict with each other, Ross argued that in general it is more important to avoid harm than to create positive benefits. So, for instance, fidelity normally overrides beneficence, and non-maleficence normally overrides all other duties. Ross also believed that the pursuit of some long-term positive qualities like knowledge and moral character, a goal covered by the duty of Self-improvement, can sometimes override the pursuit of short-term pleasures or the avoidance of short-term harms. Ross named these rules 'prima facie duties' precisely to emphasise that all of them can have exceptions. In this way he hoped to avoid the problems and abuses that often arise when we think our rules are absolute.

Kantian deontology is probably the most influential rival to utilitarianism. As examples of where it is used, almost all religious thinking in ethics is some variety of deontology, and modern jurisprudence and legal thought still stems from deontological principles. Moreover, almost all discussion of human rights is deontological in character. The categorical rejection of slavery, racism, sexism, hate crimes, war crimes, cruel and unusual punishments, etc., and the protections of basic civil liberties like speech, association, privacy, *habeus corpus*, and freedom of conscience and religion, etc., all stem from deontological thinking.

Criticisms of the theory: Probably the most widely mentioned criticism of deontology is that it might be wrong to always ignore the actual consequences of our choices. When we do things, our intentions do not always coincide with the results. One can do a lot of harm even when one means well. And there is always a possibility that doing the right thing can sometimes bring about harm to people who don't deserve it.

A second criticism has to do with conflicting moral laws. It is conceivable that situations may arise in which two or more moral duties conflict with one another. Should you always tell the truth, even in a situation where doing so might lead you to break a promise, or fail to protect someone in danger?

And finally, Kant's categorical imperative is perfectly capable of supporting various trivial or silly rules, for instance 'Always wear a clown hat when visiting the Queen.'

9.5. Areteology / Virtue Theory

Aristotle (384–332 BCE)
Elizabeth Anscombe (1919–2001)
Rosalind Hursthouse (b. 1943)
Philippa Foot (1920–2010), Onora O'Neil (b. 1941)
Alasdair MacIntyre (b. 1929)

Statement of the theory: An action is right if it demonstrates the virtue that is appropriate for the situation; a virtue is a quality of character necessary for success in the pursuit of the good life.

Virtue theory is the oldest but also the trickiest of the theories. It tends not to ask if such-and-such an action is the intrinsically right one, or whether it will produce the best consequences. It asks, instead, what kind of life is most worthwhile, what it means to live well, and what we must do to flourish as human beings. The usual answer that a virtue theorist supplies when asked these questions runs like this: To live a worthwhile life, we must develop certain virtues. So, what is a virtue? It is 'a settled disposition of habit', as Aristotle defined it; it is a special quality of character, a behavioural or psychological disposition, even 'a way of being in the world'. Each virtue has a certain object of interest: For instance, courage is concerned with the management of fear, temperance with the management of pleasure, etc. Each virtue also has a certain role in one's pursuit of a worthwhile and meaningful life.

Now there can be disagreement among various theories of virtue about just what a worthwhile life actually is; and there may also be some disagreement about what virtues are useful and necessary to achieve that worthwhile life. Indeed, there are different lists of virtues, from different cultures and different times in history, such as:

Just as 'one swallow does not make a spring', as Aristotle said, one good action by itself does not make one virtuous.

- *The Heroic Virtues* (from the mythology of early Bronze Age and Iron Age Europe): Courage, friendship, generosity.
- *The Classical Virtues* (from the works of Plato and Aristotle): Courage, prudence, temperance, justice.
- *The Seven Grandfathers* (from Anishnabe and Ojibway culture): Wisdom, Truth, Humility, Bravery, Honesty, Love, and Respect.

Although there are different lists of this type, there is usually enough general agreement among those differing theories for their supporters to get along with each other. Some theories of virtue claim that the virtues are necessary for the attainment of ethical goals like 'leadership', or 'happiness'. Some emphasize that the virtues are closely tied to the maintenance of a certain kind of community, and the preservation of various personal and civic relationships. But all, or perhaps nearly all, theories of virtue hold that the having and the practicing of a virtue is self-rewarding: By acting and living in a certain way, the virtuous person creates for herself and her associates a better quality of life than she could create otherwise. Similarly, all, or nearly all, theories of virtue hold that a vice, the opposite of a virtue, is self-punishing; the vicious person gives to himself a stressful, difficult, and unhappy life. Thus, a quality like courage is clearly a virtue because a person wishing to lead a worthwhile life would have to know how to face danger and how to swallow fear once in a while. And a quality like cowardice is clearly not a virtue, because the cowardly person is effectively controlled by his fear.

Aristotle defined virtue as 'an excellence in the service of a function or a purpose.' There's a moral and a non-moral meaning implied here: A knife can be 'virtuous' if it is sharp, for instance, and that's not a moral statement. But Aristotle thought there was a purpose to being human: it is to use the 'faculties' or 'endowments of nature' which he thought are unique to us, and not shared with other animals. Using those talents and skills, and developing them to excellence, is what makes us happiest in life. The most important of these talents, he says, is our power of reason. The

important task which reason plays among the virtues is to show how much of a virtue is too much, and how much is not enough. This principle is now called the **Doctrine of the Mean**. A vice, Aristotle would say, is manifesting too much or too little of the particular quality that a situation calls for. Courage, to continue the example, goes between rashness or recklessness (which is too much courage), and cowardice (which is too little.) The idea is often compared to archery: Your arrow can fly too high or too low, and in either case miss the target.

And finally, most theories of virtue emphasize that developing virtue takes time. Just as 'one swallow does not make a spring', as Aristotle said, one good action by itself does not make one virtuous. Virtue theory requires one to *practice* a certain form of behaviour over the spread of one's life. One becomes courageous by making courageous choices and doing courageous things. Eventually, habit takes over and then you don't need to be quite as calculating about your choices. But even so, the virtues must be deliberately chosen, in each moment that calls upon you for a moral response.

Criticisms of the theory: One of the obvious problems with virtue is that the theory may not appear well suited to solving practical problems. When faced with a specific practical question such as is likely to arise in a business environment, a hospital, or an art venue, virtue theory tends to return rather unhelpful answers. It isn't impossible to apply virtue theory to practical ethics problems, but neither is it easy. (Imagine a conversation like this one. A client says, 'We are having a fiscal imbalance. Should I fix this problem by cutting workers' wages or laying some of them off?' The philosopher replies, 'Only if doing so would be virtuous…')

Some critics have pointed to deficiencies in the definition of a virtue itself. Aristotle's definition of a virtue as 'a settled disposition of habit' might not be a good enough explanation of what a virtue is. Every moral theory faces a criticism like this one; that is, a question about the meaning of its core concepts. But as it faces virtue theory, the problem lies in the conundrum of 'deliberately choosing' that which we

have a 'settled disposition of habit' to do.

9.6. Social Justice

As noted already, the ethics of justice is not about individual choices. It is a theory of social and sometimes political choices; it's a theory of how wealth, resources, and power are shared (or not shared!) in a community. One theory might say that all the wealth should be shared as equally as possible; others say there might be some benefits for everyone if we allow some degree of inequality.

Often, questions about justice are also questions about what individuals owe their communities, and what those communities owe their individual members. The answers can range from 'nearly everything', as in some radical forms of communism, to 'nearly nothing', as in some radical forms of libertarianism.

And to complicate it even further, some questions about justice are also questions about who counts as a member of the community, and thus who deserves a share of its wealth and power, no matter how it is divided. This, too, ranges on a spectrum from 'everyone', as in most conceptions of human rights and most conceptions of religious ethics (think of Jesus' statement that we must love our neighbours), to 'only the deserving people', such as only men (as in a patriarchy), or only the able-bodied members of some nationality or ethnicity (as in most forms of fascism).

Theories of social justice are also as ancient as any other moral theory, and they are as diverse as the ancient cultures they come from. The Confucian principle of the Five Relations, the Hindu caste system, Plato's model of the ideal Republic, and Augustine's model of the City of God, are perhaps the best-known examples. The constitution of any modern nation is also, in its own way, a theory of justice, since it is (among other things) a statement about what kinds of powers may be exercised by governments, who gets to be in charge of government, who supervises them, and possibly what must happen if governments exercise their powers wrongly.

There are, of course, many theories of justice; here in this text I will focus on two of them, one from Europe's early modern period, and the other from

20th-century America.

JEAN-JACQUES ROUSSEAU: THE SOCIAL CONTRACT

The early modern theory of social justice is called **social contract theory**. First proposed by the Swiss philosopher Jean-Jacques Rousseau in his book *The Social Contract* (1762), this is the idea that the relationship between an individual and the community he lives in should be likened to a kind of contract. In this contract, individuals owe certain responsibilities and duties to others, and they are required to accept various burdens; in return, the community offers ever member various benefits which make everyone better off than they'd otherwise be.

A simple example of a social contract would be something like the 'rules of the road'. Everyone who wants to drive a car must obey certain simple rules, such as taking a driver's test and getting a license, driving on the right side of the road (or on the left, in Britain and Ireland!), stopping at stop signs and traffic lights, keeping their speeds below posted speed limits, signalling their turns, and so on. There might be some people who find these rules annoying: The speed limits or the traffic lights occasionally make them late for work, or make them feel like driving is no fun. But in return for following rules like these, all drivers are safer than if they did not. There are fewer traffic accidents, and when accidents do occur there are fewer injuries and deaths; and so on. Compulsory vaccinations for various diseases could be seen as another kind of social contract. Every child, shortly after birth, receives several injections of vaccines for diseases which, historically, spread quickly and killed thousands of people every year. Sometimes more vaccines are delivered later; some, like the annual flu shot, are voluntary and are delivered to adults of any age. People take on the burden of queueing up at a health clinic, enduring the momentary pain of a needle, and paying the taxes which cover the costs of the program. The contract might include accepting the possibility that one out of every thousand recipients (a hypothetical number for the sake of the example) will have an adverse reaction. In exchange for these burdens, we no longer see thousands of people each year dying from painful or disfiguring diseases like measles, mumps, rubella, smallpox, whooping cough, polio, and others.

The widest possible social contract includes nearly everything people do which might in some way be regulated by the state, and perhaps quite a few other things besides. In such a wide social contract, everyone is required to take on responsibilities like obey the law, vote, fill in their census forms, and pay taxes. In return, the state provides services like infrastructure, police protection, courts of law, free or low-cost schools and universities, public health services, parks and gardens, public broadcasting, the regulation of interest rates and stabilization of the value of money, and so on. If this social contract obtains in a democracy, its benefits will include the opportunity to revise the contract from time to time, through various devices like elections, referendums, lobbying work, court judgments, and even protests and demonstrations. So, one country might have a very wide social contract, involving more responsibilities for citizens in exchange for more services from the state; another country might have a narrower social contract, with fewer responsibilities and fewer services.

Rousseau himself regarded the social contract as an exchange of rights. When you enter an organized community, you give up your natural rights, such as your natural right to take whatever you want, and to personally punish those who hurt you. In exchange, you get in return civil rights, which include the right to equality under the law, and the right to the assistance of the entire community for the protection of your person and your possessions. Here's how Rousseau himself described the benefits of this exchange:

> The passing from the state of nature to the civil society produces a remarkable change in man; it puts justice as a rule of conduct in the place of instinct, and gives his actions the moral quality they previously lacked. It is only then, when the voice of duty has taken the place of physical impulse, and right that of desire, that the man, who has hitherto thought only of himself, finds himself compelled to act on other principles, and to consult his reason rather than study his inclinations. And although in civil society man surrenders some of the advantages

that belong to the state of nature, he gains in return far greater ones; his faculties are exercised and developed, his mind is so enlarged, his sentiments so ennobled, and his whole spirit so elevated that, if the abuse of his new condition did not in many cases lower him to something worse than what he had left, he should constantly bless the happy hour that lifted him for ever from the state of nature and from a stupid, limited animal made a creature of intelligence and a man…What man loses by the social contract is his natural liberty and the absolute right to anything that tempts him and that he can take; what he gains by the social contract is civil liberty and the legal right of property in what he possesses… We might also add that man acquire with civil society, moral freedom, which alone makes man the master of himself; for to be governed by appetite alone is slavery, while obedience to a law one prescribes to oneself is freedom.[2]

JOHN RAWLS: THE DIFFERENCE PRINCIPLE

Since John Rawls published his book *A Theory of Justice* (1971), nearly all discussion of social justice among philosophers has somehow revolved around his ideas: Promoting them, modifying them, criticizing and rejecting them, but nonetheless talking about them.

The first line of Rawls famous theory confirms the ancient orientation of justice toward the public realm: 'Justice is the first virtue of social institutions, as truth is of systems of thought'. So, when we speak of 'distributive' justice, we're speaking of the fairness of how we distribute those social goods. Rawls claimed that social goods must be distributed in a way that is advantageous to everyone. Note that he does not say they have to be distributed equally. There could be advantages for everyone gained by an unequal distribution. This leads to what Rawls calls the **difference principle**: Any inequalities in the distribution must be acceptable to those who receive the smallest share. To put it another way, the difference principle is the idea that whenever anyone is working on a big political or economic or social problem, the best answer is the one which gives the most benefit to the marginalized, the disempowered, the worse-off party. In his words: 'The social order is not to establish and secure

the more attractive prospects of those better off unless doing so is to the advantage of those less fortunate.'

From this position, Rawls claims that some forms of inequalities may still be just: This is the case if they are to the benefit of the least well off. Under such a principle, injustice is not simply inequality, but rather any kind of inequality that is not to the benefit of everyone, and especially that is not to the benefit of the least well-off person.

This is, he says, the system of distribution which all rational parties would choose if they were in an 'original position', standing 'behind a veil of ignorance'. That is to say, it is the system of just distribution everyone would choose if no one knew what his or her social position would be, nor what share he or she would receive. In the 'original position', one can know the basic structure of society but one can not know whether one will end up rich or poor, male or female, black or white, well-educated or poorly-educated, and so on. Rawls claims that someone in such a position would bet that they might end up as the most marginalised and deprived person—and would therefore want that person's share to be as large as it can be.

It's worth noting at least one criticism of the theory. Rawls presupposes that in the 'original position', people are still self-interested, and they want to maximize the size of their own share; and this Rawls identifies as rational behaviour. Some of Rawls' critics have questioned this assumption about rationality. There may be other models of rationality that do not presuppose self-maximization: For instance, it may be rational to be charitable, sympathetic, and caring.

9.7. Ethics of Care

Do men and women view ethics in different terms? One philosopher who thought the answer to that question was 'yes' was Carol Gillian (b. 1936) in her book *In A Different Voice* (1982). Gillian is now widely regarded as the founder of a branch of feminist ethics called Ethics Of Care. The basic idea is that the traditional moral theories of Utilitarianism and Deontology are too abstract and impersonal, and can lead to indifference about the suffering or the vulnerability of people who

---

2 M. Cranston, trans. Rousseau, <u>The Social Contract</u>, Book 1, Chapter 8. (Penguin, 1968) pp. 64-65.

are presently in front of you. So, the Ethics of Care proposes, as the solution to that problem, that one's moral choices should be informed by empathy and compassion, especially for those you are in an actual and immediate position to help, in proportion to their vulnerability, and in proportion to the significance of their relationship to you. So, according to this theory, it is more important to help or support a family member over a stranger, or an injured person over a fully healthy family member, or an injured person who is nearby over an injured person who lives far away, etc. It is a flexible theory, which can be framed in the terms of all three moral theories I've already discussed (and so it's difficult to place it on the taxonomy).

Although it resists discussing ethics in the abstract, Ethics of Care can apply to some broad-ranging social and political principles. For example, philosopher Sara Ruddick argued that if a politician thought about war as a mother would think about it, instead of as a military planner, then he might be less willing to declare a war.[3] As further observed by Virginia Held, the ethics of care might have a kind of priority over other ethical theories, such as justice, because 'There can be no justice without care... for without care no child would survive and there would be no persons to respect.'[4]

The theory has also found application in professions like nursing, early childhood education, and psychological counselling. One's patients and clients deserve care not simply because they are your patients, but also because they are human beings in need. Moreover, besides their medical or developmental needs, patients and clients may also be in need of the kind of human recognition and compassion which a medical doctor or a clinical psychiatrist might be unable to provide.

9.8. Discourse Ethics

Discussions, debates, and arguments are among the most ancient and most useful ways in which people sharpen their intellectual skills and learn from each other. Yet many debates quickly become useless shouting matches or festivals of hate. Online debates are especially vulnerable to this problem, because online debaters need not face each other directly

and so need not see or bear the effects of verbally harming others. Some philosophers have therefore proposed principles of **discourse ethics**, the purpose of which is to keep debates productive and gainful for everyone. Paul Grice's principles of **implicature,** noted already in Chapter Four, are one such group of principles. Another is Jurgen Habermas' theory of discourse ethics: Habermas said that these rules are 'necessary for a search for truth organized in the form of a competition'. Speaking personally, I think the search for truth does not need to be *competitive*. Still, I do see the need for a few basic guidelines, lest the most aggressive or angriest voices dominate a conversation, or other participants feel compelled to go along with the views of the aggressors at the cost of suppressing better ideas. Rather like the rules of the road, where every driver obeys traffic lights and speed limits and so more people reach their destinations safely, the rules of discourse ethics allow everyone's voice to receive a fair hearing, and the best ideas can rise.

Here is a proposed set of rules for your next discussion circle, whether it's in your classroom, your church study group, your online community, your political forum, or wherever you find yourself discussing ideas that are important to you.

- Everyone who comes to the discussion may speak. The circle may not disband until everyone who wants to speak has had a chance to do so.
- Everyone who speaks must also listen.
- Everyone shall assume that all participants are rational, and they shall interpret each other's words in the very best possible way.
- Everyone shall debate for the sake of progress and knowledge; not for the sake of dominance and victory.
- Speak clearly, consistently, and rationally.
- Speak only what you actually believe.
- Speak what you understand to be true.
- Speak from the heart.[5]

What should you do about people who break those rules? Perhaps one useful thing to do is to give offenders a warning, and to remind them of the rules. Those who break the rules too often may have to be excluded from the discussion. This may seem to

3 S. Ruddick, "Maternal thinking", in J. Trebilcot (ed.), Mothering: Essays in Feminist Theory, (Totowa, NJ: Rowman and Allanheld, 1983) pp. 213-30.
4 Virginia Held, The Ethics of Care (Oxford University Press, 2006), p. 17)

contradict the basic principle of creating a space for discourse which is open and welcoming to everyone. Philosopher Karl Popper called this contradiction the **paradox of tolerance**:

> If we extend unlimited tolerance even to those who are intolerant, if we are not prepared to defend a tolerant society against the onslaught of the intolerant, then the tolerant will be destroyed, and tolerance with them. In this formulation, I do not imply, for instance, that we should always suppress the utterance of intolerant philosophies; as long as we can counter them by rational argument and keep them in check by public opinion, suppression would certainly be unwise. But we should claim the right to suppress them if necessary even by force; for it may easily turn out that they are not prepared to meet us on the level of rational argument, but begin by denouncing all argument; they may forbid their followers to listen to rational argument, because it is deceptive, and teach them to answer arguments by the use of their fists or pistols. We should therefore claim, in the name of tolerance, the right not to tolerate the intolerant.[6]

Popper published this in 1945, so it's likely he was thinking of Europe's experience fighting the Nazis—a political movement which, during its rise to power in the 1930s, took advantage of other people's tolerance to popularise intolerant (militaristic, murderous, hateful) political views. The paradox of tolerance leaves us in the logically difficult position of having to exclude certain (intolerant) people in the name of preserving an open and inclusive society. The enemies of the open society sometimes point to this paradox as evidence that the open society is full of hypocrisy. They might then suggest that some other value program should replace it: A program which, while it might be elitist or even violent, at least has the virtue of being logically consistent.

There are several ways to try and resolve this paradox. One is utilitarian: It might be argued that an open society, haunted as it may be by this paradox, is still better than the alternatives. Another is to do with justice: For instance, Rawls said that an open society requires its members to defend the practices and insti-

tutions which are necessary for the preservation of its openness: 'While an intolerant sect does not itself have title to complain of intolerance, its freedom should be restricted only when the tolerant sincerely and with reason believe that their own security and that of the institutions of liberty are in danger.'[7] This is not much different than asking drivers on public roads to obey speed limits and stop signs, and taking away the licenses of those who flout those rules. Our observance of such rules makes it easier for everyone to drive. (I'm getting lots of mileage from that metaphor, eh?)

I think virtue ethics offers another possible resolution to the paradox: A model of discourse ethics which includes the possibility, however small, that an excluded person could someday be welcomed back. In such a model, intolerant people would remain outside the conversation for as long as they remain a danger to it. But those inside the conversation move to exclude them in the manner of an educator, rather than the manner of a gatekeeper. They should preserve the hope, however faint that hope may be, that someday the intolerant will learn that intolerance is no path to any kind of good and worthwhile life. If and when the intolerant demonstrate that they've learned that lesson, we might have a reconciliation with them. This is virtue-ethics because it presupposes that everyone, even the very worst people, can change their habits of character and become better people if they decide to, and if they find (or if they're shown) a better path to a worthwhile life. Now, I think it's undeniably un-virtuous to enjoy the sight of someone being excluded: That would be schadenfreude, not virtue, even if the intolerant deserve their exclusion. Yet like every other ethics theory we've looked at so far, some critical questions can arise. Whose job is it to educate the intolerant? Might the safety of those inside the conversation matter more than the effort to include as many people as possible? What if the excluded person doesn't learn anything—should he be excluded forever, and if so, would that only strengthen the paradox instead of solve it? And what if the view of human nature presupposed here is not supported by enough evidence in human behaviour?

I leave these questions in your capable hands.

5 These rules are a revision of those which first appeared in Myers, Circles of Meaning, Labyrinths of Fear (Moon Books, 2012), pp. 357-365.
6 Popper, The Open Society and Its Enemies, (Routledge, 1945), Chapter 7, Note 4. 7 Rawls, A Theory of Justice, p. 220.

Chapter Ten: Activities!

10.1. Finding Your Online Diversity Quotient

I have nearly two thousand people on my Facebook friends list, so I see lot of memes every day. Memes are ideas, expressed in pictures and videos and quotations and so on, which people share with each other, and the more they are shared the more their movements seem to take on a life of their own. One day I thought it would be fun to save them to a database and tag them according to the kinds of messages they express. What would I discover? Were there some kinds of memes that are more popular than others? What are these things really telling me about the thoughts and feelings of the people around me—or, the thoughts and feelings they want me to believe they're thinking and feeling? And what are they telling me about myself?

The original idea was to make records of the content of my (online) intellectual environment over four days, to see what was in there. My basic procedure was very simple: I would only sample the memes that appeared while I happened to be online. That way, I wouldn't have to be online all day. And I also promised myself not to deliberately change my internet habits during those days, so that I wouldn't get an artificial result. I also didn't track the links to blog posts, news articles, videos, or other online media. To keep it as simple as possible, I only tracked the photos and images. And I only tracked the ones that someone on my friends list shared after having seen it elsewhere. That way, each of these pictures had passed a kind of natural selection test. Someone had created the image

and passed it on to someone who thought it worthy of being passed on to a third person, and so on.

After the first few hours, I had about 50 memes for my collection and had already noticed a few general trends. I started tagging the samples into what appeared to be the four most obvious categories: Inspirational, Humorous, Political, and Everything Else. The Humour category was already by far the largest, with more samples than the other categories combined. At the end of the first day, there was enough variety in the collection that I could create sub-categories. The largest of these was "Humour involving cats or kittens". No surprise there, I suppose: The internet is well known for being cat-obsessed.

But at the end of the second day, with about 200 samples in my collection, I started to notice something else that was much more interesting. A small, but significant, number of these samples were connected with social, political, or religious causes other than those which I personally support. Some promoted causes that were reasonably similar to my values, but I have never done all that much to support them. For instance, I've got nothing against vegetarianism, but I'm not a vegetarian myself. So, I labelled those memes as 'Near' values because they are not my values, but are reasonably close, and I felt no sense of being in conflict with them. Then I noticed that some of my samples were for causes almost directly opposed to the ones I normally support. I saved and tracked those political statements just as I did with the others, but these statements received a label as 'Far' values because they expressed values fairly distant from my own.

Now I could look at all these images and put them in three broad groups: Common Values, Near Values, and Far Values. And in doing so, I had discovered a way to statistically capture the real variety of my intellectual environment, and the extent to which I am actually exposed to significantly different worldviews. Let's name this measurement your Intellectual Environment Diversity Quotient. Or to keep it as brief as possible, your DQ.

At the end of four days, I had 458 pictures, and I had tagged them into six broad categories: Inspirational, Humour, Religion, Causes, Political, and Foreign Language. Here's how it all turned out. (Note here that if some of these numbers don't seem to add up, that is because some samples were tagged more than once, as they fit into two or (rarely) three categories.)

Total size of the dataset: 458 (100.0%)
Inspirational images: 110 (24.0%)
Humour: 225 (49.1%)
Religion: 36 (7.8%)
Causes: 148 (32.3%)
Political: 47 (10.2%)
Foreign language, any topic: 11 (2.4%)

And by the way, only 5 of them explicitly asked the recipient to 'like' or 'share' the image.

Now, for the sake of calculating how much real variety there is in my intellectual environment, we have to look at just the images expressing social, political, religious, or philosophical values of some kind. This doesn't necessarily exclude the inspirational or humorous pictures that had some kind of political or moral message, because as mentioned, there were many pictures that got more than one tag. As it turned out, around half of them were making statements about values. (That, by the way, was also very interesting.)

Here's the breakdown of exactly what my friends were posting pictures about. And as you can see, there's a lot of variety. But what is interesting is not how different they are from each other, but how many of them are different from my own point of view. You

can figure this for yourself by comparing the memes streaming in to your own news feed to what you say about yourself in your own social media profile, or by just deciding with each image, one at a time, to what extent you agree or disagree with it. Whichever way you do it, you have to be really honest with yourself. In this way, calculating your DQ is not just about taking a snapshot of your intellectual environment. It's also about knowing yourself, and making a few small but serious decisions about what you really stand for.

Total Religion, Causes, and Political: 231 (100.0%)

Total religious: 36 (15.5%)

Buddhism: 4 (1.7%)
Christianity: 6 (2.5%)
Pagan: 8 (3.4%)
Northern / Asatru: 6 (2.5%)
Aboriginal / First Nations: 3 (1.2%)
Taoism: 1 (0.4%)
Hindu: 1 (0.4%)
Any: 6 (2.5%)
Atheism: 1 (0.4%)

Total causes: 148 (64.0%)

Against cruelty to animals: 3 (1.2%)
Against religious proselytization: 3 (1.2%)
Support education, science, critical thinking: 19 (8.2%)
Pro-vegetarian: 1 (0.4%)
Organic and/or backyard gardening: 3 (1.2%)
Feminism / anti-violence against women: 3 (1.2%)
Feminism / sexual power relations: 7 (3.0%)
Feminism / body image: 5 (2.1%)
Anti-war: 4 (1.7%)
Israel-Iran anti-war solidarity: 3 (1.2%)
Support for soldiers / war veterans: 8 (3.4%)
Support for retired military dogs: 2 (0.8%)
Support gun ownership: 3 (1.2%)
Race relations, anti-racism: 1 (0.4%)
Support gay marriage / LGBT pride: 10 (4.3%)
Support environmentalism: 5 (2.1%)
Support universal health care in America: 1 (0.4%)

Support the student protest in Quebec: 3 (1.2%)

Against fascism and neo-Nazism: 1 (0.4%)

Total party political: 47 (20.3%)

Right wing: 8 (3.4%)

Left wing: 36 (15.5%)

Centre: 3 (1.2%)

Now for the sake of calculating the DQ, we need to look at the percentage of value-expressing memes that are near to my values, and the percentage of those which are distant. That's the measure of how much of the intellectual environment you live in could really challenge you, if you let it.

Total: 231 / 100.0%

Common values = 150 / 64.9%

Near values = 64 / 27.7%

Far values = 17 / 7.3%

So, my DQ, rounded off, is 28 and 7.

Now, you might be thinking that if I did the experiment on a different day I'd collect different samples, and I'd get a different result. This was especially clear in the humorous pictures, because some of them depended on the time of year for their effect. For example, I got a lot of Douglas Adams references, because one of the days I was collecting the images was 'Towel Day'. I also got a lot of Star Wars images because I was collecting my samples on May the 4th. Similar effects can also influence the memes that were expressing values; for instance, if the dataset is collected during a religious holiday. Friends who are religious might post more faith-supporting memes on days that are close to their significant holidays. Therefore, the figure I just quoted above might not be very accurate. Therefore, to address that possibility, I ran the experiment again two weeks later. And here's what I got the second time.

Second set = 470

Total Religion, Causes, Political, Second Set: 243 (100.0%)

Common values = 157 (64.6%)

Near values = 77 (31.6%)

Far values = 9 (3.7%)

As you can see, it's a slightly different result. The total collection was larger, and there were a lot fewer distant values represented. And among the humorous pictures, there were a lot more references to *Doctor Who*. But overall it wasn't a big difference. In fact, the percent of pictures expressing some kind of value was still about 50%, just as before. So, if I add the second set to the first and do the math again, I can get a more accurate result, like this:

Both sets combined = 474 (100.0%)

Common values = 307 (64.7%)

Near values = 141 (29.7%)

Far values = 26 (5.4%)

New DQ = 30 and 4.

Now, I don't know whether that figure is high or low, because I do not have anyone else's data to compare it with. And I also cannot (yet?) judge whether it would be good or bad to have a high DQ, or a low one, because, well, that's a value statement too!

But what I do know is that I can now accurately measure the extent to which my intellectual environment has a real range of different ideas and opinions. I can measure how much social or religious or political 'other-ness' there appears to be in my world. Now, this isn't a measure of *why* I might have that much diversity in my world. Do I value diversity? Or am I merely tolerant of it? If I have less diversity, is it because I prefer people who are like-minded, or easy to deal with? The search for answers to those questions would be the basis for a different kind of research project. But my DQ might be a good place to get started.

10.2. The Socratic Dialogue Game

The game requires at least two players, and in experimenting with this game in my classroom I found that it can work in small groups of no more than five members. It does not require either any specialized knowledge of philosophy as a discipline, or any specialized knowledge of logic apart from what's described in the rules. However, I do ask my students to observe the principles of good and bad questions, and good and bad thinking habits, as described in Chapters 2 and 3 of this book.

The first thing to do is to buy a stack of index cards, and then write a different philosophical question on each of them. Here are the questions that I used; of course, if you think of more, feel free to add them to your set of cards.

- What is love?
- What is justice?
- What is courage?
- What does it take to live a worthwhile life?
- What does it take to be a woman? Or a man?
- What is friendship?
- What is the significance of death?
- What is the best kind of government?
- What is education?
- What is greatness?
- What is truth?
- What is the significance of sex?
- What is civilization?
- What is a family?
- What is the point of sports and games?
- What is our moral responsibility to the Earth?
- Should people always obey the law?
- What does it mean to be an authentic individual?
- What is God?
- What is the Divine?
- What things are most sacred?
- What is a community?
- What is our duty to the community?
- What is our duty to your nation, or the state?
- What is reality?
- What are art and beauty?

- What is wisdom?
- Do living beings have souls?
- Where does knowledge come from?
- What kind of people should we be?
- Do we human beings have free will?
- What are the best kinds of stories?
- What is the true value of money?
- What is health?
- What is fairness?
- What is the significance of history?
- What is happiness?

It may appear as if some of these questions are a little vague. To the question, 'What is our duty to the community?' for instance, someone might wonder: Which community? Does it mean people who live nearby? Does it mean those who share values with you, no matter where they live? Does it include online communities? To the question, 'What is God?', one might wonder: which one? I left a few of these questions vague like that on purpose, in the hope that these clarification discussions would emerge in the course of playing the game.

Here are the rules for the 'Agora Variation', so called because it's close to how Socrates himself used to do it around the Agora of Athens.

Find a partner. One of you will play the role of 'Socrates' and the other will play 'The Expert'. The person playing Socrates asks The Expert a question, chosen by a random draw from the 'Deck of Many Questions'. The Expert answers.

If the Expert's answer is something evasive (a description or an example instead of a definition, or a weasel-word answer, etc.), Socrates may gently ask for a more direct answer.

When the Expert gives a direct answer, Socrates thanks her for it. Then Socrates asks the Expert to clarify any undefined or poorly-defined terms. Socrates may also raise counter-examples or analogies, if necessary, to show that a term is too broad, or too narrow,

1 Douglas R. Hofstadter, "About Nomic: A Heroic Game That Explores the Reflexivity of the Law" in his column "Metamagical Themas," Scientific American, 246, 6 (June 1982) pp. 16-28. Suber's first rule set also appears as Appendix 3 in his book The Paradox of Self-Amendment (Bern: Peter Lang Publishing, 1990). **2** Peter Suber's web site URL is: https://legacy.earlham.edu/~peters/writing/nomic.htm

or circular, or in some other way unsatisfactory. The Expert can also object to a question if it appears vague or irrelevant, or if Socrates commits a fallacy.

When the Expert has clarified everything that needs clarification, Socrates can ask questions that explore some of the likely consequences and implications, especially those which seem to lead to contradictions. If it can be done respectfully, also explore any implications that the Expert may find uncomfortable.

Continue this back-and-forth, question-and-answer exchange until 1) you both agree you have a satisfying answer to the original question; 2) Socrates runs out of questions; or 3) the Expert admits to having no idea how to answer the original question. Then switch roles, and start again with a different question from the deck.

Here's the 'Symposium Variation'. Players choose a question from the deck. Each player then prepares a five-minute speech to answer it. Then someone else in the group (perhaps chosen in advance, at random) presents a three-minute rebuttal to one of those speeches, possibly followed by a reply to the rebuttal from the first speaker. This variation can be used as a 'flash essay' classroom assessment activity. It also makes for a fun dinner party activity among friends, especially when the 'answers' are prepared in advance, and the 'counter-arguments' are off the cuff.

10.3. Nomic: The Game of Self-Amendment

Imagine a game in which the point of the game is to figure out exactly what game you are playing. Nomic (from the Greek word *nómos*, 'law') is such a thing: it is a multi-player game in which a change in the rules of the game is, in itself, a move in the game. It was invented by philosopher Peter Suber in 1982.[1] He got the idea while studying the provisions in real-world laws, such as national constitutions and acts of parliament, which govern how laws can be changed. The game demonstrates how those laws work, and how people reason and negotiate among each other in the process

of following them and changing them.

The structure of the game is deceptively simple. It begins with the presentation of a small number of initial rules. Suber's own initial rule set had twenty-nine rules, some of which were deliberately boring so that players would have an immediate wish to change them. Each player, one at a time, proposes to change, add, or remove a rule, and then the other players vote on that player's proposal. Players earn points when they successfully create the change in the rules that they want. *Every* rule in the game, from how to determine the winner to the very idea that people are obliged to obey the rules, is open for revision and removal (and re-adoption and re-revision and— you get the idea). As a result, a given game of Nomic can become very complicated very quickly, and can even continue for years.

Suber's initial rule-set is easy to find online, including on his own website,[2] so I will not reproduce them here. In my classes I have used my rules of Discourse Ethics, noted in Chapter 9.8, as an initial rule-set, along with some of Suber's rules about how to propose and vote upon changes to the rules, and how players may accumulate points toward victory. (I framed it for my students as a game whose purpose was to explore the idea of Discourse Ethics, and to decide how class discussions should be run.) The game has numerous other philosophical and personal applications. As Suber himself described it:

> Nomic has been used to stimulate artistic creativity, simulate the circulation of money, structure group therapy sessions, train managers, and to teach public speaking, legal reasoning, and legislative drafting. Nomic games have sent ambassadors to other Nomic games, formed federations, and played Meta-Nomic. Nomic games have experienced revolution, oppressive coups, and the restoration of popular sovereignty. Above all, Nomic has been fun for thousands of players around the world.[3]

---

3 From Suber's own website at Earlham College, Richmond, Indiana, USA. https://legacy.earlham.edu/~peters/nomic.htm Retrieved 1st October, 2018.

10.4. Thought Experiments

As we saw in the discussion of creativity and imagination (see Chapter 3), philosophers often use thought experiments to bring issues under a new and sharper light.

An ancient and famous experiment called 'The Ship of Theseus' is one of this kind. Imagine a wooden sailing ship setting out from Athens. Each day of its journey, Theseus and the crew remove one plank and replace it with a new one. By the time they return, every plank on the ship has been replaced. Now, is it still the same ship as the one that first set out? If it's not, then could a definite time be fixed as to when the ship became no longer the same? As you have probably realized, this experiment is not really about ship building. It's about selfhood, and personal identity over time, and the Greeks who invented this story knew that. It's a way of asking questions like this: Given that your body and perhaps your thoughts are not the same now as they were in the past, and given that the material which makes up your body is changing all the time, how do you know you are the same person now as you were an hour ago? A week ago? Ten years ago? As an aside, something similar could be said about the game of Nomic, described above. Is it the same game, one round to the next, when some or all of the rules have been changed?

Here are some thought experiments from twentieth-century philosophy:

THE TROLLEY PROBLEM (by Philippa Foot and Judith Jarvis Thompson). Imagine you are at the controls of a runaway trolley, and it is about to strike and kill five people who are tied to the rails ahead. You cannot stop or derail the trolley, but you can switch it to a different track, where it will hit and kill only one person. What would you do?

THE COW IN THE FIELD (by Edmund Gettier). Imagine that a farmer is worried that his cow has wandered away. He asks a neighbour to check and see if it's still there. The neighbour checks, and sees the cow, then reports to the farmer that the cow is fine. Later, the neighbour checks again and notices that the cow was hidden behind some bushes, and that what he thought was the cow when he checked the first time was actually some black-and-white plastic bags that got stuck on a wire fence. So, even though the cow was actually in the field, was the neighbour right when he told the farmer it was there? Is the farmer right to believe it's there?

THE CHINESE ROOM (by John Searle). Imagine there is a locked room with two windows on opposite walls. There is a girl in the room who has a book about how to manipulate the symbols of Chinese writing, but she does not know how to read or speak Chinese. People outside the room write questions (in Chinese) and insert them into one of the windows. The girl receives the papers, and using the rules of her book she changes them into new symbols, and then sends the new symbols out the other window. The people outside received the changed symbols and find that their questions were answered. Does the girl in the room understand Chinese or not?

THE BRAIN IN A VAT (by Hilary Putnam). Imagine that a mad scientist abducted you while you were sleeping, and surgically removed your brain. He places it in a vat full of nutritious chemicals, and connects it to electrodes controlled by a computer, which simulates the signals of your eyes and ears and other physical senses. Assuming there are no obvious glitches or faults in the simulation, how will you know that you are not seeing the real world?

THE TELETRANSPORTER (by Derek Parfit). Imagine a machine that can disassemble the molecules in your body, then beam the information to another location where a similar machine can reassemble you. Suppose you step into the machine in order to beam yourself to Mars. The machine does its work, and then you step out and find yourself still on Earth. A technician tells you there has been an accident: Instead of transferring all your information to Mars the machine only copied it. There is now another 'you' on Mars. The other you calls you on a video phone to and says, 'I'm terribly sorry about the accident, but since I have all of your your memories, feelings, and values, I will carry on with your life the same way you would have done.' Which is the real you?

As noted above, the real purpose of these thought experiments is to stimulate thought about difficult philosophical questions. The Trolley Problem is about ethics: It asks us to compare one of our moral convictions, the wrongness of killing (i.e., deontology) against another, the duty to cause the least harm to others (i.e., utilitarianism). The Cow in the Field is about what counts as knowledge, and whether we can know something accidentally. The Chinese Room is about computers and artificial intelligence. The Brain in a Vat is about the trustworthiness of our physical senses, and whether we can know what reality is. (Descartes' version, by the way, involved an evil demon instead of a computer.) And Parfit's Teletransporter is perhaps a science-fiction version of the Ship of Theseus.

As you consider each of these experiments:

- List as many possible answers to its questions as you can. Look for the best argument in each answer's favour. (If you don't like some of those arguments, still try to present them in the best possible light. Remember your **Principle of Charity!**)
- Consider whether any of those arguments hold any unexamined presuppositions. If they do, that by itself does not make the answer wrong. But it does invite some investigation into whether those unexamined presuppositions are reasonable.
- Consider what values, moral or epistemic or otherwise, are in play, and whether those values are competing with other values that are important to you. In this respect, a thought experiment is not only a way of answering weird questions—it's also an exercise in self-awareness.
- Find variations of these thought experiments in which one or two seemingly minor points have been changed. (For example: What if someone tied to the tracks in the Trolley Problem is someone you personally know? Or

very young, or very old? Or a convicted criminal?) How do those changed parameters change the questions involved? How do they change the answers?

As an aside: Some people believe that philosophy is more difficult than economics or physics. I don't know if that's true. But with all these runaway trolleys, brains in vats, teletransporters, and things, philosophy is surely weirder. But I digress.

Epilogue: Why Can't We All Just Get Along?

WHY IS THERE so much violence, conflict, fear, and hate in the world? Why can't people just get over it and be friends? These are, of course, among of the oldest and most difficult of moral questions. There are hundreds of answers, and none of those answers were easily discovered. It might be that there are just not enough of the good things in life for everyone to have as much as they want. So, as people discover this they end up distrusting each other, and competing to get as much of those things as they can. (This is what Thomas Hobbes argued.) It might be that most people cannot stand the presence of others whose thinking and reasoning is radically different from their own, as David Hume once claimed. Or perhaps it is as Plato said, that as people grow accustomed to pleasures and luxury goods, they eventually become unable to restrain their appetites for those things. Therefore, like 'a city with a fever', they turn to their neighbours, to take by stealth, or even steal by force, what they think they need to satisfy their feverish demands. Perhaps some people are indoctrinated by murderous political or religious ideologies, so they believe that by fighting destructive wars or by exterminating everyone in their region who thinks (or merely looks) different, they will purify the world and bring about a Judgment Day. Or, it might be that some people are just naturally, inexplicably evil, and there's no other reason for it: 'Some men just want to watch the world burn,' as Alfred said to Bruce Wayne in *The Dark Knight* (2008). But I have never been satisfied with that idea: It seems too superficial, too quick, and too easy. People have reasons for what they do—reasons that are irrational, faulty, silly, or perhaps demonstrably insane—but these are their reasons, nonetheless. In 2017, there were 307 mass shootings in the United States between January and November of that year, in which four or more people were injured or killed. The shooters' reasons ranged from the coldly calculated, such as the desire to terrorize people who held differing political beliefs or different lifestyles, to the absurd, such as the desire for media fame.

Let's re-phrase the question a little. What must people do to have at least a chance, even if only a small one, of getting along with one another? That's a question I think I can answer: We have to talk to each other. We have to be willing to speak truly and listen attentively. There is a logical disjunction between speaking and hating; there's a gulf as wide as the ocean between dialogue and murder. You might want to 'send a message' to someone (as the euphemism goes) by beating him up, or depriving him of his rights or his dignity, or even by killing him. But the recipient of that kind of message is never in a position to hear it: The very means of delivery itself logically excludes meaningful communication. Think of old Lucretius here, who taught us to have no fear of death because 'While one lives one does not die; when one dies there is no one there for death to claim; thus, death never reaches you.' In the same way, a message whose means of delivery kills the recipient finds no one at the point of delivery able to receive the message at all. I'm thinking of Emmanuel Lévinas here, who wrote that the presence of another person 'commands justice' and 'forbids murder' because of the logical contradiction between speaking and killing. I'm also inspired here by the Huron-Haudenosaunee philosopher who founded the Iroquois Confederacy, and who taught that 'thinking shall replace killing' in his new society. Perhaps someone could 'send a message' by killing one person in order to terrorise another. Or, someone might deliver a message by by shouting, threatening, bullying, stealing from, hating, or performing any other act of cruelty short of killing. The message whose means of delivery terrifies, dehumanizes, or otherwise oppresses the recipient, quickly strips away the recipient's ability to *reply* with any meaningful sense of autonomy. The recipient might accept the message because of fear, instead of understanding and rational consensus. (We might usefully invoke Hegel's master-slave dialectic here, but that will take us beyond the scope of this coda so I shall explore it in another project, already in preparation.)

It could be argued that cruelty sometimes does, and sometimes does not, acknowledge the humanity of others. But *speaking*, without threats, without violence, without belittling anyone, and without oppression, always acknowledges it. This is because to speak to someone that way is to assume that the other person can hear and understand what you are saying, and to further assume that the other person is capable of responding to you. The ability to understand and to respond, so it seems to me, is an important part of what it is to be human. Even to criticize and to disagree with someone (again, without threats, without belittlement, etc) is still to treat that person as a human being with a mind of her own, because criticism and disagreement still hope to persuade the other person to change her mind. (To wit: to criticize and disagree with someone is not the same as to take away that person's right to speak.) Similarly, to listen to someone is to assume that the other person has a mind of her own, and that she has something to say, and deserves a hearing. Even when someone has nothing much to say—such as an elder who rambles about his past or a small child who never seems to get to the point—listening can be a human kindness. Listening is not merely the opposite of silencing, marginalizing, ignoring, or fighting the other person; listening is also a way of showing respect. While we are speaking to another, we might also be confronting, competing, distrusting, manipulating, dominating, hurting, or even lying to each other. But

we are not directly killing each other. And that, it seems to me, is no small thing. It introduces a moral dimension into the very structure of logic itself. That moral dimension remains tiny and fragile, almost too infinitesimal to notice. It might disappear if someone's hurtful words drive another to suicide. Nonetheless, it is not nothing. It appears on a scale of intensity: The less fear and hate there is in our dialogue with each other, the more humanity there is.

There may be reasons to reject this rosy picture I've painted. For example, Jean-Jacques Rousseau observed, correctly I think, that rationality has just as much power to separate people as to unite them, and that one can use reason to care less about people rather than to care more.

> It is reason that breeds vanity and reflection that strengthens it; reason that turns man inward; reason that separates man from everything that troubles or afflicts him. It is philosophy that isolates him and prompts him secretly to say at the sight of a person suffering: 'Perish if you will, but I am safe'.

But surely the problem here is not with rationality itself, but it is found in a kind of reductionism that identifies reason with self-interest. But rationality is more than that! Reason can, indeed, find ways to reject the moral claims of others and secure itself in its own world, as Rousseau claims. But reason can also show us the moral worth of our neighbours and create new ways for people to be friends. Rousseau correctly grasps the former but not the latter, and thus his understanding is too narrow. Moreover, Rousseau portrays reasoning as an activity that takes place entirely within one's own mind, and nowhere else—but this is not always true.

Reasoning, especially in matters of ethics, is also a social event. It enters into dialogue with others; it speaks to people and it hears what they have to say; and it tests its arguments against the criticisms of others. And if talking to each other does not guarantee that we will get along with one another, at least it opens the possibility.

Glossary of Terms in Logic and Philosophy

Aletheia. Revealing, disclosure, un-hiddenness; the opposite of *lethe*, 'forgetfulness' or 'oblivion' (and the mythological river whose waters cause souls to forget their past lives before they are reborn); a theory of truth popularised by philosopher Martin Heidegger.

Alternative Facts. A neologism coined in 2017 by a spokeswoman for US President Trump, intended as a euphemism for lies, half-truths, **Disinformation**, and/ or Bullshit.

Analytic Proposition. A proposition which expresses only one thought. (See also: Synthetic Proposition.)

Analytic Tradition. One of two dominant paths of Western philosophy in the twentieth century, characterised by Pragmatism, Empiricism, Epistemology, and Utilitarian ethics. (See also: **Continental Tradition**.)

A Fortiori. (Latin: 'From what is stronger'). An indicator word used to show that some **Conclusion** follows with stronger reason than another one.

A Posteriori. (Latin: 'After experience'). A proposition which gains its truth because of evidence, observation, or the experiences of our bodily senses.

A Priori. (Latin: 'Before experience'). A proposition which is endowed with truth because of its logical structure alone.

Aporia. A state of puzzlement, confusion, or impasse; a problem in logic which appears impossible to solve.

(See also: **Pickle.**)

Areteology. Also known as virtue ethics: A branch of ethics which emphasizes character values and moral identity; the account (*logos*) of what is excellent (*arete*) in human affairs. The basic promise of areteology is that by living a life of moral excellence one may be successful in the pursuit of eudaimonia, flourishing, happiness, worthwhile-ness of life. (See also: **Logos, Ethics, Doctrine of the Mean**.)

Argument. A collected series of statements intended to establish a proposition; any two or more propositions in which there is at least one premise, and the premise(s) lead to a Conclusion according to logical rules. A typology of common arguments is given in Chapter 5 of this book.

Argumentation. The process of debating the worth and merits of a proposition.

Begging the Question. A type of logical **fallacy** in which a conclusion says exactly the same thing as the premises; an argument which presupposes the conclusion instead of providing reasons for it.

Bias. In general, a belief or a value to which one continues to subscribe even after that belief or value has been shown to be wrong, harmful, illogical, etc. Bias can also imply unfair judgment or contempt of something. (See also: **Observer Bias, Mere Repetition Bias**.)

Biconditional Statement. Two propositions which are treated as a single proposition, having been joined together by the relation of 'if and only if'.

Boolean Operators. The three main logical operators 'And', 'Or', and 'Not', which are used in the fields of analytic logic and computer programming. Did you see how I used one of them, right there?

Bullshit. A discussion of events or facts about which the speaker lacks knowledge; a discussion of events or facts in which the speaker doesn't care whether his claims are true or false.

Burden of Proof. The responsibility to bring forth evidence or an argument that some proposition is true or false. This responsibility normally falls on the person who has advanced the proposition. (See also: **Extraordinary Claims**.)

Categorical Imperative. A principle of ethics proposed by Immanuel Kant: 'Act on that maxim which you can at the same time will that it shall be a universal law'. (See also: Deontology, Practical Imperative, Ethics.)

Categorical Logic. In formal logic: A branch of **Deduction**, involving **Syllogisms** and **Categorical Propositions**.

Categorical Proposition. A type of proposition which has two parts: A Subject (the thing under discussion) and a Predicate (a property attributed to the subject, or a classification in which the subject belongs), united by the copula verb 'is/are'. (See also: **Proposition, Categorical Logic, Formal Logic**.)

Circular Fallacy. See Begging the Question.

Cognitive Dissonance. The condition of unease or discomfort arising from holding two contradictory thoughts at the same time.

Conclusion. The 'point' of an argument; that which a speaker wishes to persuade others to believe; a statement which is logically supported by one or more premises.

Conditional Statement. Two propositions that are treated as a single proposition, having been joined together by the relation of 'if' [first proposition], 'then' [second proposition].

Confirmation Bias. The preference for evidence which confirms one's assumptions; the deliberate resistance of evidence-which goes against one's assumptions.

Conflict of Interest. A situation where some person or organization has multiple interests (plans, duties, wants, etc), some of which are incompatible with each other; a situation where one interest may improperly influence how someone makes decisions regarding another interest. For example, a manager might hire a family member to a job, instead of a better-qualified candidate. The interests in conflict here are his professional duty to his employer, and his family responsibility. The presence of a conflict of interest can usually serve as a **prima facie** reason to cast reasonable doubt upon someone's decisions.

Conjunction. Two propositions that are treated as a single proposition, having been joined together by the Boolean Operator 'And'.

Conspiracy Theory. An explanation for events that depends on a story about a nefarious organization working in secret to harm the public and/or conceal facts from the public. The evidence for this story tends to be vague, ambiguous, explainable in simpler terms, or otherwise open to doubt. (See also: Extraordinary Claims, Reasonable Doubt.)

Continental Tradition. One of two dominant paths of Western philosophy in the twentieth century, characterised by Existentialism, Phenomenology, Hermeneutics, and Postmodernism. (See also: Analytic Tradition.)

Contradictories. Two propositions which cannot both be true at the same time, but also cannot both be false at the same time. (See also: Contraries, Subcontraries, Subalterns.)

Contraries. Two propositions which cannot both be true at the same time, although they can both be false at the same time. (See also: Contradictories, Subcontraries, Subalterns.)

Conversational Implicature. See Implicature.

Cultural Relativism. The belief that an idea is true, right, etc., because it is generally believed to be so by the members of some culture or society. In social science: The belief that everyone judges what is true, right, etc., according to their own culture(s), and no one stands outside of all cultures in a position of pure objectivity or neutrality. (See also: **Relativism, Personal Belief Relativism**.)

Dasein. Being-in-the-world; the particularly human experience of existence. A concept in metaphysics proposed by Martin Heidegger.

Deepity. A statement that sounds wise and important but actually has little or no meaning; a statement that has two meanings, one of which is true but trivial, and the other one sounds wise and important but is actually false.

Deduction. (adj.: Deductive). A type of argument in which, if the premises are true, the conclusion must also be true. (See also: Induction, Argument.)

De Morgan's Theorems. A set of theorems in formal logic that show how some types of complex propositions can be swapped with simpler ones without loss of meaning. (See also: **Formal Logic.**)

Deontology. A branch of ethics that emphasizes duties, which may be imposed by nature, pure reason, God, or a similar source of moral authority.

Dialectic of the Absolute. A philosophical system developed by G.W.F. Hegel, in which all of history is framed as the work of a world-soul becoming aware of itself, and, in a series of iterations, expressing itself with increasing clarity, completion, and perfection.

Difference Principle. A theory of justice proposed by John Rawls, which holds that any inequalities in a society's distribution of wealth and power must be acceptable to whoever gets the smallest share; the most just distribution is that which gives as much benefit as it can to the society's worse-off members. (See also: **Thought Experiment,** Matthew 25:40.)

Dilemma. Ambiguous propositions; an argument with two or more possibilities which nonetheless lead to the same (usually unwelcome) conclusion.

Discourse Ethics. Principles of discussion or debate designed to ensure that argumentation is friendly, progressive, enlightening, and inclusive, and to prevent discussions from becoming unproductive shouting matches. (See also: **Argumentation**, **Paradox of Tolerance.**)

Disinformation. A form of propaganda that deliberately lies to the audience, in its content and/or its apparent source; a form of Propaganda that aims to capture its audience in a fictitious reality. (See also: **Fake News.**)

Disjunction. Two propositions that are treated as a single proposition, having been joined together by the Boolean Operator 'Or'.

Doctrine of the Four Causes. A procedure of scientific reasoning developed by Aristotle. It involves explaining things and events in terms of four 'causes': Efficient, material, formal, and final. (See also: **Science.**)

Doctrine of the Mean. A theory proposed by Aristotle which states that for every virtue there are two vices: A vice of not enough of the corresponding virtue, and a vice of too much of it. (See also: **Areteology**.)

Doubt. See: Reasonable Doubt.

Dunning-Kruger Effect. A form of observer bias in which unskilled, poorly-skilled, or incompetent (at some task) people believe that they are smarter or more competent at that task than they really are. (See also: **Bias, Observer Bias**.)

Empiricism. A school of thought which holds that our most important source of knowledge is the experience of our physical senses, as well as the evidence of experiments with observable and mathematically quantifiable results.

Enlightenment (The). A movement in Europe's intellectual history, spanning roughly from 1650 to 1789, in which science and reason gained greater public legitimacy and prominence, and enjoyed more power to persuade. The proponents of the movement aimed to use logic and science to solve philosophical, social, moral, and political problems, instead of resorting to theology, mysticism, or superstition. (See also: **Romanticism**.)

Enthymeme. A categorical **syllogism** in which one of the premises is missing. (See also: Argument, **Categorical Logic**.)

Epistemic Values. In science, a group of values proposed by Karl Popper which help distinguish Science from non-science; including falsification, mathematical quantifiability, use of experiments. (See also: **Science, Falsification**.)

Epistemology. The branch of philosophy that studies **Knowledge**.

Epoché (reduction, suspension, leading-back). A logical procedure invented by Edmund Husserl, in which one suspends judgements about the reality of things in order to study how they appear to one's perceptions.

(See also: **Phenomenology, Continental Tradition**.)

Equivocation. A word or phrase that has two or more distinct meanings, and is used in those two or more senses within the same argument. (See also: **Fallacy**.)

Ethics. The branch of philosophy that studies moral rightness and wrongness, justice and injustice, character and virtue, and similar matters, as well as their practical applications.

Ethics of Care. The branch of ethics developed by various American feminists, which holds that one's most important moral responsibilities involve showing empathy and compassion to others, especially for those you are in an immediate position to help, in proportion to their vulnerability, and in proportion to the significance of their relationship to you.

Existentialism. A school of philosophy which holds that there is no intrinsic or pre-determined meaning in life and no pre-determined human nature, and which attributes high significance to individualism, freedom, and authenticity.

Extraordinary Claims. A proposition about facts or events which, while perhaps not impossible, are nonetheless wild, outlandish, and/or unlikely; claims which require extraordinary evidence. (See also: **Conspiracy Theory, Burden of Proof**.)

Fake News. Lies that are deliberately, not accidentally, broadcast in the mass media. Essays, articles, photographs, reports, etc., which are designed to appear like professional journalism, but which deliberately deceive their audience, for purposes such as political or commercial gain. It can come from media organizations (newspapers, broadcasters, etc.) whose entire business is to produce and spread it. It can also come from bloggers, YouTube video creators, and others who produce media content in their spare time. It is typically distributed by users of social media. (See also: **Propaganda, Alternative Facts**.)

Fallacy. A type of argument in which the conclusion does not follow from the premises because of a false premise or an invalid inference; a faulty argument; an error in **Logic**. Historically, philosophers have identified hundreds of fallacies; Chapter 7 of this textbook covers a typology of common ones. In a rational discourse, the aim of pointing out the fallacies in someone's speech should not be to embarrass or subdue that person, but rather to encourage that person to find a better argument.

Falsification. A principle of scientific reasoning invented by Karl Popper that aims to solve the problem of induction. The idea is to find the theory which is true by eliminating all theories which can be proven false. (See also: **Epistemic Values**.)

First Philosophy. A branch of philosophy considered fundamental, and of greater importance than the others; the branch whose questions must be settled before one can move on to the questions posed by other branches. Various philosophers or philosophical schools have held different branches to be 'first': Medieval **Scholasticism** held that **Metaphysics** goes first; Descartes said it's **Epistemology**; Levinas claimed it's **Ethics**. I myself think it might be **Phenomenology**, but I'm not yet sure.

Flouting a Maxim. In informal logic and discourse ethics, the act of deliberately breaking a rule of discourse ethics, without at the same time confusing one's meaning or intentions. Informal signals such as physical gestures, tone of voice, or a reference to a social context, might accompany the words which flout the maxim, in order to clarify one's intentions or meanings (and, often, to make one's conveyance of meaning funny).

Formal Logic. The study of propositions, arguments, inferences, etc., and the rules for reaching deductively necessary conclusions, and/or inductively strong conclusions. Formal logic typically abstracts the content of an argument using a symbolic notation system, in order to make the structure of an argument clearer.

(See also: **Symbolic Logic**.)

Framing Language. A narrative; a form of spin or slant placed on a story or an account of things; the words, phrases, metaphors, symbols, definitions, grammatical structures, questions, and so on, which we use to think, speak of, and understand things in a certain way; the contexts, narratives, and intangible structures of meaning which both surround our worldviews and at the same time inform them. (See also: **Worldview, Informal Logic**.)

Game Theory. In mathematics, the study of the competitive and cooperative interactions of decision-makers, where the results of each person's decisions also depend at least partially on the decisions of others, and where the people involved may or may not have information about each other's decisions. An early game-theoretical argument called Pascal's Wager goes slightly differently. In that argument, there isn't a lack of information about the other party's decisions. Rather, there is a lack of information about whether the other party exists at all.

Godwin's Law. An eponymous law describing people's behaviour in online discussion forums, coined in 1990 by Mike Godwin. It states that 'As an online discussion grows longer, the probability of a comparison involving Hitler approaches 1.' Variation: Once a discussion reaches a comparison to Hitler or the Nazis, its usefulness is over. Note that Godwin's Law may not apply to discussions about persons who really are Nazis, and/or persons who really are calling for the social exclusion or the death of some group of people because of that group's ethnicity, religion, sexual orientation, and so on. (See also: **Discourse Ethics**.)

Habits of Thinking. Patterns of using informal logic, including good habits like curiosity, self-awareness, skepticism, etc., and bad habits like saving face, Relativism, stereotyping, and laziness. (See also: **Informal Logic**. A longer list of good and bad thinking habits is the topic of Chapter 3 of this textbook.)

Hermeneutics. The branch of philosophy that studies how we interpret cultural materials, especially texts. There is a notable hermeneutic tradition among scholars of religious texts like the Bible, but hermeneutics can also apply to other texts.

Hypothesis. In science, it is an educated guess; a **Prima Facie** explanation for things or events that could be put to some kind of experimental or empirical test. (See also: **Science, Epistemic Values, Theory.**)

Implicature. In informal logic and in discourse ethics: A group of values developed by philosopher Paul Grice, which help make it easier for others to understand the meaning of one's statements and expressions. (See also: **Flouting a Maxim.**)

Incompleteness Theorem. A mathematical theorem by Kurt Gödel which shows that in any given set (of numbers, etc.) there will still be at least one axiom which cannot be defined in terms of that set.

Indicator Words. Words like 'because', 'given that', 'it follows that', 'therefore', etc., which indicate to a listener where the premises and conclusions are.

Induction (adj.: Inductive). A type of argument in which, if the premises are true, the conclusion is probably true. (See also: **Deduction, Argument.**)

Inference. The logical relations between propositions in an argument. (See also: **Validity, Strength.**)

Informal Logic. Principles of reasoning which assist one's practical everyday decisions; principles of logic which use flexible and general rules for reaching conclusions.

Information Literacy. Practical knowledge of the way that information is framed, transmitted, legitimised, shared, etc., in the mass media; techniques of **reasonable doubt** applied to information that comes from mass-communication technologies and industries.

Intellectual Environment. The site or location where thinking takes place; the ideas and beliefs that prevail in any given social group or cultural community. (See also: **Worldview**)

Justice. In ethics generally, this is the study of the rightness or wrongness of the power relations in a community or social group, including the rightness or wrongness of the distribution of wealth, honour, resources, and/or punishments. In Virtue ethics/ **Areteology** it refers to the virtue of giving to others what you owe to them and requiring from others what is owed to you; the virtue that helps individuals recognise fairness in their give-and-take relations with others.

Knowledge. Information, together with one's awareness of possessing or processing it; the substance or the material of one's thinking (as distinct from the methods or procedures of thinking); information that one accepts and embeds in one's mind by means of a process of reasoning; a kind of potentiality for thought or feeling or action, embedded in one's mind by a process of reasoning. In analytic philosophy: Justified true belief. (See also: **Logic, Reason, Epistemology.**)

Limit Situation (From German: *Grenzsituation*). A situation in life, as described by philosopher Karl Jaspers, wherein one confronts the narrowness of one's usual way of thinking; a situation in which one's usual worldview is shown to be unhelpful or faulty; an event which prompts or demands a new way of thinking. (See also: **Informal Logic, Worldview.**)

Logic. The procedures of good (correct, **Sound**, consistent) thinking; the procedure of thinking which begins with good questions and clear premises, and then moves from those premises to various deductively necessary or inductively prompted conclusions.

Logical Positivism. (See: Positivism.)
Logos. (From Greek: A saying, a speech, an account, a rationale, a word.) According to Heraclitus and other philosophers of the classical Greek era, Logos is

a name for the organizing principle of the universe; it comprises the basic patterns by which all things are governed and by which all things can be understood. In Christian thought, Logos is related to the nature of God (cf. John 1:1). The word Logos is also the etymological root of the English word *logic*, and of the suffix *-ology* (as in psychology, anthropology, etc.) (See also: **Logic**.)

Mere Repetition Bias. A type of observer Bias in which one comes to believe something only because one has seen or heard it frequently, for a long time, and for no other reason. (See also: Intellectual Environment, Disinformation, Observer Bias.)

Metanarrative. A story about stories; a story which connects other stories together; a body of beliefs or commitments which influences how events are interpreted or how discussions are framed; a major part of a worldview. (See also: **Worldview, Framing Language, Narrative**.)

Metaphysics. The branch of philosophy that studies being, human nature, freedom and free will, God, death, and other matters of ultimate reality.

Methodological Doubt. In epistemology, a procedure of reasoning developed by René Descartes, in which one assumes that if there is any reason to doubt something it should be assumed to be false. If, by this process of elimination, a thinker encounters something that they cannot doubt, that indubitable thing would become the foundation of all knowledge.

Modernism. School of thought characterised by confidence in universal values, especially those related to scientific reasoning, technological and social progress, freedom, democracy, capitalism, secularism, and individualism. (See also: **Postmodernism**)

Modus Ponens. In formal logic, a standard pattern of argument that takes this form: If P then Q; P, therefore Q.

Modus Tollens. In formal logic, a standard pattern of argument that takes this form: If P then Q; not-Q, therefore not-P.

Moral Statement. A proposition that says something about what's good or evil, just or unjust, virtuous or vicious, etc.

Narrative. A story; a body of knowledge organized in the form of a story; an interpretation of events that takes such a form. (See also: **Worldview, Framing Language, Metanarrative**.)

Naturalistic Fallacy. A form of bad reasoning, in which propositions about facts lead to inappropriate conclusions about morality. An early version of this was David Hume's Is-Ought Problem. The fallacy in its most widely accepted form was introduced by G.E. Moore in 1903. (See also: **Fallacy**.)

Necessary Condition. In science and in analytic logic, a condition which must be the case in order for a proposition to be true. (See also: **Science, Sufficient Conditions**.)

Negation. A proposition which asserts that something is not the case. (See also: **Proposition**.)

Nocebo Effect. The self-generated experience of pain, or the medical symptom of some disease when one is not physically injured or sick. This effect is triggered when the subject in a clinical trial has been administered an inert substance that she believes may have harmed her; a self-generated 'side effect' that a trial subject might experience; the opposite of a placebo. (See: **Observer Bias**.)

Objectivity (adj.: Objective). A way of thinking or a state of mind in which one is as free as possible from the influence of personal feelings, biases, expectations; a way of thinking which observes events as an uninvolved or disinterested third-person observer would see them. Note that objectivity in this **sense** has no relation to 'Objectivism', the worldview of American novelist Ayn Rand. (See also: **Bias**.)

Ockham's Razor. A requirement of logical simplicity, attributed to William of Ockham; the requirement that in argumentation there should be 'no unnecessary repetition of identicals'. In Bertrand Russell's formulation: 'The explanation with the fewest assumptions tends to be the truth'. In pop culture: 'The simplest explanation tends to be the truth'.

Overdetermination. In science, a theory which is confirmed by more evidence than is needed. (See also: **Science, Underdetermination**.)

Parable. A work of intellectual imagination, in which a story is told in order to teach something or draw attention to facts and concepts that the speaker wishes emphasized, or which serves as part of a Thought Experiment.

Paradigm. A worldview in relation to science and scientific method. As defined by Thomas Kuhn, it is the sum of the facts, predictions, and methods which guide a scientist's work.

Paradigm Shift. The period of time during which a sufficiently large number of anomalies in the observed results of routine scientific work causes scientists to doubt, and possibly to reject, their current paradigm; this period of doubt (a 'crisis', to use Kuhn's terminology) often leads to the adoption of a new paradigm.

Paradox. An argument which has true premises and valid inferences, yet nonetheless appears to produce a wrong conclusion.

Paradox of Tolerance. This is the situation described by Karl Popper in which it can become necessary to exclude a belligerent person from a discussion in order to preserve the inclusiveness of the discussion. It is part of **Discourse Ethics**.

Pareidolia. A psychological phenomenon in which one perceives patterns in the world which aren't really there. Usually, pareidolia is associated with visual perceptions, such as the appearance of a human face in the bark of a tree. It can also apply to the perception of non-existent or poorly-evidenced patterns in a social world or a media environment, leading to conspiracy theories, prejudices, etc. (See also: **Skepticism, Observer Bias**.)

Parrhesia. (Greek: Bold speech). A true statement which incurs some danger for the person who utters it. A person who utters bold speech is called a Parrhesiastes. (See also: Whistle-blowing.)

Pascal's Wager. An early form of **Game Theory** developed by Blaise Pascal, which purports to show why it is rational to believe in God. A simplistic version of it might go like this: It is better to believe in God because if God does exist and you don't believe, the consequences for you would be worse than if God does not exist and yet you do believe.

Perceptual Intelligence. An intellectual exercise which takes place beneath one's conscious notice, in which present events are compared to similar past events, and then a conclusion is drawn about what is likely to follow from present events; this conclusion is reported to the conscious mind in the form of a 'hunch', an 'instinct', or a 'gut feeling'.

Personal Belief Relativism. The belief that an idea is true if someone believes it, and further that it is true only for the person or people who believe it. (See also: **Relativism, Cultural Relativism**.)

Phenomenology. The philosophical study of the structures of consciousness, from the first-person point of view. (See also: **Continental Tradition**.)

Philosopher. Broad meaning: Any person who practices philosophy. Narrow: A professor of philosophy; a person who has earned or is pursuing a graduate degree in philosophy. Historical: A public menace, a threat to all social and moral values, a corruptor of the young. Socratic: A gadfly who rouses a sluggish society into a more examined life. Nietzschean: A terrible explosive that endangers everything.

Philosophy. (From Greek: *Philia sophia*, the love of wisdom; the friendship with knowledge). The pursuit of answers to the highest and deepest questions by means of logic and systematic critical reason.

Pickle. An especially vexing problem; an unpleasant social or interpersonal situation that seems hard to escape from; an unexpected turn of events which makes it harder to accomplish something. Actually, I just thought it would be fun to include the word 'pickle' in this glossary. (Synonyms: Fine Kettle Of Fish, Sticky Situation, Bind, Box, Jam, Tight Spot.)

Poe's Law. Identified in 2005 by Christianforums.com participant Nathan Poe, this law states that: 'Without a winking smiley or other blatant display of humour, it is utterly impossible to parody a Creationist in such a way that *someone* won't mistake for the genuine article.' More generally, Poe's Law states that without some obvious indicator of the author's intent (such as a smiley or an emoticon), parodies of extremist views in any field might still be mistaken for a real view.

Poisoning the Well. A variation of the Genetic Fallacy and the *ad hominem* fallacy; a way of **framing** a debate to ensure that all ideas and arguments from a particular person or source are pre-emptively dismissed, or treated with unnecessarily severe suspicion. It is a way of attacking someone's honesty or reputation before that person presents any of her ideas, and so undermining the possibility of continued rational discussion. (See also: **Fallacy, Framing Language**.)

Positivism, Logical Positivism. A position or a tendency of analytic philosophy which holds that propositions are meaningful only if they refer to something in the observable world, and if they can be shown either true or false.

Postmodernism. Incredulity toward metanarratives. A position or tendency of philosophical thought characterised by radical skepticism of any truths, worldviews, narratives, and values which claim to be 'universal'. Also characterised by the analysis and criticism of those universal values by way of historical or social contexts, outsider positions and experience, relativism, and irony. (See also: **Modernism, Continental Tradition**.)

Post-Truth (Era of). Some cultural critics say that in our times, objective facts are less influential in shaping public opinion than appeals to emotion and personal belief. (See also: **Fake News, Alternative Facts, Truthiness, Rhetoric**.)

Practical Imperative. A principle of ethics proposed by Immanuel Kant: 'Act in such a way that you always treat humanity, whether in yourself or in another, as an end in itself, never as a means to an end.' (See also: **Deontology, Categorical Imperative, Ethics**.)

Pragmatism. A theory of truth developed by Charles Sanders Peirce, which holds that propositions can be true if they happen to be empirically useful to believe. Note that this theory of truth was meant to apply especially to empirical propositions (that is, propositions about observable facts), and not social or ethical ones. (See also: **Theory of Truth**.)

Premise. A proposition given in support of a conclusion. (See also: **Argument**.)

Prima Facie. (Latin: 'At first glance' or 'on the face'). A conclusion one might draw about things or events from a brief or superficial inspection before investigating more deeply.

Principle of Charity. A professional courtesy among philosophers: The assumption that other people are rational unless there are good reasons to assume otherwise; the practice of interpreting other people's arguments in the best possible light.

Problem of Induction. A logical puzzle identified by David Hume. It states that all inductive arguments that aim to predict something about the future rest on hidden and indefensible premises about past experiences. (See also: **Falsification, Skepticism**.)

Propaganda. A communication from any political organization (government, churches, corporations, charities, etc.) intended to raise public support for its projects. Most people today use the word in a pejorative or ironic sense.

Proposition. A statement; a claim. In analytic logic, a simple sentence that has only one meaning, which can be either true or false.

Propositional Logic. A branch of formal logic involving propositions and argument structures of various kinds, some Deductive and some Inductive; any type of argument in formal logic that doesn't fall under **Categorical Logic**.

Questions. You already know what questions are, but I think it's awesome that you're reading this glossary. Cheers!

Reason, Rationality. Organized curiosity. The capacity of the human mind to understand the world and to make deliberate responsible choices ('responsible' in the sense that one is 'able to respond' when asked to explain oneself); the process of rendering the world intelligible. As a singular noun ('a reason'), it is an explanation or a justification for one's ideas or beliefs. As a verb ('to reason') it is the activity of investigating and understanding; the activity of discussing things with others so that participants can teach and learn from each other, and/or come to agreement with each other.

Reasonable Doubt. Healthy skepticism; the suspension of acceptance of some statement or proposition, due to an absence of sufficient support for it. (See also: Skepticism.)

Rectification of Names, The. An ethical and logical principle attributed to Confucius, which requires

people to use appropriate and correct words to describe their plans and situations.

Reference. The contribution to the meaning of a proposition that derives from the definition of words, and from the events or things in the world those words indicate. (See also: **Sense**).

Relativism. The belief that a claim is true or false only in relation to some other condition; the belief that no claim is absolutely true for all times places and people, nor absolutely false for all times, places and people. Relativism is often well-intentioned: For instance, it may help people with different worldviews understand each other and coexist in peace. However, it can also obscure or derail the search for truth, and it can serve as a justification for prejudice, bad thinking habits, and value programs generally. (See also: **Cultural Relativism, Personal Belief Relativism**.)

Rhetoric. The art of effective persuasion, especially in speaking and writing; the use of composition techniques and figures of speech to impress or influence an audience, possibly with little concern for what is truly right or wrong, and/or what the speaker actually believes.

Rhetorical Question. A proposition phrased in the form of a question, for which the speaker usually expects a very specific answer. (See also: **Rhetoric**.)

Romanticism. This was a movement in Europe's intellectual history spanning roughly from 1750-1850, which served as a counterpoint to the Enlightenment. It held that art, passion, feeling, imagination, and especially struggle, were the most important sources of knowledge and meaning in life, both personally and politically. (See also: **Enlightenment**.)

Sample Size. In inductive logic, and especially in inductive arguments concerning statistics, the sample size is the number or the fraction of the members of a group one studies in order to draw conclusions about all members of the group. Errors in logic follow when the sample size is too small to be indicative of properties of the larger group. (See also: **Induction**.)

Scholasticism. The dominant school of thought in Europe's Middle Ages, which demanded strict logical deduction and aimed to unite classical Greek and Roman philosophy with Christian theology. (See also: **Doctrine of the Mean, Logos, Syllogism**.)

Science. (From Latin: *Scientia*, knowledge). Procedures for reasoning about the nature of the world using evidence, experiments, mathematical quantification of experimental results, and the testing of Hypotheses.

Sense. The contribution to the meaning of a proposition which comes from the context in which the proposition is uttered. (See also: **Reference, Worldview, Intellectual Environment**).

Self-interest. In economics, this is the central assumption about human nature and rational decision-making. In logic, this is a type of bad thinking habit, typically leading to observer bias—especially when disconnected from ethics or from objectivity. (See also: **Habit of Thinking**.)

Skepticism. Unwillingness to accept that (some) things are (always) as they appear to be. Unwillingness to accept that which is not obviously evident, or that which requires extraordinary evidence, without further investigation. Unwillingness to accept the views of others, no matter how earnestly those views are believed and no matter how numerous the believers, if one finds the reasons for those views are not strong enough, or if there are simpler reasons backed with better evidence that supports different views. (See also: **Habits of Thinking, Reasonable Doubt, Informal Logic, Ockham's Razor**.)

Social Contract. A theory of Justice proposed by Jean-Jacques Rousseau, which holds that all the members of a given society are involved in a contract relationship with one another, in which individual members owe various responsibilities to the group, and the group provides various benefits to the individual members.

Socratic Dialogue. This method of logical enquiry was developed by Socrates: One person poses philosophical questions to the other, not only to discover acceptable answers, but also to find logical inconsistencies or other **Aporia**.

Socratic Wisdom. The knowledge of one's own ignorance; the knowledge of the limits of one's knowledge; the knowledge that one knows nothing of great importance.

Sophistry. The use of Logic, and also logical Fallacies, to dominate debates and/or to deceive people; argumentation which, on a superficial level, appears sound, but upon closer inspection is shown to be unsound. (See also: **Rhetoric**.)

Statement. See Proposition.

Stoicism. (adj.: Stoic.) A school of thought in classical Greece and Rome, founded by Zeno of Citium (336-264 BCE), which holds that the cosmos is governed by an all-unifying rational order, comparable to the Logos but perhaps closer to *Nous* (Greek: 'Mind'); and that happiness comes from letting go of that which we cannot control.

Strength. In analytic logic, a property of correct inferences in **Inductive** arguments.

Soundness. In analytic logic, a property of arguments as a whole; a property of arguments which have true premises and valid (or strong) **Inferences**.

Subalterns. In formal logic, this refers to two statements which can both be true at the same time because one of them is a universal statement and the other is particular statement that is implied by the universal. (See also: **Contraries, Contradictories, Subcontraries**.) Note that 'subaltern' in this sense has no relation to the theory of the same name proposed by philosopher and sociologist Antonio Gramsci.

Subcontraries. Two statements which could both be true, but which cannot both be false. (See also: **Contraries, Contradictories, Subalterns.**)

Subjective Relativism. (See also: Personal Belief Relativism.)

Sufficient Conditions. In science and in analytic logic, a condition which—if fulfilled—is enough to make a proposition true. (See also: **Necessary Conditions**).

Syllogism. A type of formal argument pattern that was the most important type of argumentation from the time of its invention by Aristotle until the rise of Empiricism. It consists of three categorical propositions: The first is the major premise, the second is the minor premise, and the third is the conclusion. (See also: **Categorical Logic, Categorical Proposition, Scholasticism, Argument.**)

Symbolic Logic, Symbolic Language System. A procedure of simplifying and clarifying arguments using symbols to represent propositions and logical relations, first developed by Gottfried Leibniz and further developed by various philosophers in the analytic tradition.

Synthetic Proposition. A logical proposition which expresses two or more thoughts, combined (synthesized) together. (See also: **Analytic Proposition.**)

Tautology. A proposition or argument which is true because of its logical form alone; an argument in which the premises and conclusion have exactly the same meaning, and therefore nothing may be concluded.

Theory. In science, an explanation of things or events which has thus far resisted all attempts to prove it false; the best explanation of things or events scientists presently work with. (See also **Science, Hypothesis.**)

Theory of Truth. A theory that attempts to explain how one might find out whether a given proposition is true.

Thought Experiment. A work of intellectual imagination, in which concepts or problems are clarified, special attention is drawn to unexpected or unusual facts, or questions are cast into a clear light. Questions posed by thought experiments are not always easily answerable; there can be more than one good answer, and there could also be no answer at all. (See: **Parable.**)

Truth. In analytic logic, a property of propositions. (See also: **Theory of Truth, Deepity**, your nearest **philosophy** professor, or your nearest source of overwhelming beauty. I prefer meadows and forests, art galleries, live music shows, and some of Einstein's field equations. You might prefer a well-played goal in your favourite sport. Or tomorrow morning's sunrise. The **Romantic** poet John Keats said: 'Beauty is truth, truth beauty—that is all ye know on earth, all ye need to know'. Was he right? Or was T.S. Eliot right to say that line was meaningless? I should get back to writing this glossary.)

Truthiness. A property of sentences, arguments, discussions, ideas, etc., that feel like they're correct, regardless of facts, evidence, or Logic. A tactic for appealing to intuitions, feelings, 'gut feelings', and prejudices, to make someone believe that something is true.

Underdetermination. In science, an observation that confirms more than one theory. (See also: **Science, Overdetermination.**)

Undistributed Middle. A **fallacy** that arises when the middle premise of a **categorical syllogism** has not been placed in its proper position in the first and second premises.

Utilitarianism. A branch of ethics that emphasizes consequences, outcomes, and results.

Validity. In analytic logic, a property of correct inferences in **Deductive** arguments. Not to be confused with **soundness**.

Value Program. A type of worldview, as described by philosopher John McMurtry, that allows for no critical examination of its most important moral values, and which justifies the harms caused by its believers. (See also: **Worldview, Ethics**.)

Venn Diagram. A visual method of testing the soundness of categorical syllogisms, that uses overlapping circles.

Virtue, Virtue Theory. (See Areteology.)

Weasel Words. Statements or phrases that are deliberately ambiguous; statements or phrases which, while not actually false, nevertheless give the listener a misleading picture of the facts.

Whistle-blowing. A form of Parrhesia; the act of drawing public attention to some kind of moral wrongdoing or illegal act in one's workplace, or a community.

Worldview. In informal logic: The sum of one's answers to the highest and deepest questions in life; the intellectual narrative in terms of which the actions, choices, and purposes of individuals and groups make sense; a mindset; a way of perceiving and interpreting things; a way of thinking; that which is revealed by the use of a framing language. Attributed to Albert Schweitzer, who defined it as: 'The content of the thoughts of society and the individuals which compose it about the nature and object of the world in which they live, and the position and the destiny of mankind and of individual men within it.' (See also: **Narrative, Metanarrative, Framing Language, Limit Situation, Intellectual Environment, Philosophy**.)

Zeno's Paradoxes. A group of contradictory and/or perplexing sayings, attributed to the early Greek philosopher Zeno of Elea, which seem to show logical problems in everyday events such as motion through space. (See also: **Aporia, Paradox**.)